Who's that Girl?

Confessions of a Stargazer

Odyle Knight

SELESTIAL PUBLISHING

Copyright © 2024 by Odyle Knight

All rights reserved. No part of this publication may be reproduced, distributed, or transmitted in any form or by any means, including photocopying, recording, or other electronic or mechanical methods, without the prior written permission of the publisher.

 A catalogue record for this book is available from the National Library of Australia

Cataloguing in Publication Data: 22 November 2024
Author: Odyle Knight
Title: Who's That Girl? Confessions of a Stargazer.
Published: Selestial Publishing, Australia, 2024
Subjects: Memoir, biographical, astrology, spirituality, historical

Who's That Girl? Confessions of a Stargazer, Odyle Knight.
Paperback: 978-1-7637940-9-2
eBook: 978-1-7637940-1-6

Disclaimer:

This is a true story of my life experiences but some of the names and identifying details of the characters have been changed to protect the privacy of the people involved.

The use of images of individuals included in this publication does not imply any association with or endorsement by these individuals or their estates. The use of these images is presented without any claim of endorsement, sponsorship, or approval.

*

***

THIS BOOK IS DEDICATED

TO THE MUSICIANS, COMPOSERS AND DANCERS,

THE SEEKERS OF TRUTH AND PEACE, THE STARGAZERS,

ALL BLESSED WITH A TOUCH OF MAGIC AND BRILLIANCE.

AND TO ALL THOSE SOULS WHO RAISE THE FREQUENCY OF

****** THE EARTH, SIMPLY BY THEIR PRESENCE ON IT. ******

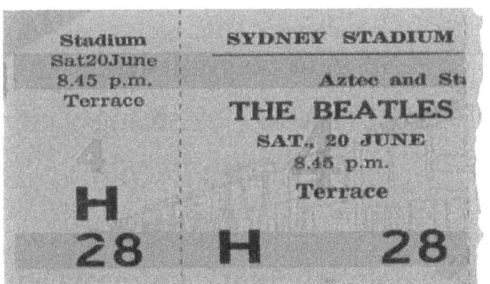

Beatles Concert – 1964 – Sydney

Cover photo – Odyle Knight with Keith Moon, the wild drummer of the Who, one of the best drummers of all time. This photo was taken in 1968 with consent and joy on a street in Potts Point in Sydney, Australia.. Keith passed at 32 in 1978 leaving behind a glimmer of his greatness. *** Copyright © 2024 Odyle Knight

WHO'S THAT GIRL

Confessions of a Stargazer

ISBN 978-1-7637940-9-2

Also by Odyle Knight:
BALI MOON – A Spiritual Odyssey
BALI MAGIC – Reflections of a Reluctant Psychic
BALI HAI – A Woman's Journey
HIPPOS EAT GRASS – Busting the Fat Myth

Soon to be published:
PEOPLE OF THE STARS – Astrology and the History of the Jewish People

www.odyleknight@hotmail.com
www.odyleknight.com

© Copyright Odyle Knight 2024

SELESTIAL PUBLISHING 2024

CONTENTS

THE SWINGING SIXTIES 1
HAPPILY NEVER AFTER 22
LIVING IN THE SEVENTIES 34
THE LITTLE GYPSY 41
TURNING POINT 51
THE POWER OF LOVE 59
LOST ON A DESERT HIGHWAY 67
HOMEWARD BOUND 87
BALI HIGH 97
A MYSTICAL REALM 108
FANTASTIC TALES 118
SILENT SENTINELS 129
IN THE SPOTLIGHT 135
LOVE IN THE JUNGLE 144
MOUNTAIN MAGIC 153
STAIRWAY TO THE STARS 167
FLOATING ON THE MOON 176
THE KING AND I 189
MIND GAMES 201
HAWAII BLUE 213

DREAM WEAVER	221
THE LOST CONTINENT	232
DARK PASSAGE	244
THE ETERNAL FLAME	249
INTO THE ASTRAL	269
COME SAIL AWAY	280
I'VE GOT THE MUSIC IN ME	287
HOLY OF HOLIES	304
SEA OF HEARTBREAK	318
OCEAN OF LOVE	331
ABOUT THE AUTHOR	338

CHAPTER ONE

THE SWINGING SIXTIES

I was born with stardust in my veins. It first exploded in 1964, at the age of 14, at the Beatles concert in Sydney. My screams of ecstasy were swallowed up by the collective roar of the audience, the mass teenage hysteria drowning out any hope of music or reason. The Beatles were reduced to four figures of fantasy, lost among the heaving crowd, as the revolving stage at the old boxing stadium at Rushcutters Bay whirled them in never-ending circles.

The Beatles hated the venue, the usual manic scene amplified by flashes of crazed fans and loud pandemonium. Like countless others, I felt compelled to run down the aisle and jump onto the stage, but my best friend Isabel kept me grounded, her hand firmly clenched in mine. As I glanced across at her, tears rolling down her cheeks, we were forever bonded. All those hours we shared sticking pictures of the 'Fab Four' on our bedroom walls were worth it.

Meanwhile, my parents waited patiently in their Peugeot car, in shades of silver, to drive us home across the Sydney Harbour Bridge. Who knows how we found the car amongst the frenetic crowd after the concert but we tumbled into the back seat in a state of euphoria. Speech was impossible as we had screeched ourselves hoarse and were in a transcendent state having been in the presence of British demigods. No words would suffice. Nothing could match that magical night when the world transformed into a place of sheer wonder.

The torch was lit and there was no turning back, and two cultures were about to clash headlong. My father, bless him, had any trace of his faith drained from him during World War II but still he drove me on a Saturday night to the Jewish youth dance on the other side of Sydney, to the eastern suburbs. Isabel was French and Catholic, so instead I went with my friend, Rachel. With the final wave goodbye, we hopped onto the first bus to Kings Cross, the happening part of the city, and headed straight for the hot night spot, Surf City.

To the throbbing beat of the Aztecs, we stomped the night away and watched the crowd get lost in the music and the debauchery of it all. Bleached Surfie blondes in skimpy minis and towering stilettos danced beside super cool Rockers in tight jeans and leather, their hair as slick as their egos. Peeking behind the stage curtain, I spotted one of the guitarists enjoying several of the adoring female fans who flocked around him. Here, there were few limits, and it was exciting. When it came to the stars, I wanted to walk on the wild side.

There were some rules I didn't break, well almost. To keep my curfew, after the night out, I rushed inside the house from the taxi and ran into the kitchen to turn back the clock before my father roused to check the time. Satisfied, he went back to bed. I raided the cupboard for chocolate to continue my high. Excitement, danger, and chocolate – a preview of times to come. Some things in life are as tempting as they are forbidden.

It was a habit formed from an early age when my family lived in a residence above their mixed business shop in the inner city. Late at night my sister, Elly, and I would take turns creeping down the stairs, after our parents were asleep, to dip into the candy cabinet.

Sneaking back with a handful of fizzy Clinkers, with insides the colour of a rainbow, and chewy caramel Fantales wrapped in fabulous stories of movie stars, we enjoyed our spoils. It took a while before my father discovered the loose floorboard in our bedroom where we hid the remains of our stash and he continually complained that's where all his profits went!

Our pursuit of sweets was the only thing that bonded me with my elder sister because we clashed both in personality and volume. A messy Virgo, not the usual neat freak type, with a loud Leo roar, Elly was grating at best. My mother continually tried to push us together, which only drove us further apart. We were best that way, for being family is no guarantee of connection. In many ways, I was a loner, a sensitive Libra lost in a rich fantasy world.

It was Mrs Strange's garden, across the road from our house that enchanted me most as a child. With its superb display of roses and scented jasmine, I stepped onto the threshold of beauty in a neighbourhood dipped in grey and asphalt. Elderly Mrs Strange had the palest skin and gentlest heart and talking to her was a relief from my home which was turbulent at best. Memories of the war still troubled my parents, casting a shadow over us.

My family arrived in Australia from Greece in 1951 when I was two, several years after the conflict of the Greek Civil War ended. My father had been conscripted into the Greek army not long after he returned from the degradation of the Second World War, and the terror of a Nazi concentration camp. How he survived is a miracle. It was in these sordid conditions that he first laid eyes on my mother, a 15-year-old girl from Hungary. Both their families were murdered at Auschwitz but their fate was sealed. They belonged together.

I escaped my parents' haunted past by colouring in flimsy paper doilies by myself, playing fiddle sticks with my sister while fighting over a special doll or hiding under a blanket on the sofa on the porch. I also loved stacking empty bottles in the backyard into neat crates, as if tidying them up brought some sense of order into my life. I was best left sitting alone behind the shop counter, dipping into the bread barrel while reading the latest copy of True Confessions magazine, imagining that I had something interesting to confess to.

Full cream milk was my nemesis, especially bottles left out on the hot school porch all morning which students were forced to drink, to stay 'healthy'. The butcher's children next door drank milk by the gallon until they became bovine in appearance, fleshing out and rotund like the cows we saw on weekend drives to the country.

Memories of feral cats on the roof screeching a lover's lament in the dead of night ensured a restless sleep. They remain fixed in my mind, as does the deafening silence when a burglar crept by our beds one night to rob the shop downstairs.

By far my worst fear was darkness. I slept with a light on because the darkness was threatening. Murky, empty, and perilous. Not a chink of light to dispel my fears. On the rare nights my parents had time to themselves we slept over at Mrs Miller's house. A fine Australian lady, she insisted we drink a warm milky cup of Ovaltine before sleeping and then turned off all the lights. It was a restless night with my stomach churning and my eyes shut tight, hoping to avoid any potential thief or dark entity lurking nearby.

Noise also rattled my sensitive soul. In a photo of me as a seven-year-old at a party, I was kneeling alone in front of a table with my fingers stuck firmly in my ears, trying to block out loud sounds. Stirred by an acute sensitivity to all sensory stimuli, it was an early warning sign of an issue gathering force inside me. It took years to uncover and many decades before the harsh truth was learnt.

When noise transformed into music it had a healing effect. Noise shaped by structure and creativity had the potential to raise my spirit. Lyrics were a doorway into parts of my soul not yet discovered. On the long voyage from Europe to Australia in 1951, my mother's memory was of me, an active two-year-old, perched on the edge of the stage gazing up adoringly at the musicians in the band. In my mind, notes and colour emerged from their instruments, shaping meaningless space into a brilliant symphony. The wonder of music remained with me all my life and those who created, or performed it, were my inspiration.

My mother fanned that love of music. Despite a moderate budget she ensured there were 'special' moments. My sister and I were treated to ballet and theatre and rare performances by a visiting flamenco troupe. She spoiled us with dresses from exclusive Mark Foys, lovely pink or sky-blue taffeta set off by shiny black patent leather shoes. Her only fault was insisting that my dark hair was cut short in a fringed basin style which I detested. My shiny hair was my joy and I hated the hairdresser even more than visits to the dentist, many considering my sordid chocolate past.

Music of another kind influenced me in the 1950s. During lessons on religious study at Marrickville Primary School, I sat on a bench outside in the sunshine listening to Christian hymns echoing across the playground. Sydney was in its early phase of immigration and our area was mainly Anglo-Celtic, true blue Aussies. My family was one of the first immigrants there so I was content to sit alone under a tree and daydream. A few other children sat around me, all from different backgrounds, who were equally difficult to place.

In retrospect, it was hard as a child to gauge my identity. My parents did not practice the Jewish faith when I was growing up. There was no Sabbath spent at the synagogue, no lighting of the candles, or celebration of the festivals or holy days. Instead, not wanting us to miss out, we were ensured a happy Christmas, like all our friends. My father snuck up the stairs the night before to leave a pile of presents by our beds so we could share in the joy.

On Sundays, we often went to the beach at Ramsgate where I joined in with the Christian Sunday school because of the stickers they handed out. I also sang along to some of the hymns I'd heard in the school corridors. My parents seemed to have no objections to this giant leap of faith, probably because they distanced themselves from their religion, having suffered greatly because of it.

They were also happy for a respite from my constant questioning. Whatever I was told or asked to do, I invariably asked, 'Why?' to the point of driving them mad, especially on car rides.

My Greek birth documents stated only the year I was born but not the date. So, my mother got inventive and lied about my age to get me into school a year earlier, switching my birthdate from October to January, to qualify for the first enrolment. Cunning.

At school, I thrived on mental stimulation and became irritatingly clever, making the others feel behind. So they got rid of me by sending me on errands around the school. I felt cheated because I never got to celebrate my birthday. My fictitious date in January fell during the school holidays and my real birthday went unnoticed.

I wasn't scared when I got lost among the crowds at The Royal Easter Show. With my independent spirit and love of animals, I wandered off to admire the stalls of pot-bellied pigs and prize-winning bulls proudly showing off their blue ribbons. My parents' panic turned to relief when they tracked me down to the Lost Children's tent where I was enjoying ice cream surrounded by a group of policemen. Hence my later love of men in uniform and sweets. After all, I was born a romantic Libra with an indulgent Taurus moon.

My sense of self was moulded through layers of recorded time, within the music. In the mid-1960s, I wanted to transform into the ethereal blonde Michelle Phillips of the Mamas and the Papas and glide across the stage, and the universe. Instead, I was grateful for their singer, Mama Cass, with her ample size, flowing caftans, and mellow voice. In looks, Cher, with her long dark hair and exotic racial blend, helped define my identity as 'different'.

Shapely brunettes were rare so I was forced to alter my looks to fit in. On my weekly ferry trip to Manly to lie on the beach with friends, I hid behind dark sunglasses and a long blonde wig. Unable to see from under it, I hacked off the front to make a fringe and with the first gust of wind it stood up at attention but I didn't care.

At last, it felt like I belonged. I got a lot of mileage from that wig, especially on a party night, where stud Russell, known for his kissing prowess, liked to practice on my face. Apart from some lip bruising, it felt good to be the chosen one. I wasn't a natural blonde, couldn't fit into tight blue jeans, was a failure on steep stilettos but still, I was the chosen one!

With the emergence of Twiggy, the big-eyed blonde British model with the body of a waif, my life was ruled by the scales. Every day, with great solemnity, I weighed myself. My reaction ranged from ecstatic because I had lost half a pound or dejected because all my best efforts had failed. I was still me. No grapefruit diet or lemon fast was going to change the fact that I was me. I never realised till much later just how important that was.

Fashion was designed for lean lasses and not girls with curves and it evolved little over the decades. So I was forced to get innovative and make many of my clothes, using my mum's old Singer sewing machine. It was a skill that proved beneficial in the future, a stepping stone to a valuable life path. However being invisible or outside the norm, especially as a teenager, is not easy.

It was my first boyfriend Boris who saved me from society. A six-foot-tall beatnik with a black beard, grey cashmere sweater and pencil trousers, Boris possessed a subtle intellect. It had become mildly fashionable to 'think', a cool trend for the non-conformist. I reverted to being dark and intense, wearing loose jumpers and leggings. In a defiant act, I grew my straight dark hair to my waist and lashed bold black kohl eyeliner onto my eyes.

Every Saturday night Boris met me at The Bowl disco, a trendy place in the heart of Sydney. Before making my entrance I scrutinised myself in one of the mirrors, checking that I looked chic and super-disinterested, as was the mood of the times.

When Boris wandered off to get drinks from the non-alcoholic bar I grooved to great bands like the Easybeats. It was a fab place to be but predictably our romance fizzled out because Boris loved French kissing and I preferred British, far more restrained. I learnt my lesson with voracious Russell. Less is definitely more.

Through all the challenges I was bolstered by a strong ego. I enjoyed high school, especially the drama and art classes where my creative side found expression. My family had moved to the north side of Sydney, a more affluent area on a bushland retreat where my parents built a modest home with the sale of their business.

Here Judaism was more in vogue and at Willoughby Girls High School there was a Jewish religious class with Rabbi Katz. I still felt just as alien as I did in my first school because I still could not relate to my faith. The sense of connection was lost on me.

While there were few gestures at home of our Jewish religion, we sometimes went to the Passover celebration at a friend's house. There we relived the ordeal of our ancestors' journey through the desert in search of a new home, as Moses led his people from slavery in Egypt to the 'Promised Land' of Canaan, thousands of years ago. From the bitter herbs to the unleavened bread, *matzah*, I was far too young to understand the depth of such collective angst.

Instead, I focused on indulging in teenage dreams. School remained a positive outlet, except for the dreaded gym class. The teacher screeched my name whenever I tried to merge into the background during sport, so I forged notes to get out of the class or did a disappearing act. Swinging a bat or scaling objects was far too heathen for me and running in circles around an oval was pointless.

One physical activity that I loved was dance. It was an extension of music and the ultimate expression of self. I was not the ballet type, but I loved to shimmy and groove for the camera on the show Saturday Date, hosted by Jimmy Hannan. Isabel and I lived close to Channel 9 studio and it was our week's highlight. I even 'borrowed' one of the programs, but Jimmy carried on regardless.

The bands featured on the show were great, and so began our quest for autographs, although this was limited to homegrown talent. International was to come later. Three young guys who performed there regularly, greeted us by name but we never thought to get their autographs, thinking they wouldn't go far. Bad mistake. They went on to become a worldwide phenomenon – *The Bee Gees*.

As aspiring groupies, our love affair with rock gods gained force with every new arrival from Britain. Nothing matched the feeling as I sat in the classroom, hiding my radio, listening to the faintest report that the Beatles had just landed in Sydney. The earth stopped turning for a fraction of time, at least mine did.

The Beatles arrived in Australia in the early hours of 11 June 1964, to frantic scenes at the airport. They were paraded around, in capes, on the back of a flatbed truck, despite the heavy rain and strong winds, so the screaming fans would not be disappointed. The band was drenched in the process. Their drummer Ringo Starr was absent, having been hospitalised in London a week earlier with tonsilitis. Jimmie Nicol was the stand-in drummer until Ringo was well enough to rejoin the band just in time for the Melbourne concert.

The Beatles stayed in a suite at the Sheraton Hotel in Potts Point. At their press conference, they impressed the hardened reporters with their off-the-cuff comments, sharp wit and charm, and won them over. Their Australasian tour was a success, and although few fans got the chance to hear them through the avalanche of screams, they were overwhelmed just to be in their presence. The Beatles tour marked the beginning of the British invasion, an onslaught of British talent and concert tours to sweep the country.

The Beatles were musical genius, and their impact can never be replicated for they represented a singular moment in time. As they matured, their music evolved through a series of phases one more inspired than the last. They pushed me, and millions of other besotted fans, over the edge of adoration onto the precipice of ecstasy.

I watched the Beatles movie *A Hard Day's Night* 11 times, screaming along with Isabel. Other people in the theatre yelled obscenities and hurled orange Jaffa balls at us but we could not stop.

It left such an indelible imprint that years later I married a British guy who reminded me of Paul McCartney, such was my infatuation with his soft brown eyes. When he sang 'And I Love Her' on the movie screen it felt like he was singing it just for me.

The next group to excite were the Rolling Stones whose first tour to Australia was in the summer of 1965. The Stones had sold millions of records by then, becoming one of the most powerful musical influences of the times. While the Beatles were clean-cut and appealing to parents and the press, the Stones were scruffier, bohemian and overtly sensual which was far more provocative.

The Rolling Stones created headlines, fighting with press and photographers, trashing dressing rooms and other wild behaviour inviting scandal and calls for them to be banned. Singer Mick Jagger's gyrations on stage prompted moans of rapture from the adoring fans.

At their hotel, the Chevron, directly opposite the more sedate Sheraton Hotel where the Beatles stayed, guitarist Brian Jones hid girls in the room service trolley at the hotel and smuggled them onto their floor. Not that he needed to. Many besotted fans would have been happy to give themselves willingly to their rock gods if only they could get to them. Isabel was one of the few who succeeded.

Isabel left school at 16 to go to secretarial college but neither of us lost our lust for the British rock gods. Isabel made it into the Chevron Hotel and stowed away in the dumb waiter winching her way up to the barred floor of the Stones. Fortunately, I wasn't with her because I probably would have got stuck halfway up.

Isabel met Mick Jagger, Keith Richards and the late Brian Jones. As a souvenir, she grabbed a chunk of his hair from a brush in the bathroom, strands she still treasures today. I managed to score

Mick Jagger's autograph at the airport from a policeman who saved it for the most deranged fan he spotted on the day.

The Rolling Stones concert was held at the Manufacturer's Auditorium in the Agricultural Halls of the Sydney Showground, a strangely inappropriate venue for such a dynamic force. Sitting two rows from the front was like being sucked into the eye of a hurricane.

With every slick move, each drawn-out vowel and sexy twang of the guitar, the crowd roared. Their first song, 'Not Fade Away', was prophetic as the band is still going strong today, while the last one, 'It's All Over Now', was misleading. I was so excited that I ran out to buy tickets to the second show so I could do it all again.

The 1965 Far East tour was an odd package and included on the bill were American Roy Orbison, the Newbeats, and New Zealand's Ray Columbus and the Invaders. Somehow I managed to get to Roy Orbison after the concert. As he walked quickly by, he left a magnetic aura and scribbled my name and those priceless words, 'Love Roy Orbison'. I hope that I was one of his original 'Pretty Woman'.

In my quest to acquire the signatures of the super-talented and famous, my autograph collection grew. Few pop stars escaped, and none complained or refused my request. With each signature, I tried to decipher the elements required for greatness. What made someone stand out from the rest, and shower them with glitter and fame?

In astrology, the planet Neptune governs music. A pale shade of blue, Neptune rules Pisces, the final sign of the zodiac. With its sensitivity, Neptune can inspire and confuse so reality can be confronting for musicians who can tap into a higher frequency. That's why many reach out for alcohol and drugs to cope. Some meet a sordid end, their death as volatile as the way they lived, while others reign on or simply fade from view.

Like many pop stars, the Stones guitarist Brian Jones died far too young, at the age of 27, the completion of one Saturn life cycle. He was found drowned in a swimming pool with a concoction of alcohol and drugs in his system. Two days after his death, a free tribute concert was held for him in London's Hyde Park. Over 250,000 people sat silently as Mick Jagger recited a touching poem by Shelley and a mass of butterflies were released, fluttering above the crowd to guide the musical minstrel on his way to a better place.

One British band that caused near riots in America was the Dave Clark 5 with their hit 'Glad All Over'. They were a handsome bunch, and I was glad all over when they toured Australia in May–June 1965. When it was announced that they would be guests on the show Bandstand on Channel 9, I alerted Isabel. We loved meeting up for our 'star encounters' and, dolled up in our flashy outfits, we rushed to the studio to hopefully catch a glimpse of our idols.

Soon to be 16, and having perfected the Cleopatra flick on my eyeliner, my teal eyeshadow made me look older than my years. Isabel was pert and pretty, her blonde hair cut into a cute bob with a fringe. Undeterred that all the tickets to the show had been snatched up, we headed for the back lot of the studio looking for action.

We were not disappointed. Just as we did, two black limousines pulled up and out jumped five fabulously groomed young men. On impulse, I grabbed the closest one, Dave, the drummer and leader of the band, by the arm. Isabel latched onto Lenny, the lead guitarist.

The boys did not protest as we strode into the studio together. It didn't hurt to have two cute 'dolly birds' by their side. As the lads went off to be interviewed, we were served canapes and drinks as we watched them from the green room, the crew presuming we were their girlfriends. To be part of the band's entourage was thrilling.

Proximity to a rock god was like manna from heaven and in years to come my pursuit of musical gods was relentless. Instead of scaling fire escapes or other such brazen acts, I learnt an important lesson that day. If you don't have 'it', fake it. If you've already got it, shout it loud and proud. Instead of sneaking into a hotel, strut in as if you belong there – or even better date the guy at reception so he can let you know the bands' schedule.

Then, with all the dates sorted, it was simply a matter of turning up on the day and wearing something fabulous to catch their eye. It was the 'Swinging Sixties', so the bolder the better. If I breathed in hard, I could wriggle into my emerald paisley mini, canary yellow crepe frock, or purple flocked velvet from vogue designers John and Merivale. The bands were gaudier, in marvellous frilled satin shirts and spangled sequin jackets. The '60s was a psychedelic era, full of rainbows and unicorns, imaginary or induced.

It was not only the British musicians who left an impact. Of the American singers, none were more iconic than Bob Dylan. I was gifted a rare poster of his Australian tour in 1966. Arriving at the Stadium early for his concert I chatted with a security guy at one of the doors. Responding to my adoration of the star, he disappeared for a while and then returned and handed me the prize poster, supposedly signed by Bob Dylan himself. I was ecstatic. Only years later did I find a message written on the back: 'Give me a ring at the Stadium sometime, Reg the man with the beard. 323331.'

Del Shannon was another American rock star I met, his song 'Runaway' was my first pop disc. Until today, it triggers a response, with its electronic keyboard and dynamic vocals. Other US stars also signed their autograph for me. Like Gene Pitney, with his plaintiff 'It Hurts to Be in Love'. Having never been in love, I wanted to plunge headlong into it, so I could share in his angst. The Newbeats, with their hit 'Bread and Butter', happily signed while Wayne Newton wrote my name with 'All My Love, Wayne Newton'.

Decades later, I nabbed an autograph from superhero Flash Gordon, scribbled on my pay slip, the only paper I could find. He was in Sydney for the Logie TV awards and was coming up the Hilton escalator when I was going down. Instinctively I reached out to touch him. When his security team tried to fend me off, I said with a sultry smile, 'Don't worry, I won't hurt him.' He smiled back and happily signed. Then he was gone in a flash.

There were many Aussie greats that I tracked down for their signature. The likes of Johnny O'Keefe, a raging presence who made me want to 'Shout'. The Easybeats had more than 'Friday on my Mind'. The late Barry Humphries signed as he swirled past me with his cape in the corridors of a Sydney radio station. It was one unique personality after another. The '60s were ripe with talent.

Ray Columbus and the Invaders had a hit with 'She's a Mod' and I aspired to be one. Style was paramount for this trendy subculture but the mod's love of short geometric hairstyles and Vespa motor scooters was my undoing. I suited neither.

My passion for all things British remained. Tom Jones, a true gentleman, first came to Sydney in 1966 after his hit 'It's Not Unusual', winning the Grammy Award for Best New Artist. The original 'Sex Bomb', he invited Isabel and me to join him for afternoon tea at the hotel with his band, the Squires. Several lads wanted to see Bondi Beach, so we acted as their guides for the day. Herman's

Hermits were too tame for me but I still have Herman's luggage label as a souvenir. I hope the suitcase eventually made it to his room.

You knew you were in the presence of greatness with British stars like Jimmy Page of the Yardbirds who toured in 1967, spurred on by the band's hits 'I'm a Man' and 'Heart Full of Soul'. Jimmy went on to found Led Zeppelin and is considered one of the greatest guitarists of all time. When he wrote 'Love Jimmy Page xx' under my name, I felt blessed. Along with the autographs of so many other stars, it was a fantasy come to life for a teenage girl.

With every written tribute it seemed like the spark within me was gathering force. These stars were recognising me, and so was the universe. On the bill for the same show in 1967 were the Walker Brothers from the US, with their hit 'The Sun Ain't Gonna Shine Anymore', but those guys cast enough light that it just didn't matter.

The year 1967 also saw the tour of Eric Burdon and the Animals. The band were intense, gritty, and brilliant in their own right, and their hits, 'Don't Let Me Be Misunderstood' and 'The House of the Rising Sun', are rock classics. I clicked with guitarist Vic Briggs who signed his name and then wrote down his address in London in case I wanted to visit. He later became immersed in music with an Eastern influence, changed his name to Anton, converted to Sikhism and played classical Indian music as he assumed his true identity.

Performing along with the Animals, were the band Dave Dee, Dozy, Beaky, Mick & Tich whose hit 'The Legend of Xanadu' topped the British charts. Another hit for the band was 'Bend It', a real groover with its suggestive lyrics and 'Zorba' beat.

After a frantic call to Isabel's office, memories of the past stirred, and feigning illness she made a beeline for the exit, much to the disapproval of her boss. Ours was a long overdue reunion and worth it because Isabel clicked with Dozy. The last I saw of her, he had picked her up, literally, and she was being twirled around in the street. Her smile lasted for weeks, and the memory a lifetime.

My attention was captured by Tich, hard to resist in his silky hot pink shirt and heavy gold bracelets. We sat on the sofa in the hotel lobby and chatted, his arm draped casually around me as he took drawn-out puffs of his cigarette. He was just so cool. Tich played guitar and strummed mandolin and flamenco guitar on all their hit records. When Tich wrote down his London address and insisted I visit, I swooned. I was 17 and blossoming. All the guys in the bands I met never made lurid suggestions or came on too strong.

There was little doubt that I was a groupie, but I remained innocent, at least in body. That was put to the test in 1968, when I met suave Paul Jones, headlining with The Who. When he snuggled up beside me on the lounge in the hotel lobby, I had to suppress the urge to mount him. Paul however remained a true gentleman.

He looked great in the black T-shirt I bought him as a gift from my university, The University of New South Wales. *Scientia Corde Manu et Mente* was their motto, Latin for 'Knowledge by Heart, Hand and Mind'. If my hands had acted on what my mind was thinking, Paul was unlikely to have emerged unscathed.

There was a definite magnetic aura about Paul Jones, one that made him stand out. On a previous tour in January 1965, Paul had performed as the singer for the band Manfred Mann and even then he stood out from the rest. As he sang, there I was walking down the street in my short mini, looking fab and looking fine, singing 'Do Wah Diddy Diddy'. The mood was uplifting and a whole lot of fun.

Another British group who oozed sex appeal were the Kinks, who hit the UK charts with 'Tired of Waiting'. They had it all. Sheer grit, pounding beats and taut pelvis. They *really* got to me and most of the girls on the planet. On their way to Australia, the band stopped in Singapore, where the fans became so frenetic that the police fired warning shots into the air. They were an attractive lot and their music generated a high-octane response. In person, when they looked into my eyes and signed their names, they were hypnotic.

Unlike the other bands, the Small Faces, on a later tour, seemed aloof. They had reason to be. The Australian press berated them, having a field day with shock headlines. Excited fans, dressed as mods, screamed as the revolving stage at Sydney Stadium stopped turning, leaving half of the audience with a back view. When a gang outside their hotel tried to hassle the band, the thugs fled when confronted by the wild drummer of the Who, Keith Moon.

The Who was the headline act for that 1968 concert, which included Paul Jones and the Small Faces. An incident on a plane from Adelaide to Sydney, mild by today's standards, had them vowing never to return to Australia. Add arrests, confrontations with the press, and Keith Moon chucking a snare drum out the window of his hotel room in Melbourne, then the battle was on. A telegram from the then Prime Minister, John Gorton, warned them never to set foot in Australia again, and it took almost 40 years for them to do so.

Despite what proved to be a disastrous tour, Roger Daltrey, the lead singer of the band, was ever so polite when we met in the lobby of the Sheraton in Sydney, as were bassist John Entwistle and brilliant songwriter and lead guitarist Pete Townshend. Their songs remain rock classics, including 'My Generation' and 'Pinball Wizard'. Their track 'I Can See for Miles' became a hit again in 2024.

While the rest of the band seemed staid by comparison, drummer Keith Moon was as crazed as his reputation. Moon was a rock legend, considered to be one of the top drummers of all time. He was not only super cool but also completely out of control. A touch of madness is often the prerequisite of musical genius, separating the great from the ordinary. Moon's eccentricity was reflected in the planets when he was born, for each acted as a mirror to his soul.

My passion for astrology provided incredible insights, even in my early years. Moon's birth chart was loaded with high-voltage energy and a path fraught with challenges. Erratic Mercury, the ruler of the mind, joined forces with destructive Pluto in Leo when he was born, prompting dark thoughts and extremities of behaviour. Morbid Saturn close by added a layer of depression, a bitter pill to swallow.

This heavy combination triggered spurts of vandalism, for which he was renowned. Moon often smashed his drum kit on stage and destroyed hotel rooms while on tour, hurling TVs out the window and blowing up toilets with dynamite. With these outrageous acts was Moon trying to shut the door to a troubled mind rather than risk falling back into the dark Plutonic hole from which he struggled to break free? It was a confronting combination to deal with.

The planet of music, Neptune, locked in the sky with dynamic Mars, meant its fiery energy was pumped into his drums which he often destroyed, detonating explosives on stage. Moon had to vent this volatile force so as not to self-destruct. The unstable planet Uranus, linked to his present lifetime, pushed him to the edge. It seemed like there was never enough time and the world just wasn't big enough to contain these extreme bursts of energy.

For a split second, and a tiny fracture in the universe, our energy attuned. Keith put his head on my shoulder and our planetary merging struck a mighty chord. Despite his showy antics, with four planets in the sign of love, Libra, including Venus and Jupiter, squaring a sensitive moon in Cancer, he was a man with lots of love to give, albeit distorted. Tuning into my Libra essence, he grabbed my autograph book and in a rare act, he dedicated his love to me.

I spread the love by gifting my university's T-shirts to each member of the Who. Roger Daltrey's signature, thanking me from the band, was appreciation enough. My heart soared when I saw Keith Moon strut on stage wearing the black T-shirt with the university logo. Part of me was on that stage with him and there could be no greater glory for this was one band that left a lasting impression.

The Who are English rock legends considered one of the most influential rock bands of the 20th century. Their music struck a mighty chord with millions of fans, opening the door to an inner vault of the senses and reflecting the exciting mood of the times.

Keith Moon died at 32, leaving behind a grand legacy and one more broken heart. He was inducted into my Rock and Roll Hall of Fame and his page in my autograph book remains one of my most prized possessions. His signature is rare and highly sought after. Our photograph together, head to head, is even rarer, for we shared a fleeting bond. To this day, memories surface as I scan my autograph book, which remains a fabulous catalogue of my youth.

The British invasion in the 1960s infiltrated not only the mind but also the soul of its time. The music was electric, almost orgasmic, because it reached an untouched part of the body and spirit, incredibly pure and wanting. The collective brilliance shone light upon the earth, rousing the mood of the times and eclipsing the long shadow of the Vietnam War. The bands who shaped it were mesmerising, carving the '60s into a definitive period of history.

It was not only the talent but also the electricity of the times. So many of us wish we could relive them and still have the bodies to dance as we once did. To see life, once more, through a psychedelic lens. As much as we would like to turn back time, to relive those wonderful moments, the clock rarely goes backwards. Unless, like me, you want to escape the wrath of an overprotective father after a hectic night out at Kings Cross, for a 16-year-old girl in the 1960s.

CHAPTER TWO

HAPPILY NEVER AFTER

I blame it on Uranus. Blazing bright in the middle of the heavens when I was born, it fed my craving for excitement and change. I was never good at keeping jobs or staying in one place for long. Easily bored, I liked a challenge. Born an air sign, learning was my passion and knowledge my goal, hoping to enjoy myself along the way.

Between semesters at university, I held a string of casual jobs but none lasted long. My first position was with The Australian Record Company, filling order forms mindlessly. I whizzed through my stack and then asked for more, and more.

My supervisor was not impressed. He cautioned me not to be so speedy and show up long-time employees. It reminded me of primary school when I was sent on messages so I did not outshine the others in my class. This lot frowned upon me too so after a few weeks of restraint, like a bolting horse tied to a heavy cart, I handed in my notice. It was a precedent for the future.

The next step on the career ladder was a job at Curzons Department store. Located on Pitt Street in the heart of Sydney, it is long since gone. I was placed in the Manchester section where I learnt to fold towels, a skill that remained with me for the rest of my days. It was probably the most useful job I ever had. There are only so many towels you can fold before you get bored, so I left for bigger and better things. A thirsting mind needs stimulation.

It was off to Horwitz Publications in North Sydney, the publisher of popular pulp fiction books. Keen to make an impression, it was not the one I was hoping for. My boss Cynthia came looking for me one day in the warehouse while I was searching for some titles.

The guys there, joking around, offered me a ride on the forklift platform and Cynthia was halfway down the stairs when I zoomed around the corner raised to her height. She was not impressed, her face as red as a beetroot, and needless to say, I was fired.

I was equally erratic in the boyfriend department but things were about to change. It all began in a basement nightclub in Martin Place in the city. After stumbling down darkened stairs, a table was chosen around the dancefloor. Each table was complete with a pole, and a lit-up number. With telephones on the tables, you dialled the number of anyone you fancied, avoiding the humiliation of walking across the floor. If your phone rang you squinted to get a look at your caller, then feigned indifference or a huge sigh of relief.

That's how I met Peter. It is often a convoluted path to love, and Pete was one of four friends, young British guys, who immigrated to Australia under the 'Ten Pound Pom' plan. It was part of the Assisted Passage Migration Scheme that over a million Britons took advantage of between 1945 and 1982, in a bid by the government to populate the vast continent of Australia with a workforce.

After I went out with Pete a few times, he took me to his unit in the eastern suburbs where I met two of his mates from the mother country, Fred and George. It took a while for the third one to emerge. Love at first sight is a curious thing. One look at Luke and the hair on the back of my neck stood up, along with a surge of feelings.

I had fallen into lust several times but love was another matter. Granted Luke was British and looked like Paul McCartney, but he was also intelligent, polished, and well-spoken, as only the British can be. He often corrected my use of the English language because he went to the Chislehurst and Sidcup Grammar School for boys in Kent, apparently akin to Eton. I thought I was quite clever up till then, but there was room for improvement.

So began a roller-coaster of romance. Slow dancing to Otis Redding's 'I've Been Loving You Too Long' was sultry enough to melt into Luke's arms. It was a turning point, from a carefree and wild teenager to a young woman on the path of maturity. Love was a serious matter, one that required commitment and devotion.

In the final year of my degree, it was fortunate that the boys lived close to my university. I hated driving the long distance each day from my home on the north shore. To cope I rose at 5 am to miss the morning traffic on the Harbour Bridge. Scooting off in my mint green Morris Mini, crunching the long gear stick, I often overshot the toll booth on the bridge, forcing the toll man to run after me.

Arriving far too early, I studied in my car to pass the time before classes began. Close by was Randwick racecourse and the horses trotted by for their morning exercise, steam on a frosty day flaring from their nostrils. I found my Psychology course interesting while my second major, History, concentrated on Australia and parts of Asia, and I didn't realise the significance until later in life.

Sociology was lost on me. Most of the time was spent sketching palm trees during lectures and dreaming of greater things. Close to exam time I realised how little I knew on the subject. A painful case of shingles on my face, stress-induced, confined me to bed, and I was able to defer the final exam till I was better versed.

An Arts degree required one science subject, and my choice was History and Philosophy of Science. It included a little stargazing and astronomy, so I was in my element. It was my fascination with stars, both earthly and heavenly, that fired my imagination.

My bedroom had been transformed from a sprawl of pop royalty to the boudoir of a wandering spirit. I painted a large mural of my zodiac sign, Libra, on one wall and next to my bed, I pinned up postcards of P&O cruise ships. Wedged between my love of astrology and the ocean, I conjured up a fabulous future.

The call of the sea remained with me all my life. There was little socialising on campus, as many students were too academic. My one good friend was Sue. Her only flaw, as an Aquarian, was her weak ankles, and I was kept busy picking her up from the pavement when one gave way, or off the gravel at the nearby hot dog stand.

Sue indulged my love of the ocean by meeting me at Sydney Harbour whenever a cruise ship was in port. In those days, before I met Luke, passes were available to visit the ship and it was on board P&O UK's *Oriana* that I first met British crewman Chris. He fed my lust for travel, writing me letters from foreign ports, firing my imagination. There was so much I wanted to do and so much to see.

I took Luke home to meet my mum and dad just before my graduation. They were relieved, as the only guy I'd taken home before was Sammy, one of the few Asians on campus in the late '60s. Sammy was Malaysian Chinese, hip and long-haired, and right outside their comfort zone. Unsure of how to act, they adapted and over the years they got used to and accepted my diverse preferences.

Luke was attractive and polite and looked and acted like the perfect son-in-law. Never mind that Luke was Christian because my father had become an atheist, and an angry one at that. At worst, when he was troubled by horrific scenes of the past, he yelled, *'There is no God! Where was God in Auschwitz?'* venting his rage by hurling the odd plate or two. His memories were locked away and he would never speak of them. There was nothing to be said. No response eased his pain or caused a dent in his armour. My mother teetered on the edge of a deep depression, a wall of books on the Holocaust a testimony of her lifetime obsession.

My home could be tragic and being with Luke calmed my soul. Luke was self-assured, the product of a loving family and a 'normal' upbringing. I was unsure what *normal* was, having never experienced it, but I was sure my family did not fall into that category. Ironically, the first lecture of my Psychology course was on the subject, 'What is normal?' There never was a right answer.

Holocaust survivors were rarely going to be normal, the numbers tattooed on their forearms a reminder of the torture they endured. Then again, their fractured emotional responses would be deemed 'normal' for those who endured such brutality. It was a deep wound and like a cancer, it spread insidiously through the soul.

After graduating from university, Luke and I got engaged. There was no formal marriage proposal, romantic overture or bending down on one knee. Rather we drifted into it, as if it was just a matter of time. We celebrated our engagement in the function room at the North Sydney Leagues club and on the night the place was buzzing with friends and laughter. I felt elegant in black with a long silver jacket while Luke was the epitome of the English gentleman in his well-fitting suit, with his soft green eyes and perfect smile.

The following year Luke went through the daily paces of his job as a public servant while I accepted my first teaching assignment.

With a shortage of teachers, university graduates were accepted without a teaching diploma. I was appointed to a boys' high school, a long bus, train, and bus ride to the west. Even worse was the fact that I was to teach Economics and Business Principles, subjects I had never studied in my life and didn't have a clue about.

It was overwhelming, especially in a boys' high school where some students were only a few years younger than me. Reaching desperation point, I marched into the Principal's office advising him that his Leaving certificate students would fail if they kept me on.

That afternoon, when I got home, exhausted from the trip and flooded with anxiety, a telegram was waiting. I had been relocated to a girls' high school close to my home. What an enormous relief.

I loved my new school. No matter their grade or level, the girls wanted to learn. I was in my element, teaching Social Sciences and Geography. I brought the lessons to life, plunging my students into the jungles of South America or the arid desert of the Sahara. Learning should be fun and I did my best to inspire the girls on so many different levels. They reciprocated with their enthusiasm.

1970 was a good year. My career was rewarding, and I had found my calling in teaching. It was also the year that Luke and I married. As a couple of mixed faith, neither of us religious, our wedding took place in the Registry Office in Sydney, with our family and friends present. I wore an emerald green mini, its hemline skimming the bounds of decency, with a cream crochet vest, while Luke looked gallant in his suit. It was a perfect backdrop for the confetti showered on us as we walked down the stairs, onto the street.

No way would I let my wedding go by without a touch of romance, so we celebrated that evening in the posh Blue Room of the Menzies Hotel. All glittering chandeliers and silver service, the buffet was superb. Changing into my flowing long white wedding dress, specially made in the style of Juliet who had found her Romeo, I danced with my husband and celebrated with our friends. When I looked at the photos of the night, it was the one when I danced with my father that struck me most because he was smiling at last, genuinely happy.

Our honeymoon was spent on Lord Howe Island. Taking off in a seaplane, we skimmed through the water heading for a touch of paradise. Listed as a World Heritage site, this rich volcanic remnant is the world's most southern true coral reef. Rich with subtropical forests, its sandy beaches were tinged with the clearest blue ocean. As we waded through the turquoise water, studded with coral, colourful fish swam around our feet. In the throes of passion, we climbed the slope of a mountain and made out, as lovers often do.

Next on our wish list was a world trip so Luke could reunite with his family. He sorely missed them and I would meet them for the first time. My students were heartbroken when I told them that I was leaving and they showered me with love and gifts.

A few days before I left there was constant knocking on my staffroom door. A deluge of flowers, cards, homemade cakes, and other gestures of appreciation spread across the desks. All the teachers came to look, never having witnessed this outpouring of affection before, and the principal was beside herself because many of the students were crying in the playground. I was greatly touched.

My exam class all passed with top honours and they wrote letters of thanks to me, as well as the congratulations I received from the department head. One class performed a play they had written for me which was so moving. With a heavy heart, I left my beloved students, but the image of their faces remains entrenched within me.

A few weeks later we set sail for London. As a Sagittarius, Luke gave in to my desire to cruise to England taking the long way to see some of the world. On board P&O's *Arcadia,* we set sail from Sydney to the UK, across the Pacific to Tahiti and Hawaii, up to Vancouver, and through the Panama Canal to the island gems of Bermuda and the Bahamas in the Caribbean. There were two classes on the ship, remnants of a bygone era, and we splurged and booked first class. On board, we snuck through the iron gate to the tourist section because they seemed to be having more fun down there and Luke did not need to wear a tuxedo.

When we reached Southampton after six weeks, Luke's parents were standing on the docks waiting for us. His mum embraced him for the longest time and welcomed me into the fold. His father was rather more detached but an extremely decent man. When we arrived at their home in Kent, it was cups of tea and biscuits and long talks, with his mum showing me photo albums of Luke at different stages of his life. He was cute as a baby and even cuter now. When his lovely sister Sally turned up we had an instant connection.

After weeks spent reminiscing with Luke's family and friends, we drove through the English countryside, past green meadows, visiting historic sites along the way. Medieval castles drenched in fields of bluebells and daffodils, grand cathedrals, writers and poets of old, and a powerful monarchy all attested to its power.

The country's spiritual presence stood out, dating back to the mystical tales of Merlin, King Arthur and his knights, and the mystery of Stonehenge. A Taurus country, with its national day on April 23, it was blessed with the musical genius of singers and groups who changed the world. Till today it remains a source of incredible talent.

A few months passed before we headed off to explore Europe. In the trail of many Aussie expats, we bought a VW campervan and crossed the English Channel by ferry to France. Of the wonders to unfold as we traversed the continent, apart from the splendid and diverse scenery, were the amazing works of art. Sprawling galleries showcased a treasury of beauty, and statues created by master sculptors mirrored each unique culture with its distinctive history and heritage. Australia was such a raw country by comparison.

As always with travel, there were a few incidents along the way, including the theft from our van on an isolated road in Italy, and the turbulent night the van shook so hard that its canvas roof almost ripped off in the wake of the strong mistral winds in southern France.

Then came the heated argument that caused Luke to hit a pothole at speed in the Greek countryside. We spent the next hour combing through fields of red poppies, looking for the four hubcaps that flew off in his rage. The rug I crocheted a different colour for each country we drove through was lost long ago but the memories remain. So many others vied to take their place over the years.

To complete our circumnavigation of the globe, we boarded the *Fairstar*, a Sitmar liner transformed from troop carrier to cruise ship in 1964, to return to Sydney from Southampton. Our first port of call was sunny Tenerife in the Canary Islands, part of Spain. Then we skimmed down the west African coast, round the Cape of Good Hope to Cape Town, perched beneath the iconic Table Mountain.

What I witnessed in the city of Durban, at the time of Apartheid, was distressing. Luke and I felt uneasy as we sat on a bench in the park, labelled *Whites Only*, and drank from separate bubblers, among other obvious signs of racial discrimination. This was not a state I was used to and sensitive to the similar plight of the Jews in the past, it left me feeling regretful and apologetic. That's what travel does. It's a journey into the recesses of the human mind.

Our trip ended when we reached Sydney and even though the excitement was over, it was good to be back home. The first to greet me was my fluffy black cat, Pippa. She was a rescue from the RSPCA and was a wise old soul. Years before, on the way to her new home, she sat on my lap in her carrier for the long trip on the double-decker bus. At the time I still lived with my parents, and our home was on the edge of a bushland retreat. Pippa hid among the bushes but when I called her she always ran up two flights of stairs and jumped into my arms. Pippa was my soul animal.

My mother loved her gentle spirit while my father feigned indifference but secretly grinned when the cat poked her head around the corner to see him walking down the hall and beat a hasty retreat. Pippa followed me wherever I moved, from city life to country barn, she came along for the ride. Her final resting place was under her favourite lemon tree in the family garden, in her own special spot.

The first home Luke and I moved into in 1971 was a lovely terrace house in the desirable suburb of Glebe Point. Central and near the water, the location was perfect. We bought it for the measly sum of $11,900 which today seems inconceivable. Pippa loved it because she could run down the hallway and skid around the corner, competing with the little dog that lived on the other side of the wall.

The house became a place of mixed feelings, and months later, my heart was wrenched from my chest when I woke up one morning in a pool of blood. I had miscarried our first child and, with Luke close by my side, I was rushed to hospital. Mourning the loss, I had time to introspect. Was being a teacher enough or did I need my own children to feel fulfilled? In the years to come, the decision was made for me. My life was meant for a different purpose.

After two years, we sold our house and moved into a leafy area in the northern suburbs. With several large gum trees and a huge garden, we added to our menagerie with a small white poodle, named Loopy Loo. It suited her greatly because she was forever running in circles and driving Pippa nuts. I spent my days decorating our home and learning how to cook. I became adept at preparing a good meal and a delicious cream caramel dessert. On the surface I was happy but something deep inside me was restless.

That feeling was nothing compared to those stirring in Luke. He was holding on by a thread. His job had become mundane and he missed his family greatly. The horsemen of Sagittarius are restless creatures, so after a difficult year, Luke snapped and chose the easy way out, devastating me in the process. He simply disappeared.

That morning, he dropped me off in the city to shop. Then he turned the car around and drove back home. He took his passport, cleared out his belongings, and then vanished. He did not even leave a note. *Gone without a word.* Our relationship was sound, and we were still very much in love, so I deserved much better.

All that was left for me was heartbreak. The humiliation of reporting him as missing to the police, a half-renovated house with mortgage payments, little money, two pets who depended on us, a wife who loved him and a minefield of despair. I had no clue where he was. The cascade of tears I shed drained my soul dry and I was spent. There was nothing left and I felt empty inside.

Weeks later a postcard from Luke arrived from Bali, explaining that he 'needed to find himself'. From there, he flew back to

England. Soon after he bombarded me with letters, drenched in kisses, begging me to join him. I stood firm, playing by my own rules.

Was it worth trying to salvage our marriage? The man I thought I knew seemed so far from reality, and Luke had crushed me. I was young and naïve and believed in the power of love to overcome anything, not yet familiar with the brutal toll love can inflict. I doubted that I could ever forgive Luke for such a massive betrayal.

Taking a job in a solicitor's office, I saved up and then booked passage on a ship to England, through Asia, to see some of the world along the way. On a cold grey day in London, Luke and I finally reunited but our spark had dimmed and the trust was gone.

Months later, we returned to Australia to try to revive our marriage but our efforts were wasted, as we went through the motions of what might have been. Once trust is lost, it can never be regained. Eventually, we decided to part and go our own way. It was time to carve out a new life but I had no idea what direction it would take.

.

CHAPTER THREE

LIVING IN THE SEVENTIES

Ah, the 1970s. Not a patch on the '60s but the decade still had its moments. I answered an ad for a room in a shared apartment in Mosman, right on the water. It turned out to be on the top floor of a grand old house with sweeping views over Sydney Harbour. From the white sails of the newly completed Opera house to a glimpse of the Harbour bridge it was ideal. All that for the princely sum of $22 per week, the price for a piece of paradise in the mid-70s.

The two guys I shared the flat with were friendly and very laid-back. In the mood of the times, nothing seemed too urgent or dramatic. The group of hippies who lived next door came over occasionally to sit in a circle and pass around some weed but I never indulged. It was not my scene but it suited the rest well, making them even more mellow than before.

Walking down a steep hill, I caught the ferry across to the city for my new job with an overseas shipping company. Their office was near the Rocks, overlooking any visiting cruise ship. It gave me the perfect vantage point and I never tired of the streamers and fond farewells as the ship set sail, and the excitement was contagious.

My supervisor at work was the delightful Sarah who taught me the correct procedures and protocol. There was an instant rapport between us because Sarah possessed an abundant spirit and a wicked sense of humour. We ate lunch each day together and talked incessantly. It's amazing how kindred souls lurk in the corridors of life, just waiting for the right cue to make an entrance. It may be a temporary bond or prove lifelong.

Sarah's cousin, Helen, soon became part of our entourage. The artistic type, she was vulnerable and gifted. Sarah was all science, Helen was all creativity, and I was somewhere in between. We formed a gang of sorts. Most weekends I stayed at Sarah's place, a lovely unit on the cliffs of Tamarama with a stunning view of the ocean and the sound of crashing waves on the rocks. I loved that Sarah indulged herself, her unit was always full of beautiful flowers and large bowls of fruit. She was a woman who knew her worth.

Each Saturday we headed off for a night on the town. We loved to have a good time, so we named our group after the seal on the dashboard of Helen's car, the Rootes Group. In keeping with our crazy spirit, we changed our names each week, always part of a theme. Gemstones were our favourite. Sarah chose Ruby, Helen a sensitive Pearl, while I stuck to Topaz. It was the birthstone for the sign of Scorpio, where my Venus was firmly placed.

Our night spot of choice was the Bondi Lifesaver, at its peak in the 1970s. It was the hip place to be and listen to great Aussie bands like Skyhooks, AC/DC, Little River Band, Cold Chisel, Dragon and the super hip blues and rock band, Jo Jo Zep and the Falcons. The venue was always packed and the music was thumping – the epitome of life in that era. 'It's a Long Way to the Top (If You Wanna Rock 'n' Roll)' as we all know, and a slow descent, and a slippery slope, on the 'Highway to Hell' for those who don't make it.

I scored a coup one night when I chatted with one of the band's singers, whose identity remains my secret, and he ended up coming home with us. Crammed into Helen's car we headed for the cliffs of Tamarama. I spent the night in deep conversation with him and although we shared a bed, we took it no further. I was in my mid-twenties, no longer a naive teenager, and mature enough to make my own decisions. It was not always about sex but rather a sensual merging of the minds and an exciting exchange of energy.

The following morning, my rock star left with scarcely a word and was spotted walking along the cliffs heading to Bondi but alas he was heading in the *wrong* direction. Helen, who worked at an advertising firm as a graphic artist, sent me a mock-up of the band with my photo pasted in the middle, so for a moment in time I was an honorary band member. My life was a cavalcade of postcards, from the whimsical to the bizarre.

The group split up in years to come and the singer was the headline act at the Star Theatre on the Gold Coast where I made my home later in life. I waited till he came out after the show to meet his fans. I reminded him of the escapade and he jokingly yelled out 'Remember Tamarama!' several times. It was obvious that he had forgotten but he was forgiven. The night meant more to me because no doubt he had many memorable nights. Mine were far more precious and, thankfully, there were plenty of good times still to come.

In 1975, I took the next step on my life journey and enrolled in a teaching diploma course at Sydney Teachers' College, a requirement to teach Primary and Infant school. This had been denied to me previously because candidates with a bachelor's degree were considered overqualified for these grades. Attending the lectures, I went through the motions, but there was little sense of connection with my fellow students or socialising of any kind.

As part of the course, one day a week was spent at a primary school doing teaching practice. My goal was to open up endless possibilities and in one lesson I used psychedelic eyeglasses from the '60s, one emerald green Perspex, the other pretty in pink, as my props. Each student, in turn, was asked to put them on and imagine they had crossed over into a make-believe world of their own creation. As they shared their vision, each one fascinating, I recall the smile on the inspector's face as she sat in the back of the room.

I was set to discover my own magical realm after attending the John Denver concert at the Horden Pavilion in the same year, 1975. His music was mellow, his words meaningful and his voice lush like a mountain in springtime. I was so moved that I relapsed into the 1960s and turned up at his hotel the following day.

The Sebel Townhouse was buzzing with activity, the lobby full of eager fans waiting to catch a glimpse of John. Being one of the pack was not my style. Outside the hotel, it was just as frantic. Media were grabbing their equipment out of cars to attend a scheduled press conference. There was a lot of controversy surrounding the tour, with the dreaded word 'marijuana' being bandied around. It was the frantic '70s and the press wanted a scoop.

It was time to be resourceful and come up with a plan. Checking out the news crews, I decided on the ABC because they looked the most amenable. Without hesitation, I walked over to their car and asked, 'Can I come into the press conference with you?'

The cameraman looked sceptical 'Only if you're press.'

'Yes,' I said, thinking fast. 'Sydney University Press.' Currently studying at the Teacher's College there, it was a somewhat authentic if not accurate version of the truth.

'You can try.' It was obvious from the man's look that I had little to no chance. It was worth a go, so I headed in with them.

To add validity to my cause, I pressed against their sound equipment as I reached the door of the press conference, where a rather officious woman stood, brandishing a list. I knew this would be a test of my *chutzpah*, a term in Hebrew that meant gall, nerve and supreme self-confidence. You couldn't get far in life without it.

'ABC?' she asked, assuming I was with the rest.

'Yes, Sydney University Press,' I replied, taking on the stance of a hardened reporter. The university's motto in Latin couldn't have been more apt: *'Sidere mens eadem mutato.'* 'The stars change but the mind remains the same.' Spot on! The coat of arms bore a lion for courage, an open book for learning, and stars. Perfect.

'Go through,' she said, the door opening to an alternate reality.

All the camera crews were setting up their gear so I rummaged through my handbag looking for something that would give me credibility. All I could come up with was a small notebook and a pen. Looking rather conspicuous, I was unsure of my next move.

Just as I considered making a run for it, John Denver's manager walked into the room. 'John won't be long' he announced. 'He's on the phone to his wife, Annie. When he comes in, you will each have the chance to interview him, one at a time. No rushing.'

Shivers. Now I would surely be exposed. Looking for the closest exit, I was blocked when the door opened, and John walked in. A trail of moondust followed him into the room. One by one each of the reporters interviewed him and then left. To get out of the way, I stood beside John and stared at him, pretending to look at a spot on the ceiling. The time of reckoning was getting closer as each of the film crews left and I was the only one left standing in the room.

The manager eyed me suspiciously and asked his aide, 'Who's that girl?'

As there were no words to explain my presence, I confessed. 'I was at your concert last night, John, and I simply love you.' The manager looked irate until John leaned over and gave me a giant hug. I could feel the love pumping through me. I was in the presence of greatness and it sure felt good. Then John turned and waved as he walked away. The cloud I had been floating on drifted from the layers of mortal earth to a place far, far away.

Alas, John's life ended on 12 October 1997, when the plane he was flying plunged into the Pacific Ocean. His was a turbulent lifetime of depression and alcohol abuse but the songs he wrote touched many lives with their sensitivity and poetry. Beneath a troubled soul lay a heart of sunshine and he *finally* did leave on a jet plane.

The evening after the press conference, I was glued to the TV, changing from one channel to the next. I freaked out when I realised that I'd been standing next to John the whole time and now my face was blown up next to his in all the news reports.

It could have been my path to stardom in the right circumstances except that I had made up an excuse rather than attend my weekly one-day teaching practice at the school. Hopefully, no one was watching the news, on *any* of the channels. My hopes were dashed when I arrived at school the next week.

A group of girls ran up to me in the playground, shrieking 'Miss, miss, you were with John Denver last week!' When I tried to convince them otherwise, hoping to salvage my reputation, they were having none of it. 'But miss, you're wearing the same dress.'

Sprung, I basked in the notoriety that only fame can bring. I was only one of two who received a distinction for teaching at the end of the year, so maybe the inspector was watching the news too! Perhaps I got top marks for initiative, and the ability to reach for the stars.

No matter the year, my love of music never wavered so I included it in my lessons. When I was appointed to my first position as an infants' teacher in an inner-city school, it became part of my program for my Grade 2 class. With 42 students aged seven, and 30 boys among them, many of whom had limited English, it was no mean feat to keep them focused. Music was the key.

Using my 'magic bell' the tinkle reminded them that it was quiet time to concentrate on their work unlike the class next door which was running riot. Each day notes were left on my desk, praising my writing on the board or how lovely I looked and other sweet messages. Each child was delightful and unique, coming from a variety of backgrounds and cultures. During breaks when I was on duty in the playground, I had rings of children circling me, making it difficult to walk. They were an absolute joy to teach.

In 1977, Abba mania hit Australia and my class sang along to 'Mama Mia' and other hits, creating a happy vibe in the classroom and opening up a world of possibilities. Their voices sounded angelic when they sang 'Fernando', for there *was* something special in the air at the time, and the stars *were* shining bright.

CHAPTER FOUR

THE LITTLE GYPSY

The only reminder, a keepsake, of my childhood, is not a doll, teddy bear, or blanket. Rather it is a small book, carefully wrapped in brown paper, with a cut-out picture pasted on the front cover of a young girl staring out into the distance, over green fields and valleys. Gazing far into the unknown, she was yearning to begin her journey. The title of the book is *The Little Gypsy*.

After several years of teaching, I grew restless and the lure of adventure and travel beckoned once more. My next trip was planned for Noumea, the capital of New Caledonia, an island group in the Pacific under French sovereignty. It turned out to be a brief holiday with a friend from college, Jody, cut even shorter by a pilots' strike.

We still elected to go even though it meant only four days on the island. *Best four days ever.* On the first day, while lying on the beach opposite a topless bar, I was approached by a man who whisked down over the sand while Jody was swimming. 'How would you like a job?' he asked, gesturing to the topless bar. Buxom was not the norm for the French, who were often of slight build, far less round and with more panache. Busty, I was something of a find but I refused his offer, considering it not a good career choice.

That night we went to a rather posh casino. Jody was slim in a straight black gown while I wore a silky long dress, patterned in yellow magnolias. We proved quite a hit. Approached by a sophisticated gent named Yves, in a white tuxedo, I sat beside him as he played blackjack. He bought me drinks while professing that I was his good luck token. It was a chic night, straight out of a James Bond movie, and something I could get used to.

The next day, in a small bus coming back from town to the hotel, Jody and I were squeezed in next to several Aussie reporters on the island covering a friendly yacht race between two contenders for the America's Cup. They invited us on board the favourite the following day for the race. I was in my element sailing around the island with the wind in my hair, inhaling the salty scent of the Pacific, along with lively company and interesting conversation.

That night we attended the trophy ceremony held at the yacht club, the memory blurred by the steamy events that followed. One of the reporters, Steve, was an attractive man and we hit it off immediately. After some mild flirting and witty conversation, we went for a stroll along the beach. Moonlight and magic, the soothing sound of the waves and a charming escort. It was an affair to remember, one that crossed the ocean to continue back home in Sydney.

Over the years my interest in astrology grew and apart from personal research, I completed a correspondence course from the Faculty of Astrological Studies in London. The more I learnt with each birth chart reading, the more intrigued I became. My birth chart revealed that astrology was not a new study for me, but rather one drawing on experience in past lives. It was reawakening an old spark.

Especially fascinating were the planetary lines that tied one to certain places in the world. My Venus line ran through the Pacific and the islands of New Caledonia, an optimum place for romance. Cruising became my passion and on one cruise we berthed in Noumea, arriving in the morning and leaving late at night. Sifting through the market, I stopped to check out some trendy gear when a young attractive French guy emerged from the back.

With the bluest eyes and cheekiest smile, Jean-Claude started a conversation and then asked if he could take me to dinner that night, offering to bring a friend if another lady on the ship would care to join us. I didn't hesitate. Others did. When I asked some of the ladies I befriended on the cruise, they were too cautious and missed a great opportunity based on suspicion that it would end badly.

It certainly didn't. After a delicious meal, we drove to the top of a hill and, with the ship in the bay below us, its lights competing with the twinkling of the stars, we slow danced. Mood music oozed from the car's radio, an invitation to make out. How could you resist in such a setting, with a gorgeous French man with the firmest body, pressed against yours? The men back home lacked his charm and finesse, and musky scent, and there was no mutual attraction.

Here, in this romantic setting, I flared back to life. It might have gone further if it was not for the smoke billowing from the ship's funnel, ready to set sail. The car tore down the road and I just made it on board. Jean-Claude rang me when he arrived in Sydney months later but it wasn't the same without the magic and moonlight.

A year later, I revisited Noumea as the first stop on a world trip. It was meant to be a quick layover but I ended up staying longer. It was written in the stars because my Venus line, the path of the planet of romance on a world map, was firmly planted in the Pacific close to these islands. It went into overdrive once again when I arrived there, but this time it was more one-sided, full of angst.

In Noumea, I met Maurice, a Kanak – a dark Melanesian race, who was hopelessly in love with someone else. He was as intense as he was complicated. Mine was an infatuation, fed by trips to hidden waterfalls and him strumming the guitar to the sounds of nature, as he mourned his lost love. It was morose and I wrote brooding songs, *in French*, which made them ultimately more meaningful.

You have not suffered until you have suffered in French.

I carried my malaise on the wings of a plane heading for Los Angeles where I met Helen to begin a minivan tour across America. LA was intimidating, my first taste was someone being pounced on and arrested at the airport. Then the bus driver, armed with a belt full of lethal paraphernalia, leapt out of the bus at Venice beach and jumped on some guy in the park drinking booze from a bottle concealed in a paper bag, to make a 'citizen's arrest'. I was not getting peaceful vibes and was anxious to start on our tour.

The Grand Canyon was grand, followed by a noisy night at a campsite. Helen opened our tent flap and let the guys have it. Dragging her back before she could be terminated by a gang of Hell's Angels bikies, I was shocked by their response, 'Oh, sorry, ma'am. We'll keep it down.' Helen was impressive when she tried. Then I looked behind our tent, at a jeep full of park rangers, weapons at the ready. Enough said.

The trip across the US was fascinating with loads of interesting sights but there was no common bond or sense of connection. My favourite city was New Orleans with its great music and fun vibe. We went to a raging club where I met Randy, a deep-sea diver, and we enjoyed a wild flirtation that lasted through the night. It was great to add a crazy American to my list, but this time I wrote a poem in English in tribute to the night, not quite as thrilling as French!

New York was too overwhelming for me – the sensory overload and streams of people were more than I could handle. Helen loved the city, it appealed to her artistic side and stimulated her creativity. I needed somewhere infinitely more sedate, as England proved to be. Still close to Luke's sister, Sally, she and her family were always welcoming. I stayed with them for a while in their lovely home in Kent until the lure of London became too great.

My first employment agency sent me for a job interview as a receptionist in a boutique hotel in exclusive Belgravia, central to the city. It was a standing joke to send first-time job seekers there because the proprietress, Mrs Payne, was notoriously hard to please and very, very British. I rambled on about how competent I was every time she asked a question and impressed, she gave me the job, much to the shock of the agency staff.

There was an exclusive dining room in the hotel that attracted the elite and I loved escorting the distinguished guests through its doors. Even better, just around the corner at 33 Belgrave Square was the headquarters of The Spiritualist Association of Great Britain. Its mandate was to prove the existence of life after death, and among its members was Sir Arthur Conan Doyle, writer of Sherlock Holmes, with a profound interest in spiritualism. I often visited the centre for sessions with mediums, triggering a psychic connection.

Moving into a small room in the area, part of my work benefits, I'd walk through Victoria train station daily to get to the hotel. One day some brute punched me in the stomach as I entered a tunnel and the thrill began to fade. Reality stepped in with a vengeance. Mrs

Payne's façade began to crack as her racist comments became more pronounced. Shortly after I was fired for being too 'gay', my clothes were more 'Bali' than the preferred tweed and pearls. It was a blessed relief. I preferred gay to stoic and racist.

My next positions were infinitely more pleasant as an usher in several theatres in London's West End. I watched the movie *Paint Your Wagon* umpteen times, selling ice creams and humming my swan song 'I Was Born Under a Wandering Star' so often that it was implanted in my brain. I looked anything but glamorous in my lime green uniform but it was *theatre* so I was happy.

Had I known who left their imprint on the floorboards of the Dominion Theatre I would have been starstruck. In 1931 it hosted the London premiere of Charlie Chaplin's *City Lights* with the great star in attendance. In the 1950s, Bill Haley and the Comets opened their UK tour there and in 1957, the Judy Garland show ran for a month. Elizabeth Taylor was present in 1963 at the opening of *Cleopatra* which played for two years, while *The Sound of Music* set a record for the longest run of screenings at any venue in the world, over three years.

It was the place of stars. I was fortunate to see the great Gladys Knight and the Pips perform live and was ready to board her 'midnight train' to anywhere. At intermission, the theatre bar was so swamped I was called in to help. As a non-drinker, I had no idea about alcoholic beverages and so, sweaty and confused, I mixed up some strange brews as money was thrown at me in all directions. I simply guessed the price and no one appeared to be any the wiser.

Spurred on by the lure of adventure, I went to the open interviews in London for positions as Driver, Courier and Supercook for Contiki Tours. Their busy European tour schedule catered for the young market from all over the world. I applied to be a Supercook, who organised tour groups into teams, either shoppers, cooks or washer uppers, on a rotational basis during the trip. It sounded rather challenging but forever optimistic, I decided to give it a go.

Everyone at the venue looked young and exuberant and I felt like I was back competing with the leggy blondes at Surf City. When I was called into the office to meet the bosses, I was disarmed by a pair of boots poking out from under the desk. Unsure whether someone had passed out from the stress or it was just a visual prop, I carried on regardless. It turned out that the guy interviewing me was named Boots and it was his trademark.

Floored by the remark that at 26, I was older than they like, I sweetened the mix by adding that I was a bit of a psychic. 'Great,' Boots proclaimed, 'we'll take you on so you can go to our castle in France to check out if it's haunted! We've heard a few stories from groups of strange things happening there.' Now I was a ghostbuster as well as a Supercook. When I mentioned astrology, added to my list of duties was to organise bus teams into harmonious zodiac signs so they worked well together. These guys were ahead of their times.

Up for the challenge, I was sent to Holland to learn how to stir porridge and then assigned the Grand European tour with 50 hungry Aussies on board a coach for eight and a half weeks touring through most of the countries of Europe. Given the food kitty money for the entire length of the trip and having to decide how much to spend in each country, divided by the number of weeks, I was expected to change the amount into the local currency for the duration. It was daunting, especially when trying to change lira at an Italian bank.

The tour began in Paris and started reasonably well but when we reached the Beaujolais wine region in France and the Chateau

De Cruix, their 16th century castle, things got more interesting. Having imbibed too much local wine, some of the group ran wild. There were no bumps in the night or ghostly visions to scare them away. Let's face it, any self-respecting ghost, especially that of a French aristocrat, would have run for the hills as soon as this lot arrived. As for the thuds in the night and loud banging, it had more to do with the steamy antics of coach passenger Tootsie, a tall lean blonde who giggled constantly, and Tom, the over-sexed driver, than the moan of any errant spirit who had quickly vacated.

Things got more difficult by the time we reached Monaco. Who in their right mind would want to do the dishes instead of getting glammed up for a night at the Casino? Each country had its challenge and setting six shoppers loose in a Spanish hypermarket, a huge place with no signs in English, proved harrowing with our driver Tom getting increasingly irritated at the delay.

On another occasion, I was dropped off in the heart of Vienna while the bus parked far away. The only supermarket in sight was a small boutique one. The service was excellent and after shopping, five trolleys were pushed behind me on the pavement by smart young men in uniform, in an elegant conga line along the exclusive avenues of the stately city.

Arrival in Turkey was on a public holiday and we needed veggies. The only potatoes to be had were on the side of the road where a little old man, with a bent back, weighed each potato separately on his antique scales. Roland, our courier, was apoplectic at the wait.

On the Greek islands, I met my parents who were on their own travels. It was fortuitous because my mother stepped in to help one of our passengers who had a motorbike accident. With her credentials as an Australian government interpreter accepted by a Greek court, the young man was very lucky and was released.

My mother, a gifted Gemini, spoke eight languages fluently. I did not inherit her knack but understood a little Greek, even though I left as a toddler. My parents spoke Greek at home unless they didn't want me to overhear, and then they switched to Spanish. My schoolgirl French was only good enough to write tortured poetry and buy the occasional croissant in the French countryside.

On the tour, there were inevitable jealousies. Girls could be girls and guys could be jerks. On the overnight ferry crossing from Brindisi in Italy to Greece, several girls asked if I could help them meet some of the attractive Greek crew on the ship. Eager to please, I did so, but when the pick of the bunch whispered to the rest in Greek, 'That one's mine,' pointing to me, it was time to beat a hasty retreat. Handsome men meant trouble, the last thing I needed.

Istanbul had its moments too. When the tour bus arrived at the campsite, with its fixed tents, the manager Emir took a shine to me and asked me out to dinner. A little time out after a gruelling schedule of travel and stress was ideal. I got dressed and as I walked past the others, I could feel daggers pierce my back. It was a great evening – dinner and a belly dancing show. Great, except when the dancer crudely thrust me aside so she could sit on Emir's lap.

Afterwards, we drove to the top of a hill, and standing under the stars, Emir said, 'Look over there. That's Europe.' Then he turned me around. 'Now you're looking at Asia.' Perched on the dividing line between two continents, the world seemed much smaller.

When we returned to the campsite, Emir stayed in the car, parked to watch over me all night. After a few drinks, he wrote a note and slipped it into my tent, saying he would always protect me. It was an interesting, yet prophetic, choice of words.

How I made it back to London in one piece was a testament to human endurance. Laden down with heavy clogs, French perfume and other 'gifts' from outlets, I ditched the clogs before boarding the ferry back to London. After one night's sleep, I was informed my next trip was scheduled for the following day, another Grand European eight-week tour. I could barely get out of bed.

I lasted till our first stop in Paris, where the new group passed out in an alcoholic stupor in the campground. There was no getting this mob to do anything, so survival mode kicked in. Going to the closest pay phone, I rang the London office and told them to send a replacement. To my relief, I contacted my father's distant cousin in Paris and he invited me to stay in his home. Once there I fell asleep and didn't wake up for two days. They thought that I had died.

CHAPTER FIVE

TURNING POINT

With my spirit depleted more than my body, I returned to England to fill the void. At the British Spiritualist Association headquarters in London, a flyer for residential psychic courses at Arthur Findlay College caught my eye. After more than two months on a tour bus, it was exactly what I needed. It would be a relief to mix with people with a similar interest in the more evolved aspects of life.

The courses were held in a beautiful leafy setting – Stansted Hall in Essex, a perfect place to raise your consciousness. Once the country seat of the Earls of Essex, the property was later bequeathed by Arthur Findlay, a local magistrate who promoted spiritualism. He was the founder of The International Institute for Psychical Research and the newspaper *Psychic News*, and he left a grand legacy.

The stately manor house of Stansted Hall was set amongst rich lawns and sprawling oak trees. When I arrived for my course, 'Developing your Psychic Potential', I scored a charming room with a four-poster bed and a lovely view of the grounds. The first night proved restless, with lots of strange activity in the room. I was later advised that it was the province of a 'ghostly' guest.

Each of the sessions in the five-day course was fascinating but I remained reluctant to explore my psychic abilities. Perhaps I had been hung, or dumped into a creek, in medieval times, called a witch and ostracised, or worse. In England, witch trials were held from the 15th to the 18th century, and in Europe, close to 200,000 so-called witches met a gruesome end. I hoped I wasn't one of them.

I had been born into a family with a brutal history, one of racial persecution, and it was not a far stretch to believe that I had been hounded or suppressed in past lives for my psychic 'gifts'. I still felt uneasy about announcing them to the world for I had not yet truly acknowledged these powers in myself. Now it was time to begin.

It took a few days until I felt confident enough to enter a group circle, where spirits were being channelled. Rather than join in when I entered the room, I sat with two elderly ladies on a platform, who were engrossed in drawing their impressions. Comfortable with a pencil in my hand, I began to sketch, aware that it was intended for a man and his wife in the circle. They smiled in acknowledgement.

After each person in the circle gave a reading to the group, it was my turn. With all eyes upon me, I turned my drawing around for everyone to see. The couple it was intended for gasped. In the centre of the picture was a young lady, slightly veiled, who they identified as their daughter. Beside her I drew a large tree, its leaves missing with only bare branches. Beneath was a figure of the girl bowing in front of a vase of stalks with no flowers.

'I'm not sure what it means,' I stuttered. 'It's just barren.'

'Our daughter,' they replied, 'has just learnt that she can't have children. The family has been in turmoil and we are all so upset.'

Trying to interpret the drawing, I spoke as people in the room listened intently. 'There is only one apple hanging off the tree and it's gold. Yes, gold,' I repeated. 'The zodiac sign above her head, like the horns of a ram, stands for the sign of Aries.'

The couple looked even more amazed. 'Our surname is Gold,' they replied. 'Our daughter was born on March 29,' the man said checking with his wife, 'so she is an Aries.'

More bizarre were the two snakes I'd drawn, intertwined in battle. Then the wife blurted out, 'Her husband and her father,' giving him a pointed stare, 'have been fighting ever since they found out. What are those symbols above the snakes?'

'They are the signs of Leo and Libra combined to become one,' I replied. After some discussion, they confided, 'My husband is Leo and our son-in-law is Libra. That's amazing.'

They sat there stunned, as everyone in the circle started clapping. Overwhelmed by the applause, and all the attention, I wanted to sink into my chair. Then there was a knock on the door and the secretary walked in carrying a large bunch of red roses wrapped in cellophane, calling out my name. Then she walked over to me and handed me the bouquet. 'These are for you.'

Applause and flowers, in recognition of my psychic gifts. The flowers had been sent by an admirer – a young man who I spent time with earlier that week but who had to return to London. He confessed, at a later date, that I was his muse. I became the heroine in his novels and the mysterious lady who took all forms, from British spy to femme fatale. He was lovely but the spark was missing. It was set to explode when a new man arrived in the manor house.

There are those rare people who have a mighty presence, one so profound that you are forced to turn away so as not to be extinguished by their light. That was Erik. A Swedish psychic, he left a trail of beating hearts in his wake. When he walked into the room everyone stopped. The only conclusion to be drawn was that apart from being astonishingly handsome, he had been touched by a higher power and was radiating light. As hard as I tried not to look, I was as smitten as everyone around me, man and woman alike. Erik was special.

The universe has a lively sense of humour. During one session, I positioned my chair behind Erik so I could stare at him, undetected, during the talk. My plan went well until the speaker told us to move our chairs and make a circle. As we expanded outwards, I ended up sitting beside Erik. An elderly lady was on my other side. It was a trap. When we were told to form pairs, it was odds on to see which one I'd get. All the ladies in the room glared at me when I scored Erik as a partner, while I was mortified – a victim of my desire.

The next instruction was to sit facing your partner, 'Take their hands, stare into their eyes and convey, without words, what you are thinking. Your inner thoughts.' Was this some huge cosmic joke? I'd have been arrested if I expressed my thoughts, or at least branded a wanton temptress and forced to repent my ways. Erik's eyes were clear blue, like glacial lagoons, and I was being sucked into their depths, drowning in a world of shameless possibilities. Erik was gazing deeply at me and I was staring out the window.

This was not a man to dally with, this was a lifetime commitment. Many lifetimes, as he was worthy of several rides on the cosmic Ferris wheel. When I blinked I envisioned him as a Nordic king, dressed in a flowing cape and crown, walking down the stairs of his castle. I was nowhere to be seen in this picture, instead I was probably in the stable tending his horse. I was not the queen standing by his side. Flashes of my youth flooded my mind.

My high school drama class performed Shakespeare's *A Midsummer Night's Dream*. I yearned to play the enchantress queen of the fairies, Titania, all lithe and willowy, married to the fairy king Oberon. No, no queen, or even princess for me. The role went to the stunning Hedy, the svelte blonde in my class. Instead, I was cast as Bottom, the buffoon, whose head is transformed into that of a donkey. Granted it was a meatier, comic role and Bottom was courageous and confident, but I was no princess. It just wasn't fair.

That night, in the elegant drawing room of the manor house, all the guests were mingling. Erik sat surrounded by his entourage, ladies dressed in cashmere and pearls, hanging onto his every word. When I entered, there was no more room in the circle so Erik gestured for me to sit on the chaise lounge beside him.

As he continued talking, with his knees crossed, he reached out and took my hand so nobody could see. *Be still my beating heart.* I nearly swooned, keeling over in ecstasy as his energy pulsed through me. Perhaps I *had* conveyed my deepest thoughts after all.

The ladies all sighed when Erik rose to leave. Soon after I was surprised to find that the hall was full of witty conversation and cocktails. Erik was amongst the crowd, so I turned my back so he wouldn't think I was stalking him. A few minutes later, there was a soft touch on my shoulder and I spun around. It was Erik.

'If you want to say goodnight,' he said, showing me the key in his palm with his room number in clear view. 'I'll be waiting.'

The hall began to swirl under the weight of my fantasies and after Erik disappeared up the stairs, I waited a decent two minutes before I loped up after him. At last, I was Titania and had found my king. At last there was a happy ending to this fairy tale. There were no promises or illusions, just the pure magic of the moment.

When the course ended, Erik went on his way. I thought our brief liaison was over but after a week I received a letter from Sweden and tore it open. As I read his words, my chest heaved into a massive knot. He wrote that he had fallen in love with me and needed to see me again. It was so unexpected, so unreal.

Hitching a ride in a hearse, hopefully empty of its load, I made it to his log cabin in the woods of Sweden. It was all so familiar as if I had lived there before. The bond between Erik and I deepened. The log fire that burnt so brightly to keep us warm heated the lounge room while our mutual love stoked the depths of our hearts.

We walked hand in hand in the nearby forest, lost in the moment and the scent of fresh pine and mountain air. When Erik summoned his two Alsatian dogs, he did so by thought process alone. He was a man with a special kind of magic and I was bewitched.

There was a strong feeling of déjà vu and it became apparent that we had been together before, in a previous lifetime or more, and were allowed the privilege of reuniting for a brief moment in time.

To this day, whenever I close my eyes in meditation, I see Erik walking down the stairs of a castle in his cloak and crown, reaching out to take my hand. We each had different mountains to climb, and diverse paths to navigate, but our love remains eternal.

The courses I attended at Stansted proved to be a turning point, not only on a personal level but also as part of my spiritual evolution. My drawing had caused quite a stir and when Gordon Higginson, the Principal of the College, came to visit, I was one of a handful of people allowed to witness a unique phenomenon. Preparations were made in the appointed room, as the staff frantically cleaned and dusted so there were no pollutants in the atmosphere. These would prove dangerous if they were absorbed into his body.

As the select few took their place around the circle, Higginson sat on a chair in the centre and took off his shirt. The lights were dimmed and slowly a light mist emanated from his diaphragm until it formed a cloud around him. Everyone was shocked but no one dared utter a word, especially when hands appeared within the mist, as spirits tried to use the medium's ectoplasm, life force, to manifest.

Then a soft voice muttered from the void, a woman's ghostly hands moving in the mist. 'Bill. It's Elaine.'

The man sitting beside me, Bill, was speechless. 'No', he countered. 'The only Elaine I know is alive. She left here yesterday morning, driving back home.'

The spirit responded. 'No Bill, I died yesterday on the motorway.' Overwrought with emotion, Bill ran out to check after the session ended, only to find it was the truth.

Some things defy reason and go beyond our level of understanding. I had just turned 28, marking the completion of the first 27 to 30-year Saturn life cycle. It was time to go beyond the familiar and step onto a new level of personal evolution. Each year a young psychic was chosen at the college, one who showed the most promise and potential during the course. It was unreal, and I couldn't wrap my head around it, for they chose me.

It was hard enough sitting on a platform beside two old ladies, sketching my vision. Now I was expected to stand on a public platform in a large hall filled with visitors, beside the president, and give readings to an audience hanging onto my every word. Using astrological insights, I did my best, all the while wondering how this could be happening. It was the beginning of a long list of strange encounters that are my life and they never fail to astound me.

CHAPTER SIX

THE POWER OF LOVE

There are places in the world that leave a bitter taste, whether in this lifetime or the past, and their effect is so profound that they form a sacred wound in your soul. It may be the result of an incident, the people you meet or the residue of a past life that needs resolution. It could be part of an ancestral link or a trauma so severe that it is entrenched in your DNA, passed down from one generation to the next till it devours you. Perhaps it is all these elements combined.

The location of my sacred wound is in Germany and dates back to a dark time in history. My visit to the country began innocently enough. It was another in the long list of adventures that would mark my 30s. There was still so much of the world to explore, so many people to meet and places still untouched. My sense of alienation and loneliness grew during those years, as I was hounded by the need to have a partner to feel complete. It was a Libra thing.

My travels began in New Zealand, en route to Europe. There, I stayed in a hostel in picturesque Queenstown on the South Island where I met Norbert who came from a small town in Germany. We chatted away for ages and the following day took a helicopter ride up to Mount Cook and throwing snowballs, we frolicked in the snow. Before Norbert left to continue his travels, he invited me to stay at his house in Bavaria if ever I came to Germany.

The day came when I took him up on his offer and travelled through Germany, as part of my trip around Europe. Once there I met his partner Sigrid and two housemates, Fritz and Ella. They were welcoming while Sigrid, a doctor, seemed more rigid.

After a few days, she loosened up and asked me to look at her astrology chart. From the planetary aspects, it was clear that she had major issues. Whenever Pluto links with a personal planet, there is often a heaviness and dark edge that can be difficult to deal with.

Ella was quite the opposite, light and carefree, and she happily drove me around the countryside. We enjoyed brisk conversations over lunch while trying out the local cuisine. We both loved to dance and spent a few nights at the local clubs making friends.

In the meantime, the mood in the house darkened and outside it had started to snow. On Sunday, the bells tolled in the town, as the local church called its flock to prayers. I looked out the window, watching old ladies run along the cobbled path clutching their scarves around them as if tardiness would damn them for eternity.

A shudder ran through me as flashes of the past emerged. In medieval times, the Jews in Germany experienced discrimination at the hands of clergy and villagers alike. Superstition, combined with bigotry, fuelled violent pogroms against Jews that swept across Europe, through many lands during dire periods in history.

The accusations against me began when the web of paranoia that consumed Sigrid split open, and her true self emerged. There was a sharp edge to her words and like a snake that sheds its skin, the dark substance of her ego was exposed. It was disconcerting at best, and dangerous at worst. It came to a head one bitterly cold night when Sigrid, clad only in a towel, went into the sauna in their basement, smoking a joint. It was not a great combination.

After a while, she emerged ranting that she had a vision. She had seen that I was a witch. I had been called many things in my life but never a witch. 'Get out,' she screamed, 'get out of my house, *witch!*' The others tried to reason with her because it was clear that she was in an altered state, one inhabited by demons, but to no avail.

I had no choice but to leave. However, it was late at night and it was snowing. Ella came to my rescue and drove me into town. We went to the local club looking for anyone we might know, for this was a university town. With a bit of luck, several students we had met before might be able to put me up for the night.

Luckily, our new friend Ahmed offered me his room at the student dormitory because he was staying at his girlfriend's place. There was only one catch. He had a friend who would be there too but with little option I thanked him as he handed me a key.

The room was empty when I got there, so I crawled into a sleeping bag on a mattress on the floor. Tired, sleep was welcome but when the door handle turned, footsteps meant that Ahmed's friend was there. A few minutes later my sleeping bag was being unzipped. My reaction was instant. I yanked the zip out of his hand.

Was this guy crazy? He was tampering with a woman who had just been thrown out into the snow and called a witch. 'If you make another move, I'll scream so loud the whole student dorm will wake. Trust me, you don't want to end up in a German prison!' A loud sigh, followed by the sound of retreating feet and a thump on the bed. Never, ever mess with a woman of magic, or even more so the child of Holocaust survivors. They are forged out of mighty stuff.

'You don't want to end up in a German prison.' The words came to life as shocking images of the Second World War, with all its pain and misery, flashed through my mind. Six million Jews, and countless other innocent victims, lost their lives at the hands of the Nazis. They were evil personified but even worse were the normal people who followed their lead, losing any last shred of humanity.

My mother was just 15 when she was taken by force from Hungary to Auschwitz-Birkenau concentration camp in Poland and handed over to Hitler's henchmen, the dreaded SS. Her mother, grandmother, young brother, uncles, and their families, all died in the gas chambers of that hellhole and she was left with *nothing*.

No family, no home, no hope, and worse still, no reason to live. Yet she did. As the Allies advanced into enemy territory she was herded off to Germany with other poor souls, barely hanging on to life, marching through freezing cold in January towards a miserable fate. Close to 15,000 people died during these forced marches.

It was through the barbed wire of a deadly concentration camp in Germany that she first saw *him*. The man who was to become my father. They were both miserable versions of themselves having been starved, tortured, and forced to endure the worst that humankind was capable of. The hatred, discrimination and persecution of a people who possessed the knowledge of centuries of study, music and love, and who never thought to hate back.

My father had endured even more pain because the Jews from northern Greece were taken earlier in the war, and most had died. He too lost his family in the most despicable way and he was a bitter man. Rightly, for he had every reason to be enraged. Marched from Auschwitz to Germany, he was to become my mother's shield. With no common language and hope of touch, when their eyes met they fell in love, in the horrific setting of a concentration camp.

As the Allied forces progressed into Germany in 1945, men and women prisoners were taken on separate death marches to be shot in an isolated place. The Nazi cowards wanted to hide any trace of their war crimes and pretend the whole vile episode of history never existed. Proving they were aware of the sins they committed.

My father, powered by an iron will, jumped off a bridge along the way and despite being shot at by guards he escaped. My mother, and the other women, were saved by an act of God. The SS, assigned to shoot them, fled because the US army was nearby. The workings of destiny are not well understood but nothing can alter its course.

Fate dictated that I stay in Germany for a while, so renting a room I got a job as a clerk in the housing department of the US military at its Nuremberg base. Nuremberg was the city where Nazi war crimes trials were held in 1945–46. The Allies brought to justice Nazi leaders who were guilty of crimes against humanity in World War II.

Thanks to my British nationality, acquired while married to Luke, I was allowed to work in Germany for a restricted time. The office work at the military base was dull but became more interesting when I did my daily rounds, walking around the grounds to deliver correspondence. My co-workers in the office, all German locals, were dreary after years spent doing the same job.

After work, I'd spend the evening hoping for some interesting company. One night when I went to a local club, I bumped into a sophisticated man in a leather trench coat who was leaning against the wall. He drove a fancy BMW sports car and even better, he was ethical and smart. Whenever Klaus was in town on business, we caught up. It was gratifying to be reminded that there are moral people wherever you go, those who reflect on the past and want to make amends for the sins of their fathers and their fathers before them.

During my daily rounds on the military base, I noticed several posters advising that any form of discrimination would not be tolerated and must be reported. It was a serious issue, so it seemed odd that every time I phoned any department on the base, the response was, 'Corporal, followed by a title and name, "Can I help you, *sir*?"

'Actually, it's ma'am,' I replied.

Invariably, when corrected and with the sound of my voice they apologised. 'Sorry, ma'am.' An automatic reference to gender was unwise and out of line with an anti-discrimination policy.

Back then, in 1980, there were women in the military and local female staff scattered around the base. Certainly not as many as today but they deserved due consideration. It may have been just an oversight, but I had just turned 30 and was finding my voice.

With my typewriter primed, I wrote a letter to the base commander, Colonel Lee, to advise him of the matter. The staff in my office ridiculed me. 'It won't get past his aide,' they scoffed. 'Why are you wasting your time? The colonel won't even see it.'

I refused to be discouraged and sent off the letter.

A few days later, a section manager ran into the office, yelling my name. Everyone sat up straight looking diligent. I gulped, thinking I was about to be fired. Instead, she told me to follow her.

'Quick, Colonel Lee is on the phone for you!' My fellow staff looked shocked, reflecting on years of loyalty spent at the same old desk, fearful of making waves or making a difference.

Answering the phone in her office, a voice with an American drawl boomed into my ear. 'I got your letter,' Colonel Lee announced, 'thank you for bringing this matter to my attention.'

'With the military's emphasis on equality,' I replied, 'this issue has been overlooked.' Reading over the letter I sent, I was proud of my words. They were both concise and persuasive.

'There is a meeting of base commanders in two weeks. I will raise this as a matter of importance,' he added. 'All persons in our services must be acknowledged and respected.'

Walking back into my office I felt vindicated. It is important to right a wrong, no matter the case. Equally, it is vital to have a voice so that someone in authority takes notice and you are heard.

Life is a cosmic jigsaw puzzle, with all the pieces eventually falling into place. It seemed strange that I was working for the US military but there was a link of sorts. My parents defied the odds to survive the war and it was the American forces that saved them.

When my father jumped off the bridge to escape death, he hid in haystacks in the German countryside until he saw tanks with stars on their side rolling down the road. The US army had arrived.

He ran out onto the road waving wildly. From his dreadful state, they knew he was an escaped prisoner. Calling on the food supply sergeant, a Greek from New York, to translate, my father was dressed in a US Army uniform and given the privilege of riding on top of one of the first American tanks to roll into Munich in victory.

As for my mother, she too was saved by the US military, after being abandoned, along with other women on the death march, in a disused prison barrack. The SS fled when the German army retreated to avoid being captured. After several days, the doors to the barrack burst open and there stood three American soldiers.

The women, their bodies lifeless and devoid of hope, were a sight that no decent person could bear. The soldiers took one look and began to cry. My mother remembered their faces clearly. Shaking, they carried each woman outside, through the portal back to life.

I remain indebted to the American and Allied service men and women for their courage, and all those who fight for justice and decency. Without your brave efforts, I would not be here.

As an Australian, it is gratifying that the man revered enough to be the face on our $100 note, is Jewish. Sir John Monash, considered by many nations to be one of the best military generals of World War I, has a university in Melbourne named in his honour.

My father never gave up hope of finding my mother and tracked her down to a US Army hospital. They took time to recuperate at a lakeside sanctuary and gently bond, for they were wounded souls from different countries and spoke unfamiliar languages.

Despite all the hurdles, their love grew and they were married in Munich, in 1945, by a rabbi in the US Army. Their bond endured for more than 70 years, for *nothing* can deter the power of love and some things are just meant to be, emblazoned across the heavens.

CHAPTER SEVEN

LOST ON A DESERT HIGHWAY

Gazing across the hardened sands of the Judean desert of Israel there was no sign of life. The road vanished into the distance with no traffic in either direction, not even the slightest hint of the bus which was well overdue. I had been standing alone on the road for an eternity, with nowhere to shelter from the harsh sun. Jordan lay across the Dead Sea, shimmering in a heat haze, on the horizon.

How I ended up in this precarious position, alone in the desert, was a quirk of circumstance but in retrospect, perhaps it had been orchestrated by forces beyond my understanding. Even though I had travelled widely, I was still naïve and trusting in many ways.

Destiny can be tricky. This was my first trip to Israel and followed my time spent in Germany, so it was a balancing act for my soul. It was prompted by the desire to connect with my race and one of the few remnants of my family who escaped the ravages of the Holocaust. Beyond that, I wanted to explore the land of my ancestors, in a bid to find that elusive sense of belonging,

As soon as the plane landed in Tel Aviv, I scanned the faces of the officials at the airport for a connection but there was none. I felt even more alienated on the bus heading for Jerusalem, crammed among people in military uniforms with rifles slung around their necks. They spoke Hebrew, creating an even greater divide. Spoken around 1000 BCE, in the Kingdoms of Israel and Judah, it was later developed to become the official language of the State of Israel.

I was greatly relieved when I spotted my mother's aunt Lily waiting for me at the bus station. One of my few surviving relatives, she was short and sweet with a broad welcoming smile. When we reached the comfort of her small flat, I met my second cousin, Judith, and as we chatted away I looked at both women's faces yearning to see my grandmother's eyes in theirs.

I had only one cherished photo of my maternal grandparents, both of whom died tragically. There was no remnant of my father's family – no photo or words spoken, and few clues to their identity. Over dinner, we compared our lives, as Lily spread out her treasured photo albums and explained how they found sanctuary in Israel. Lily's sister, Eva, had migrated to America before the war and had raised her family there but we had never met.

My stay in Jerusalem was cut short by a sudden drop in temperature triggered by a snowfall in the nearby mountains. An icy blast swept over the city and despite my aunt's efforts to feed me bowls of chicken soup and pile blankets on top of me, I froze. Not coping well, my aunt suggested I go to a warmer spot for a few days.

So I left the ladies in the warmth of their beds, hidden under a stack of quilts and headed down south. With cups of hot chocolate and cookies to comfort them, they immersed themselves in romance novels, preferring to read about other people's exploits rather than embark on their own. It was a safer passage.

In contrast, my life was spent in pursuit of adventure which may explain how I ended up in my current predicament, in an Israeli desert with the hot sun beating down on me and a dry parched taste on my lips. I gulped water from my bottle but it was as hot as the stifling air around me. Wiping the sweat from my brow, I became increasingly agitated waiting for a phantom bus that refused to come.

The previous night was spent at a hostel at Ein Gedi, a nature reserve on the Western shore of the Dead Sea. Armed guards patrolled the perimeter, a reminder of a troubled land battling to maintain its identity. Only two buses a day headed south to the seaside town of Eilat and while everyone took the morning bus, I preferred to explore the area at my own pace. I didn't realise just how far I'd strayed along the desert road, and now with no bus in sight, I was unsure whether to go back or see where the road led.

Neither was a good option. One hour later there was still no sign of the bus. Worse still there was no traffic at all. I wasn't sure whether to panic but knew it was useless because no one was around to witness it. When I spotted a large dust cloud in the distance, one rapidly advancing towards me, I feared a camel stampede.

As the dust cleared, an Israeli military jeep swooped across the sand and screeched to a halt beside me. This had all the hallmarks of a romance novel for the driver was a striking man in uniform. However, his words were not as endearing as I hoped.

'What the hell are you doing out here alone, in the middle of nowhere?' he yelled.

'Waiting for the bus,' I replied. It was a reasonable response since it was the truth.

'The bus *isn't* coming,' he said, looking unimpressed. 'There's been flash floods. The snow has melted on the mountains in Jerusalem and further south, and the road is cut off in both directions. No traffic can get through. You're trapped in the middle.'

'Oh,' I replied, too flustered to come up with anything better.

'I can't leave you here alone,' he added, 'but civilians aren't allowed to ride on military vehicles.' Deciding he couldn't abandon me in the desert, he took off his jacket.

'Put this on,' he ordered, 'and climb on.' Placing his helmet on my head, he stunned me even more when he placed his rifle in my lap. Obviously, he didn't think I was a threat of any sort, appearing incredibly naive and rather poor in my judgement.

As the jeep zoomed across the desert, I remained silent, barely able to admire the view because the helmet had dropped down over my eyes and my arms were shaking. Glimpses of taut dry landscape flashed by and the salty scent of the Dead Sea reminded me that I was far from home, a million miles from all that was familiar.

After a time the jeep screeched to a halt at a military base in the desert, occupied by a squad of Israeli Defence Forces. It was dwarfed by a massive stone mesa jutting majestically into the clear blue sky. Daniel, my rescuer, led me through a dining area where the rest of the men were eating. They looked up in surprise as I wandered through with a cursory smile. I wanted to blurt out, 'I'm your distant cousin from Australia,' but decided against it.

Drawn from many backgrounds, these men were an attractive lot. Daniel was second in charge at the base and with his dark good looks and strong physique he was hard to overlook. When I was presented to the base commander, Rafi, he was most genial, aware that I had been through an ordeal stranded in the desert on my own.

He organised something for me to eat and ordered two men to vacate their room so I had a place to sleep. Now I felt less of a misfit, a stray who had wandered in from afar. Still, it was like walking on eggshells and this whole episode was so out of touch, so surreal.

That night I sat with Daniel under a brilliant canopy of stars in the desert sky as we shared bittersweet stories of our lives and divulged our inner thoughts, as if we were intimate partners and not distant strangers. The heavens were hypnotic but the magnetism between us dimmed even the brightest of stars. Our connection grew stronger as the night progressed and it seemed as if Daniel was a long-lost relic of my past or a welcome fabrication of the future.

It was impossible not to be swept away. It is a rare occurrence to form an immediate connection with another person. A stranger who ties you to the rest of humanity, so you don't feel so isolated or alone anymore. As Daniel spoke of his parents' ordeal in Russia and how they found their freedom in the land of Israel, it triggered an innate bond between us, forged in the fierce fires of adversity.

Their struggle for survival mirrored that of my own family, binding us not only in race, religion and bitter experience but also in the capacity to rise above evil to prevail. No greater tie exists.

A strong Israeli with the stoic determination of his Ashkenazi roots, Jews from Central and Eastern Europe, Daniel felt safe enough to share his thoughts with me. As a rule, men are insular, unwilling to divulge their feelings especially when wearing the cloaks of courage in their military uniform. They are expected to be strong but few are strong enough to admit their weaknesses. Daniel's vulnerability and honesty were his greatest strengths.

Daniel's family had lived in the Russian Empire for centuries but were never considered Russian, but rather Hebrew. In the early 20th century, the five million Jews living there comprised the biggest Jewish community in the world. After a spate of pogroms and ethnic cleansing, revolutions, repressions, two world wars, and the collapse of the Soviet Union, the Jews in Russia are represented by around

150,000 people today. If Daniel was proof, diversity forged an incredible strength and resolve, as it did with the entire Jewish race.

That strength was amplified by the aura of the mighty fortress of Masada looming high above us. The magnitude of the mighty rock, and the civilisation it once held, serve to amplify the iron will of its people and was a place of unbending courage. Even in the darkness, the visible energy that pulsed from the stone's core was immense. The glow from the full moon acted as a spotlight, casting a spell over a turbulent period in history dating back centuries.

The canopy of stars blazing above us symbolised the struggle *and* the victory. The star holds incredible meaning to the Jewish people, as a beacon of light in a darkened world. The six-pointed Star of David on the Israeli flag in royal blue portrays the splendour of the heavens while the white background represents the radiance of faith. In scorched yellow, it was used on armbands to identify the Jews during World War II by an evil Nazi regime. In truth, how can a gold star be anything but a symbol of excellence?

Huddled close to Daniel on a cool desert night, each star shimmered with a special light. As Daniel spoke, his voice hushed less to wake the other men sleeping close by, but more as a mark of respect for the solemnity of the place, the story of Masada unfolded.

A place of heroism and strange sacrifice, the flat mesa of Masada was large enough to house a settlement of close to 1,000 people. Soaring over 400 metres high on its eastern edge, the Jewish rebels who lived here shaped history, proving that while it may be one thing to live together as one, it is even rarer to die together.

These brave people of the past gazed at the same stars I looked at now, the heavens just as enticing. My lifelong mission was to uncover the starry script that provided the missing link between man and the universe. The ancient Hebrews looked to the heavens too, searching for the astrological key to this mystery.

The discovery in Israel of eight ancient synagogues with mosaic floors of the zodiac was remarkable and spoke of a deeper truth. In times to come, I came to view several of these archaeological sites and few words could express the wonder of this belief in the stars.

This attachment to astrology dates back to biblical times, as confirmed in remnants of the Dead Sea Scrolls. These ancient Jewish manuscripts discovered in 11 caves in Israel, include references to astrology and predictions, part of the ancients' quest to determine cosmic order. It was a defining factor that tied me to my ancestors.

Daniel was another, for the stars had brought us closer. Lost in the sheer magic of the moment, I turned away from the heavens to stare into Daniel's eyes. They were magnetic, and in that split second, we bonded. Everything else faded into the background as Daniel leaned over to kiss me. Then he lifted me and spun me round as if to catch any drops of moondust drifting down from the heavens. I felt weightless for Daniel was strong in body and soul.

Here, in the isolation of the Israeli desert, it was all so unreal and divinely choreographed. Longing for the comfort of Daniel through the night, it was my turn to be honest. 'I don't feel safe sleeping alone,' I said. It was a fair comment considering the risk. Beyond that, what absolute bliss to lie in the arms of such an exceptional man. And as I did, rain fell upon the metal roof, adding music to a remarkable night to remember. A symphony of the ages.

The next day I woke up to a bright blue sky with barely a wisp of cloud. Daniel left early on patrol and unsure how best to emerge in front of a squad of men, I stayed in bed despite my desire to visit the ancient ruins of Masada. The paths leading up were damaged by rock falls, so the prospect of reaching the top was unlikely. Access to Masada was also by cable car and while most days the site swarmed with tourists, the flash floods proved an effective barrier.

A knock on the door and I opened it to find Rafi, the commander, holding a tray with boiled eggs, yoghurt, and an apple. 'Your breakfast,' he said, as I grabbed my jacket. 'I've organised the cable car to take you to the top of Masada. One of our men will escort you around the ruins because only military personnel have permission to go up right now. As you don't speak Hebrew, don't say anything on the way. Our man will keep the driver occupied.'

It was an amazing opportunity so I quickly dressed. As the cable car cranked its way up to the top of Masada, my escort, Avi, chatted to the operator while I stood in the corner engrossed in the scenery. This was no ordinary journey up the solid stone edifice, and I was about to step back into history. This rocky fortress bore the scars of the loss of many brave souls. Their courage was stamped into every rocky crevice, but was the sacrifice in this ancient settlement a remarkable act of bravery or one triggered by sheer desperation?

Once we reached the top, Avi led me around the scattered remains. Herod the Great, appointed king of Judea by the Romans, chose this dramatic site overlooking the Dead Sea as his desert stronghold. He built a sumptuous palace here around 37 CE in the classical Roman style. With three terraces, it was fortified with high double walls, heavy gates and towers, along with a sophisticated water system. The site remained untouched for more than thirteen centuries, so to be given sole access now was beyond incredible.

As I wandered around the half-excavated buildings of the palace, it was amazing that some of the original mosaics were still intact. 'In the year 66 CE,' Avi explained, 'in the Great Revolt of the Jews against the Romans, Jewish rebels and their families took refuge in King Herod's abandoned palace. When Jerusalem was destroyed four years later, more Jews fled here until there were close to 1,000 people here, forming a strong community.

'A legion of 8,000 Roman troops,' Avi continued, 'led by the Roman governor of Judea, Lucius Flavius Silva, marched to Masada in 73 CE to capture the Jewish stronghold. The rebels refused to surrender so the Romans, along with Jewish prisoners of war, built a ramp of earth and wooden supports, up the cliff's western face.

'The siege lasted months and when they reached the top, a large tower with a battering ram was moved up the ramp and a volley of fireballs were flung inside the fortress. The people of Masada fought back with missiles and arrows. When the Romans broke down the gate it was not the glorious victory they hoped for. Fierce fires raged all around and dead bodies lay everywhere, drenched in blood. Slain families, holding hands to ensure an eternal bond, lay side by side.'

The story of Masada was one of self-determination. Spurred on by their leader, Eleazar Ben Yair, to never become slaves again, each man slew his wife and children. The men then drew lots to choose the last ten. They went on a killing spree turning their knives on each other until only one man was left standing, the sin of suicide his to bear alone. Two women and five children took sanctuary in the cisterns and survived to tell the tale, so it was never forgotten.

As I looked down the cliff face to the crumbling remains of the ramp, it was hard to imagine the carnage. The Romans were determined, driven by victory and conquest but the Israelis were even more resolute. Never again would they be sublimated or be bound in slavery but many innocent lives were lost here, a heavy toll.

Walking around the site I was struck by the discarded props of a film crew, yet to be cleared. Leftover scenery added authenticity to a fantastic tale. The US mini-series *Masada* had recently been filmed here, an account of the Roman siege of the Jews. It served as a reminder of the year I was there, 1980. A year of discovery.

At a gap in the battlement walls, I gazed across the vast desert sprawled out in streaks of yellow and brown ochre far into the distance. It was immense and timeless, both in the emptiness of the land and the longing for life of the Dead Sea that tinged the horizon.

Nothing could exist in the salty clenches of its waters just like the people who once lived here. As I contemplated the past, a large black crow swooped in and landed on the parapet beside me. He turned his craggy beak towards the sun, in an imperious way, and looked across the desert as if reflecting on the acts committed here.

The history of the land of Israel extends back thousands of years to the time of Abraham and an esteemed lineage of Jewish kings and prophets. It endured earthquakes and floods as nature worked to negate the battles that raged here for centuries. Israel stands on the lowest point on earth with Jordan, on the crusty shore of the Dead Sea, and the highest point to heaven for nowhere else embodies man's eternal quest for meaning as does this holy land.

The floods in the desert did not recede for three days, despite my hopes that they would last longer, not wanting my time there to end. To be marooned at Masada was an exceptional act of grace. My fleeting moment with Daniel proved to be much more – forging a profound soul connection. Packing my bag to leave the base, I realised that my diary was missing. It held all my addresses but despite all efforts, upending beds and tables, it was not found.

With no choice but to leave, I boarded the bus that *finally* arrived. With flashing scenes of rock faces and stark desert, nodding off from exhaustion, I awoke when the bus reached Jerusalem. My aunt was very relieved to see me, fearing that the floods had swallowed me up and spat me out in some remote corner of the desert.

Sitting down with a cup of tea and biscuits, my aunt and cousin Judith warned me that dry paths in the desert could turn into raging torrents within minutes, causing dangerous flash flooding that had claimed lives in the past. They listened in rapture to my amazing tale of Masada, as I relived the magic felt there.

I was not sure if they believed any of it.

'I have lived in Israel all my life and nothing like that has happened to me!' Judith exclaimed, the look on her face a mix of envy and disbelief. I kept the details of my liaison with Daniel private, for they would make any romance novel fade by comparison.

Over the years, my stories were often questioned because they seemed so implausible. It was not an overactive imagination at work but rather the fact that amazing things kept happening to me. It was great when the universe conspired to prove my point, leaving little doubt. A few days later there was a knock at the door.

Standing there was the commander, Rafi, dignified in his uniform. I gasped as he was shown into the apartment. My aunt ran off to find her finest crystal glasses and rare bottle of cognac, while Judith charged into the bedroom to change and do her hair.

'I found your diary,' Rafi said, sitting on the lounge.

'You brought it all the way here,' I said. 'How kind of you.'

Rafi smiled at me in a way that hinted that perhaps the diary *hadn't* been lost at all and after a pleasant conversation he took his leave. Never doubted again for my stories, I was admired for creating my own racy novel, worthy of a place on the shelf.

It was a Scorpio friend, years later, who set me straight. 'They were checking up on you,' she said, 'examining your diary.' I wondered how I could have been so naive but innocence is hardly a sin. Hoping I hadn't written down any intimate details of my travels, the commander's suspicions were no doubt eased when Aunt Lily offered him a nice bowl of homemade matzoh ball soup.

Decades later, talking to my second cousin, Shirley, in New York, she revealed another chapter in the story. It was after my mother's passing that she rang, and we had not spoken in many years. 'Do you remember when you stayed with me in Tel Aviv?' she asked. Vague memories surfaced, and I remembered visiting Shirley after my stay in Jerusalem, at my Aunt Lily home.

'After you left, military vehicles stopped in my street and guys kept coming up asking after you. My gay neighbour was pleased with how 'hot' they were.' I was shocked. *Who* exactly was it? *Daniel? The commander?* Had I even discussed the episode in the desert with Shirley? It was so juicy that I probably had. She seemed rather conservative so I hope I hadn't shocked her with my antics.

Now, to find out after all these years, that I was sought after was a revelation. I must have left a trail of stardust behind.

Uncovering the secrets of this timeless land was like trying to open an ancient lock with a rusty key. Jerusalem was overwhelming in its complexity with so many racial strands woven through its history. The old walled city was a web of alleyways and diverse people surging along the paths. While 74% of people in Israel are Jewish, both in ethnicity and religion, 21%, about 2 million people, are Israeli Arabs, mostly Muslim, but with Christian and Druze minorities.

Centuries of conflict were embedded in the past, and as I travelled north, to the city of Acre on the Mediterranean Sea, it was even more pronounced. One of the few natural harbours on Israel's coast, and strategically based, it is one of the oldest inhabited cities in the world. Acre had been ruled by the Persians, Egyptians, Greeks, and Romans before being conquered by Muslim forces in the 7th century.

Five hundred years later Christian Crusaders came in search of the Holy Grail, marching onwards to claim Jerusalem. In 1191, Acre became the capital of the Crusader states. After defeat by the fierce Mamluks, it took 500 years under Ottoman rule to restore Acre to its former glory. The turbulence did not end there. The Turks lost control to the British in 1918, until 1948 when it became part of Israel and was restored to its original people.

Acre had a strange, unsettling effect on me. Hidden in the shadows were warped images of the past and as I walked along the darkened road looking for a hostel, the ancient walls appeared to crumble into dust, collapsing from the weight of their strained history. Phantom horse hooves echoed in the night, followed by the clash of fighting men. My anxiety peaked when I reached the hostel and the door was slammed in my face.

The hostel was full. Tired and desperate, I shuffled down the street, looking dejected. A young Arab guy passing by, asked if he could help. When I confided that I had no place to go, Amir had no hesitation in inviting me to stay in his home for the night.

I trusted my instincts and followed him.

Trusting *his* instincts, he left me in his place as he headed out to meet friends. I spent the next hours eating ripe dates and sipping sweetened tea while going over all sorts of dreadful scenarios. The next day when I awoke, Amir was asleep in the other room.

Leaving him a note of thanks, I booked into a hostel and headed off to explore the ancient city. Remnants of the Crusader's battles still existed in the walled medieval port, as did a fortress built seven hundred years ago by the Order of the Knights of Saint John.

Grand ceremonies were held in the Knights' Hall – banquets and loud revelry as men toasted their victories and mourned their defeats. Among the banners of orders of knighthood was a flag of a red cross against a white background. It roused a memory.

It was the crest of the Knights Templar, the cross a symbol of martyrdom. I had always felt an overwhelming link to these holy knights. Knights who believed that to die in combat was a great honour and ensured a place in heaven. The Templars were a religious military order founded in 1118 that guarded the safety of the pilgrims who made the perilous journey from Europe to the Holy Land. Pope Honorius II declared them to be an army of God. Devout Christians, their headquarters was the Temple Mount in Jerusalem.

After the conquest of Jerusalem by Saladin, the first sultan of Egypt and Syria, in 1187, the Templars built their fortress in Acre, along its jagged seashore. The fortress, and its two towers, were crushed by the conquering forces. An underground tunnel remains.

Carved into the heavy stone, it led to an opening to the sea where the knights could enter the city undetected. This secret escape route, with its crypt and hidden passage, lay undiscovered for over 700 years until an issue with the underground pipes exposed it.

Tracing the knight's path, I walked through the large tunnel, along the path leading to the Mediterranean Sea. It was not hard to imagine the rustle of the Templar's cloaks as they marched through the tunnel in days gone by, the pounding of their boots hushed so as not to be heard in the street above. Spurred on by the scent of the sea, the stony tunnel became so low that I could go no further.

A mysterious link bound me to the Templar knights, dating back centuries to my ancestors. My father's maternal grandmother descended from the line of Benveniste, a noble and scholarly family who rose in rank to become Senior Advisors and Royal Physicians to the King and Queen of Spain in the 12th and 13th centuries. As the valued treasurers of the Templars, the knights bestowed the title, *Benveniste de la Cavalleria* – 'Of the Horsemen', upon their names. It was both a mark of respect and a staunch vow of protection.

A further clue to my heritage came when I travelled south to the shores of Lake Kinneret, also known as the Sea of Galilee. The place of miracles and holy men, it is the lowest freshwater lake on earth. Events that occurred there over the centuries were so profound that they impacted the course of history and shaped major religious beliefs. Unpredictable swells in these waters, caused by earthquakes and sudden storms, reflect its dynamic past.

My hostel in the town of Tiberias was perched on the edge of the lake. The first days were spent sitting at a small café, gazing across the calm of its waters. With *laffa* flatbread, humus, fresh fish, and a jug of sweet lemon juice, it would have been idyllic if not for the residue of battle on the other side of the lake. As the waiter explained, it was scarred by the imprint of countless missiles hurled into Israel by its enemies from the Golan Heights.

My roommate at the hostel was Naomi, a nice Jewish girl from New York. We got on well and talked for hours, sharing our thoughts and compulsive need to find meaning in our lives. Naomi had a serious edge and a deep quality to her words. She spoke with the gravity of an ancient, learned scholar, taking time to gather her thoughts as she mulled over them. I tended to be more frivolous, trying to add joy and remember life's blessings.

Naomi yearned to spend more time in Tiberias and hoped she could find a way to remain a little longer. One day, while at the front desk of the hostel, the manager emerged from his office to ask if I would like to work there. It came as a surprise, but with plans to move on I was about to refuse when Naomi's words echoed in my ears. When he agreed to her working there too, it was a done deal. I had forgotten how averse I was to manual labour.

We were both assigned to the bedroom brigade and while the rest whipped through the rooms at record speed, I lasted less than a day. When they switched me to the dining room, I didn't fare much better. Staying kosher was unfamiliar to me, as was the separation of meat and dairy products, with utensils and plates marked in different colours. The Israelis, being a tough lot, attacked the cleaning of the kitchen with rubber boots and a hose.

Libras are artistic types who enjoy the finer things in life, so hanging up my rubber gloves I resigned. However, there appeared to be a purpose for me remaining in Tiberias. That evening, while sitting in the dining room, I sketched a woman at the opposite table on a paper napkin. Afterwards, she strolled over to take a look.

She was the wife of the hostel manager, and after sharing my failed work efforts with her, she asked, 'How would you feel about doing some paintings? The walls could do with some colour.' It was clear a force was trying to keep me there and although I had never worked as an artist before, I had always loved drawing.

Charged with a mission, I set off the next day, with an easel and paints in hand, to capture some of the beauty of the landscape. The skipper of one of the boats on the lake offered to take me across to the Mount of Beatitudes, the first stop for the endless religious tour groups who came to follow in Christ's footsteps. The boat would pick me up later that afternoon, so it was a quiet day spent painting in the shade of the trees.

The first time I stepped foot on the holy mount, the energy was palpable. The Sea of Galilee was stunning from this vantage point, its shimmering surface lighting up the sky in an impossible way. It seemed that heaven and earth merged as one, and I was mightily blessed to be there. This was sacred land. Teetering on the edge of the deepest rift on earth, this land possessed a mystical force powerful enough to mould the spiritual direction of humanity.

During biblical times this was the scene of miracles and holy men, heavenly inspiration and absolute faith. The serenity of the area reflected its pious past for this was the place where Jesus delivered the Sermon on the Mount, powerful words with huge effect. The imprint of these words still echoed across the world.

Whatever one's faith, it is impossible to deny the spiritual presence on the mount. When the boat left and the tourists headed for the next stop on their pilgrimage, I was left alone to soak in the peaceful energy. Sitting on a shady patch of grass near the arched church which overlooked the sea, I sketched in solitude. If only I could tap into the past through the eyes of those who had stood here. Their thoughts, the deeds, and the miracles they witnessed.

On my boat trips across the Sea of Galilee, I often sat and talked with the skipper. At times he let me take the wheel, under his watchful eye, and steer the boat across the lake. Laden with Christian pilgrims from all over the world, they were eager to trace the footsteps of their saviour. Often a tour leader approached the skipper to ask him to stop the boat, 'Where Jesus walked on the water.' The skipper looked sceptical and then chose a spot on the sea to turn off the engine. The group of devotees then gathered together in prayer.

All people seek to believe. Some follow the guidelines of their religion, to the point of indoctrination, unwilling to go beyond the safety of the word. The divine word is gospel. It is their source of comfort in an uncertain world, a soft place to land if ever they were to fall. Others are cynical and sneer at any belief that smacks of established thought, or absolute faith. They refuse to invest in the idea that a higher force controls our destiny. Their view is powered by self-determination and therefore their trust lies firmly in themselves.

There are those, like me, who are on a continuous quest, open to all dogmas to draw on the aspects that resonate within them. These souls seek solace in the truth and hope to discover pearls of wisdom wherever they can. Most of their insight comes from experience as they tread on the shaky road of life, hoping that it will eventually lead to a higher path.

Next door to my hostel was a Christian mission run by a young preacher, Walter from Scotland. Most evenings I clambered over my roof onto theirs to join the group for tea and indulge in some delicious local sweets, while having a good giggle and a chat. Even then I realised the irony of the situation. I had travelled so far to connect with my people, yet I had bridged the gap by climbing over rooftops to be with the Christian folk next door.

It proved there is a common bond that exists between all people. A great gay guy in the group, Sean, shared my sense of fun and, joining forces, we drove Walter crazy as we sat at the back in his

Hebrew class and laughed at some words that sounded more like music than vocabulary. The UN personnel in the class were not amused but as hard as we tried, we could not remain serious for long. Humour was a necessary component to survive in a world that often felt like it was on the verge of its destruction.

Tiberias was settled in the first century CE and named in honour of the second Roman Emperor. It was described by an Arab scholar as a pagan city, plagued by debauchery and oppressive heat. Add plagues of insects and mud. Despite this, the town grew in size because of the hot springs close by, and it became a healing sanctuary.

My interest lay in the ruins of an ancient synagogue, on the outskirts of the town. Dating back to the 4th century, all that was left of Hammat Tiberias synagogue was its mosaic floor. When I entered the archaeological site, no one else was there. What I saw took my breath away. The mosaic floor, in all its breadth and beauty, was perfectly preserved and its large central panel rocked me to my very core. It spoke volumes about ancient Judaic beliefs.

In a circle was a vivid depiction of the 12 signs of the zodiac, exactly as they are today. Each sign, in correct order, from Aries to Pisces was graphically captured in the mosaic, and there was no doubt that the zodiac circle was the focus of the synagogue.

In the centre of the circle was an image of the sun god, Helios, riding his chariot. Four women, one in each corner, represented the seasons. The upper panel was adorned with symbols, including two ram's horn shofars and a seven-tiered candelabra, or menorah, while the lower one depicted the Ark of the Covenant, two proud lions and the insignia of the royal dynasty of King David.

Connecting the belief in astrology with the archaic roots of Judaism is inconsistent with religious laws yet these discoveries reveal the importance of star wisdom to the ancient Jews. What makes it even more baffling is the use of imagery, especially that of the human form, generally not encouraged in Jewish houses of worship.

Few words can describe how it felt gazing at this perfect work of art for it represented a page out of history. The ornate circle of zodiac signs represented much more than the skill of its execution.

It spoke of a people and a belief so intrinsic to their being – an innate trust in astrology – that it became a pillar of their prayers in the house of the Lord. It spoke of a powerful bond that tied me to this ancient land and to a faith I believed was lost to me.

CHAPTER EIGHT

HOMEWARD BOUND

On my return to London, after my adventure in Israel, the thrill of the unknown was wearing off and I longed for some stability in my life. A newspaper ad proved to be the catalyst, recruiting those with a university major in Psychology and at least two years of teaching experience for a one-year course in Australia to train as a School Counsellor, on full salary. It was a tempting offer, especially as I wanted to extend my experience in that field. So I applied for a position and was offered an interview in Sydney soon after.

Flying back home, I was approved after being questioned by a panel of three. The only problem was that all 42 places in the course had already been filled. I was advised that I would be included in the following year's intake but a year was far too long to wait. With nothing else planned, I asked if there was a possibility of applying for a special grant for a further placement that year.

The response from the Education Department was sceptical, as the Treasury would have to release a large amount to cover the costs and salary. Still, they applied on my behalf which was appreciated.

In the meantime, desperate for a purpose, I called upon a higher source. 'Please reach out,' I asked, 'to any spirits roaming around the Treasury and grant my wish.' It was far-fetched and beyond my reach but I was willing to try anything. A few days later I received a call from an incredulous guy at the Education Department. 'Can't believe it,' he said, 'but the Treasury has allocated the funds for you.' It proved the power of manifestation.

It was only on Orientation Day at the college where the course was to be held, that the truth emerged. One of the administrators scanning his list, callously remarked, 'Oh, *you're* number 43. You got in over somebody's dead body.' Then he walked away while I stood there in shock. It seemed someone from the previous year's course had tragically died and so the funds for that placement were reallocated to me. I tried to shake off a feeling of guilt but spirit reassured me that the funds were well spent. It was meant to be.

The year course went by quickly, with no highs or lows, special friends or great expectations. After graduation, it was a requirement that two years be spent working in a rural area to fill an urgent need. Most graduates requested a position on the coast with few of the hardships that remote areas might entail. When I explored a map of the state, I was drawn to the Riverina, a rich agricultural area in the south. It was not a dangling crystal that pointed it out, but rather a gut feeling tinged with a touch of providence.

I applied for Griffith, a regional city in the Murrumbidgee Irrigation area, with a strong Italian population. Known for its wine and vineyards, its hot summers yielded a variety of fresh produce. Infamous in the 1970s for its marijuana crops and ties to the mafia, it was a district with a rich history and culture, and I was allocated it.

Arriving in Griffith, I checked out the local accommodation and decided on a room, in a farmhouse not too far out of town. In a lovely rural setting, the two guys who lived there proved to be great company, essential in unfamiliar territory. Bob was gregarious and loud while Brad, a teacher at a school close by, was more introspective.

Pippa, my cat, was overawed by her new surroundings and disappeared for a few days in the barn. She soon adapted and appeared to enjoy country life, with many a mouse to chase or just lie in the shade of a sprawling tree to avoid the heat of the noonday sun.

I was assigned to a central high school, with nine feeder primary schools. They were all pleasant visits, usually once a month, to deal with any problems that may have arisen. They rarely did.

Walking into the playground, the boys, wearing their 'cowboy' hats to shield them from the harsh sun, yelled a greeting while the girls giggled and disappeared. There was a nice cup of tea waiting for me, and with a bit of luck, a delicious batch of scones, complete with whipped cream and strawberry jam.

It was only a matter of time before I drifted into a relationship with Brad, for he possessed the soul of a musician and played the Spanish guitar with great feeling. He had grown up in a tough town in the bush, one not known for its gentility, and was misplaced in a harsh setting. A true Pisces, he was like a fish out of water.

Brad played guitar and flute and sang with a local country band each weekend. We'd head off to a country barn where I danced the Brown Jug Polka with the locals while Brad performed. Watching the principal of one of my schools do the chicken dance and other such foolery was fun because city folk were more restrained.

Some of the schools in my district were a distance from town but my fear of driving was eased by the quiet country roads with the odd tractor, chugging by from a nearby orange grove. The green fields I drove through were bathed in shades of rich purple, vibrant and sprawling with Paterson's curse. An invasive weed, it was poisonous to grazing livestock, but still provided a stunning backdrop.

The heat could be oppressive. One day I returned home to find all the candles in the house wilted over the side of their holders, and I vied with Pippa for the best spot under the air conditioner. Apart from the climate, the town, with its restaurants, art galleries, social events and interesting people was a nice place to live.

After working together, I soon became friends with the school counsellor on the other side of town, Leoni. My office was air-conditioned while her older school relied on fans. Her work involved lots of testing which left Leoni stressed and depleted, while my issues were more personal. I was warned that some of the parents could be volatile but they were never more than I could handle.

I also worked with the psychologist at the Health Department in town, a pert young thing, fresh from college. As the most robust person among us, I was chosen to be Santa Claus one Christmas, and the psychologist was my elf. Unable to see under my beard, I barely missed knocking out a child skipping alongside me, with my bell. The delighted looks on the children's faces, and their giant hugs, were priceless as they looked at me through eyes of innocence.

I lasted in the Riverina for three years before Brad and I transferred back to Sydney. We rented a lovely house in the lower Blue Mountains and drove down to the western suburbs of Sydney each day. Fortunately, we were assigned to the same school because I refused to drive in the city, the traffic was far too stressful for me.

My district comprised three schools, with my base a primary school that once was the biggest in the southern hemisphere. It was a different challenge from the one I faced in the country and involved a lot of tedious testing for eligibility in special needs classes.

Instead of fulfilling me, it drained me. I thrived on personal interaction with the students and helping them face the issues that invariably arise in their school years. To transform the strained faces of children, in the middle of an emotional crisis, into a look of hope because someone listened and understood, was gratifying.

When a problem was complex and deep-rooted, I turned to astrology for a deeper understanding. A birth chart holds many clues to a life journey, providing great insight into the wounds of the past. To express these issues is very challenging and confronting, especially in the case of children, who cannot verbalise them. Even adults have difficulty facing or recognising their inner hurdles.

Mine were beginning to surface but Brad didn't notice my enthusiasm dwindling because he was far too immersed in his own world. In his youth, he was an altar boy in the local church and was better suited for the spiritual life. He found harsh reality difficult to deal with, and increasingly he let go of the physical world, where intimacy and bodily contact were important. These were a vital component of love for me and part of me felt incomplete.

It takes disillusion to tear down the foundations of the past, especially when it no longer serves you. Plagued by frustration after a year, it crippled my ability to be useful and my health started to decline. It had been an uphill battle over the past few years to deal with bouts of severe pelvic pain, which was increasing in intensity. There are few things more draining than constant pain.

Initially triggered by the brief use of an IUD in earlier years when I was married, it was followed by multiple surgeries, strong drugs and hospital stays hooked up to antibiotic drips. All failed to eradicate the condition and now the only option was a hysterectomy.

Frustration and pain joined forces until the pressure became too much. At its peak, I locked the door to my office and took refuge under the desk, ignoring all the knocks and calls. I thought back to all the children I helped and it was all worthwhile, but now I was exhausted and my worn-out body mirrored the state of my soul.

It was not an easy decision to go ahead with the surgery because I was still young, but it did not have the heart-wrenching effect it had on other women who were desperate to become a mother. I had over 2,000 children under my care and that was sufficient. Beyond that, I sensed there was more to my life and freedom was imperative.

After the operation, the head nurse came to my bedside to reassure me. 'You were a mess inside,' she consoled. The gynaecologist followed soon after, confirming his initial diagnosis. 'The surgery probably saved your life.' His words provided some solace and confirmed that I had not imagined the pain or its severity.

The suffering did not end there. Lying in bed one night, back home, I heard a terrible commotion and the wail of my beloved cat, Pippa. I ran outside, clutching my wound, to find her being attacked by two dogs. One, a nasty German Shepherd, had Pippa's head in his jaws and, without thought, I ran over and punched him on the head with my clenched fist until he released his grip. Pippa was rushed to the vet but she was never the same again.

The planets had aligned in the worst way and they were not done yet. Difficult transits of combative Mars, sour Saturn, or destructive Pluto, combined with tough angles between them, have dire consequences. Mars manifests as anger and aggression, Saturn illness and hardship, and Pluto, the god of the underworld, is karmic and life changing. Unlike the others, its effect does not pass easily. I was about to enter a dark tunnel and there was no turning back.

I tried alternative methods in an attempt to heal, many and varied. Then, one weekend, I attended a workshop on ancient Chinese healing techniques hoping to speed up the process. The tutor was a rather petulant young man who had gone to China to study these skills. His energy was mediocre at best, with occasional glimpses of a dark side hidden in the shadows. His instruction was not new to me, nor did it heal, or rock, my world but it appeared to rattle his.

During a break, the tutor confided in me that his mother was a black witch in Melbourne. My reaction was to steer clear of him. Why did he feel the need to share this with me and what bearing did this have on my life? It turned out to be critical. While the course had little impact, the repercussions altered my life. A few days later, a letter arrived from him. The message was brief but ominous.

'You think your magic is stronger than mine. I'll show you!'

It was not a subtle or well-guarded attack, rather it was brutal. After falling into a deep sleep that night, I woke to the frightening feeling of being smothered. The presence of a dark entity was hovering by my bed, followed by a deadly grip around my throat. It was petrifying. I was walking in the shadow of death and I struggled to retain my hold on life. Jerking awake, I gasped for breath.

Brad was helpless to protect me as the onslaught continued for days until I was too scared to sleep. Desperate, I needed to find a means of protection. I trolled through libraries, looking for any book, or passage, which could shed light on my situation and offer some hope. One helped. A Navajo Indian prayer of protection, 'I walk with beauty, below, around, above me,' which I repeated each night while surrounding my body in a circle of light and sealing it within a crystal shield. It provided me with a temporary sanctuary.

No church or synagogue had the answers I needed. Only the Spiritual church offered some insight. A medium stood on the platform and channelled a response, declaring, 'You have a profound role to play for the powers of light and so the forces of darkness will try to destroy you.' The words sounded like the eternal cry of my people because their light was an eternal threat to the forces of evil.

Ground down by the relentless attack each night, and frantic to escape the threat, I decided to leave the country. Fate chose the destination – the island of Bali. The person was chosen too. The grandson of a mighty healer, he was a master of magic. Few places in the world claim to accept the existence of the dark arts and magic, and few people could profess to be experts on such matters.

The purpose of my trip to Bali was to rest, a reprieve from the nightly terror. Following the well-worn trail of the seeker who goes to Bali in search of solace or inspiration, I sought refuge in the fields of Ubud. The island's mystery was still intact in those early days, and like countless others, Bali entranced me. The beauty of the lush green rice paddies was magnified by the flickering fireflies, along with the innocence of the doe-eyed cows and the tinkling of their wooden bells. The solitude and silence were a welcome relief.

Ubud acted as a barrier to negative energies because the spirits that inhabited Bali were not the sort to tamper with. However, the spell was broken only when I moved to Sanur, on the east coast. The area had a reputation as the residence of powerful men of magic that dated back centuries. Now, its past is masked under the banner of tourism, the perfect place for a sedate holiday.

It was not in a Hindu temple, draped in a sarong with flowers in my hair, that I met my priest – the man who would 'save' me. Rather it was to the raucous beat of a popular night club that our paths were destined to cross. Budding holy man by day and playboy bartender by night, Remy was magnetic in both roles. He spotted me first, on the dance floor. It was not the disco fluff popular at the time that moved me but rather the throbbing beat of Santana.

Remy instantly recognised our connection, at first more sensual than spiritual. He summoned the doorman to wait for me as I exited the Ladies. Guiding me by the arm, I was led straight to Remy's bar. Remy was a name given to him by tourists who loved his antics and considered him as smooth as the brandy. This was not his first rodeo as he took my hand and gazed into my eyes, but the spark between us was strong enough to light up the island.

In truth, fate took me by the hand that night, delivering me to the one man who had the power to save me. It didn't make me feel any less guilty leaving with Remy at the end of the night. Riding off on the back of his motorbike, we headed for the beach and a stunning display of moonlight on the ocean. The waves rippled no warnings and Remy's touch stirred feelings almost lost to me. Brad had become more of a friend than a lover. Still, we shared a bond, so I was torn because Brad was a good man who did not deserve betrayal.

It was clear from the start that Remy was a player, notching up many a tourist on his belt. To be fair so did most of the beach boys for they had their pick of girls who came to the island for a fling. Aware of the sacrifice needed to become a Hindu priest one day and devote his life to his temple, to conduct religious rites and ceremonies, Remy was determined to be carefree while he could and enjoy the freedom that would one day be denied to him.

Weeks of torment ended when we finally slept together. No devious spirit could break through Remy's force field, no demon dared defy his iron-clad shield. Safe at last, and in the throes of passion, his Mars and my Venus in Scorpio collided, causing an intense sexual attraction. What Remy didn't expect was that this time when he fooled around, he fell in love. There can be no more powerful magic.

When Remy drove me to the airport in Bali, for my return to Sydney, I turned for one final wave goodbye. Remy's face was pressed against the glass, his eyes wet with tears. It was an emotional parting because loss was not a feeling that Remy was comfortable with. He couldn't have it all, and some things were beyond his reach.

It was even more painful for me because I felt lost. Brad was at the airport in Sydney waiting to pick me up, trusting as always. We had been together for four years, and it was not a relationship to cast aside on a whim. I went through the motions of life, trying hard to pick up the pieces of the past but they just didn't fit any more.

Struggling to keep the secret from Brad, who deserved much better, I knew it would destroy him to find out the truth. Then a letter arrived from Remy begging me to come back. I never wanted to hurt Brad, but higher forces were at work. When the psychic attacks began again, the nights of horror, it was the deciding factor. A special fate awaited me, along with a pledge made in a previous lifetime.

So, I packed my bags and left. I never disclosed the truth to Brad because while it might ease my conscience, it would devastate him. It was inevitable that he found out the truth and he never forgave me. My destiny lay in Bali and deep in my heart, I knew that Brad needed a child to be complete, a child that I could never give him. There were forces at work beyond our level of understanding and we had separate lives to lead. It was written in the stars long ago.

CHAPTER NINE

BALI HIGH

The ocean breeze caressed the palm trees as the shadow of the holy mountain, Mt. Agung, loomed in the distance, streaking shades of violet and pink across the Bali evening sky. My modest room in a small hotel, set right on the beach in Sanur with the sound of the waves to lull me to sleep, gave me a long-awaited sense of peace. Gone was the pain that had racked my body and the demons that haunted me, for I was now protected by powerful magic.

The first months with Remy were idyllic as we toured the island by motorbike and grew to know each other better. Seemingly without a care in the world, I found my freedom. No more doubt, indecision, wicked spells, or sleepless nights, only happiness. The love I shared with Remy was passionate, the excitement of a forceful union. Looking into his eyes was enough to trigger an explosion and we matched each other perfectly in many ways.

A new world opened up for me, for Bali's unique culture was exotic and fascinating. My energy merged with the island because Bali has Libra sensitivity, as reflected in each word of love and every creative work of art. Its philosophy is one of balance, of the light and dark forces. The black and white checked cloth wrapped around sacred trees and temples signalled the balance of good and evil, as did offerings to the gods and demons.

Each day prayers were uttered as small baskets of flowers and burning incense were raised high in the temples, close to heaven for the gods. Those placed on the ground were intended to placate the demons. Bali was a Hindu island with a rich heritage dating back centuries to the kingdoms of Java. In their belief, both good and evil *had* to be respected. Few people were foolish enough to risk the repercussions of ignoring their spiritual duties.

Remy, a Libra born a year earlier than me, belonged on the island, descending from a long line of holy men. Before praying twice daily in his home temple, he doused himself with holy water steeped in fragrant blossoms. His scent was intoxicating and the smoke that curled from the sticks of rich incense in the offering basket for his gods completed his aura. The aroma filtered through every whisper or close embrace. It was sheer enchantment.

Remy's commitment to his temple was fired by a conviction stronger than faith. I never understood the significance until much later. While the concepts of spirit and magic are often relegated to the realm of fiction and film in Western society, Bali has an inherent belief in these things. In Remy, it was fundamental to his being.

Entranced by the culture, I began to view life through the island's mystical lens. The festival of Galungan, in the Balinese calendar of 210 days, celebrates the triumph of good over evil. Offerings, suspended on swaying *penjors* – curved bamboo poles – lined the roads, a bridge between the mortal realm and the divine.

A time of feasting, and splendid processions, it lasts for ten days. Towering displays of fruit and flowers lent even more beauty to the island, as women paraded with the colourful offerings perfectly balanced on their heads. A village procession had a special kind of magic, a stunning line of people creating a true spectacle, in matching costumes in varied vibrant shades.

Kuningan, the end of the festivities, marks the return of the spirits to heaven. It was the first time Remy included me in a ceremony, to follow an age-old tradition, making the pilgrimage across water to pray at the temple on Turtle Island, Nusa Serangan, with his family. Remy looked regal in a dark sarong and white tunic, sashed with bands of gold, with frangipanis tucked into his headband. Remy's younger sisters, elegant in Balinese dress, happily helped me into my sarong and dusky pink lace kebaya blouse. His aunt remained sullen and silent, as she battled with the presence of a foreigner.

Walking along a sandy trail on the beach at Sanur, we waited at the water's edge to board an outrigger boat for the trip across to the island. It was no mean feat getting onto the boat in a tight sarong but the ladies did so with grace, all the while balancing large offerings on their heads. I needed a great deal of help to retain my modesty.

Once ashore, we joined hundreds of Balinese in prayer at the temple. It was exciting to experience the festival the way it was intended before the island was spoiled and a causeway connected it to the highway. It was the price of progress. I was fortunate to have experienced the true face of Bali in the mid-1980s before it changed.

The glimpses of the Bali of old, with its timeless rituals, were hypnotic. My first true vision of it came when Remy's calm demeanour was shattered one day when he learnt of his grandfather's death. Remy was distraught because he was the man who had raised him, choosing Remy out of 11 grandchildren to teach the ancient ways of healing and magic. As a healer and priest, he was a man of high standing in the community and his death rites needed to reflect this.

Remy disappeared for days, his full attention focused on preparing the cremation rites for his grandfather. One week later, I watched the colourful parade wind its way through the streets of Sanur. To the beating of drums, crowds of people jostled for a view.

A line of women in deathly black slithered down the road like an endless winding snake, carrying offerings for the soul to take on its long journey. A long ribbon of white cloth, covered by cabbalistic symbols drawn by the priest, ensured entry into heaven. It floated through the air in a grand spectacle, demanding attention.

A volley of men hurtled forward, balancing a tall bamboo tower on their backs. Spinning in wild circles, they thwarted any evil spirit lurking to whisk the corpse away. The higher the tower, the greater the prestige of the departed and it was clear from its height that Remy's grandfather was a man of high standing in the community.

Standing behind a palm tree on the beach, I watched as ritual items were placed around the corpse in the bull sarcophagus – silks, brocades and ancient coins – a ransom to Yama, the lord of hell, to allow the soul to pass undisturbed. The priest stooped over the body, splashing it with holy water as the many mirrors decorating the bull glinted in the afternoon sun.

Once set alight the bull ignited in fury and a sharp crackle whipped through the air. The wooden bull groaned and then collapsed into embers and a floating layer of blackened ash. An extraordinary look of peace flooded Remy's face.

As the fire subsided, the ashes and fragments of charred bone were collected in a hollow coconut shell and then wrapped in a white cloth. Remy waded through the water following the priest, and after a prayer to the spirit of the sea to guide the soul safely, the ashes were flung into the ocean. Cleansed by all four elements – earth, fire, air and water, his grandfather's soul was now free.

When Remy finally returned to my arms he was spent, on all levels. I was equally worn out by the anxiety of not being able to reach him for more than a week. By sharing a window into his soul, the bond between Remy and I deepened but some part of him would always stay out of reach. It added to the intrigue and attraction, for there were two distinct sides to Remy – the mysterious and enigmatic holy man and the carefree playboy. Each came with their separate appeal, and both were equally perplexing.

After all the drama it was a relief to go to the club and watch Remy enter a frivolous world of fun and music. Tossing cocktail shakers into the air, he delighted people with his irresistible laugh. Girls and women hung around his bar hoping for some of his energy to rub off onto them – literally. Denying the demands of his ego, Remy never strayed with me close by. He was not taking any chances.

Remy's boss didn't appreciate me being in the club every night, dimming the allure of his number one attraction, so I tried to stay out of sight. Usually, I sat with some of the regular ladies who each had their reason for being in Bali, mostly because of a man. Conversation was essential to retain our sanity, and it was therapeutic to share our experiences. Most had their tale of woe, with rarely a happy ending, so it was good to compare notes.

The atmosphere in the club in the 1980s was a pungent mix of stale alcohol and raging hormones. The aroma was especially potent in the Ladies' room, where layers of hairspray and poufy hair combined with heavy perfumes like *Opium* and *Poison*, guaranteed to make men weak at the knees, and then pass out. An overdose of *Samsara*, a heady mix of jasmine and sandalwood, ensured that I made a beeline for the nearest exit as did Madonna's 'Holiday'.

Meanwhile, back in the club, the theme from 'Hawaii 5-0' triggered a pack of drunken Aussie lads to leap onto the dance floor, their legs splayed and limbs entwined, as they frantically rowed an imaginary canoe across the archipelago. None of them had the faintest idea where they were.

I recall an Immigration Officer at Sydney airport, on my way to Bali, commending me as the only person who knew their country of arrival. *Indonesia*. Many people never paid attention in their geography class and didn't know, or care, where they were. It would always be Bali to them, and they remained none the wiser.

That was patently clear as I watched a bevy of young lovelies push aside the rowing teams, to strut their stuff to the catchy beat of the 'Macarena'. As they pranced through the steps, half facing the wrong direction, one was impaled by a stiletto on her opponent's foot while another was being shadowed, in a most inappropriate manner, by an over-ardent canoeist who had forgotten his way back to his seat. If the gang's destination was the Pacific, he would have been thrown overboard or left behind on Pitcairn Island.

Months passed without any drama, going through the throes of an island romance. The only sore point was the amount of time Remy was gone on some excuse or other. I didn't want to demand his full attention because he had many commitments while I had none. It was hard to remain in permanent holiday mode because I had always been an overachiever, but I tried my best to relax. Just as I was getting in the groove, the bubble was set to burst.

Hidden beneath the façade of tourism, in the very core of Bali, lies a secret underbelly. The dark spirits that reside there are not to be trifled with. One day Remy took me to a far-off village to witness the ultimate battle between good and evil. To the clash of cymbals and the driving beat of the gamelan orchestra, men in a deep state of trance stabbed themselves in the chest with strong metal daggers. Some even poked them into their eyes. It was a gruesome scene.

The evil queen Rangda had cursed them but the metal blades of the daggers bent rather than pierce their skin. Shielded from harm, they were the champions of the mythical Barong, the masked shaggy lion of good. It protected them and all of Bali from evil.

While it was frightening to see the dark side in action, it was nothing compared to the dread I felt when faced with the evil forces that attacked me. I preferred not to be reminded of these dark entities. The negative onslaught was dramatic and sudden at times, at others it crept up insidiously, attacking at your most vulnerable.

Or when you least expect it.

One night at the club I was standing alone when a tipsy Aussie woman sashayed over to my side. 'All the barmen here are *married*,' Liz slurred. Then she smiled smugly and staggered away. It took a while for her words to register.

Stunned, I confronted all the barmen for answers. Each one claimed that Liz fancied Remy and was jealous. 'She just wants to make trouble,' they argued, as they joined forces to shield me from the truth. When challenged, Remy held on to the story. Lies have a way of exploding and when they do, it is time to run for cover and seek shelter from the storm. If not, you will be drenched.

It was not a subtle trickle but rather a massive tidal wave. Lying with Remy in my room one day, the sound of crunching gravel was followed by a banging on the door. As I got up to open it, Remy jumped off the bed and wrenched the door handle out of my grip, resisting the force being pushed against it. Remy yelled at me to go into the bathroom and lock the door. I hovered in fear as glass shattered, Remy's helmet hurled against the windowpane. Remy shouted for me to stay put, as he went out the door into the direct line of fire.

Warily, I opened the bathroom door just a little to watch the scene unfold. Remy was outside, grappling with a woman and shouting, words that I didn't understand. Then without a goodbye, Remy hopped onto his motorbike, with the woman clenching onto him, and rode off into the sunset. I didn't hear from him for days.

When an old man tending the garden wandered over to pick up the splintered glass, I begged him for answers. He replied, *'Istri.'* It was one of the few Indonesian words I knew. *'Istri'* meant wife. The possibilities swirled around in my head and the inner turmoil was overwhelming, especially as Remy had disappeared.

There was little comfort to be had when Remy returned. He swore that there was no love between them, having married years before in a simple temple ceremony because she was pregnant. No child in Bali can be without parents, so their son needed to be legitimate. It was a great tragedy when his son passed away at an early age. Remy claimed they had split long ago but his wife refused to let go. When she heard rumours about me it was the final straw.

Remy spent every night with me all the time I was in Bali so it seemed unlikely he was leading a double life. The icy rift between us began to thaw when he promised to divorce his wife. In a single day, it was done. Remy rescinded his marriage vows to his wife in a simple temple ceremony and they were no longer bound.

With the past behind us, our lives took on a whole new dimension. Feeling confident at last in our relationship, the physical attraction between us remained intense but the cultural divide became increasingly hard to navigate. Remy tried to include me more in his daily activities, and I often accompanied him for his morning prayer, at the temple in his home.

It allowed me to become more familiar with his extended family but affection and warm gestures were not part of their cultural norms. Coming from a European background where greetings were effusive it was a major adjustment to appear cool and detached.

The family shared a village compound, a maze of rooms with tiled porches, punctuated by a few white frangipani trees. Although Remy vaguely pointed out his father, the rest of the people just drifted by doing their daily chores and I had no clue who they were.

The elderly folk spoke only Balinese, with a complex caste system of language that I was not familiar with, and I was battling just to master the spoken language of the country, Indonesian.

Dodging a few brazen roosters strutting around the yard, I spoke some broken English with his sisters although his aunt made a point of staying aloof. There was a new baby in the compound that everyone was fussing over and it was interesting to watch the rituals as she grew. These were the essential rites of passage throughout life.

Even before birth, a ceremony is held to protect the child from bad spirits. At birth, the placenta, the spiritual sibling of the child, is placed inside a coconut and buried in the front of the home with pandan leaves to repel black magic. The umbilical cord is encased in silver or gold and hung around the baby's neck as protection.

To remain pure, the baby is not allowed to touch the ground for three months and their hair is cut only at six months, to release any sins from a previous lifetime. These rituals continue in adolescence with a tooth filing, the six upper canine teeth filed smoothly to remove any trace of evil and any connection to demons.

It was intriguing to immerse myself in Balinese culture and while some customs were clear and laid out, others remained hidden. Just like the shadow puppet play that Remy seemed immersed in, things were not always as they appeared on the enchanted island.

A year went by before the truth was revealed, a year that passed in a kaleidoscope of emotions – obsessive love, fascination with the culture and rare specks of disillusion. In the end, I was the helpless puppet being manipulated by the grand puppet master, Remy.

How the truth surfaced I'm not sure but it shot me down in a blaze of deceit and lies. If it were a plot from a movie it would be barely believable but the scenario was often repeated on the island, with many variations. Many Westerners were deceived by the allure of the island but few tales were more confronting than mine.

Remy's family, whom I had grown close to, were a fabrication. His grim-faced aunt was, in fact, his first wife, which explained her glares, and his three young sisters were his daughters. Did he fob me off as a naive foreigner, his pen pal from overseas or some tourist who wanted to learn more about the culture? Then again, he may have told them the truth and they had no choice but to live with it. Remy's father had three wives and I had no idea which one was his mother. They all sat together in an open hut, weaving offerings.

While polygamy had been accepted practice on the island in times gone by, the lies and deceit were not, or would never be, acceptable to me. There was no more forgiveness or turning back. Remy was a reckless liar and my time in Bali had been an illusion. The hurt and betrayal overwhelmed me and despite Remy's pleas, I packed a bag and headed for the bus station in Denpasar, taking the first bus off the island. It was heading for the island of Java.

CHAPTER TEN

A MYSTICAL REALM

The island of Java, west of Bali, has a haunting history that dates back many centuries – complete with Hindu kingdoms, ancient Buddhist temples and a powerful spiritual presence. Regal tigers once prowled its jungles, proud masters of the land but they became extinct by the 1980s due to the destruction of their habitat. Bali's tiger was wiped out even earlier, around 1937. Unlike these noble beasts, I had no intention of fading from view because there were still places to go, forests to roam and fields of discovery yet to explore.

After a maniacal drive down the highway in Java, I grabbed my bag and got off the bus in the town of Probolinggo. From there, I boarded a mini bus heading towards Mt. Bromo, a spectacular active volcano. A Hindu pilgrimage site, it was a place of offerings and sacrifices in exchange for blessings from the gods.

I needed all the blessings I could get because I was spent emotionally and desperate for relief. Ascending through cool greenness and a forest studded with pine trees, I reached a small homestay and a welcome dinner of nasi goreng, fried rice.

Included in the price of the room was a guide to take me to the volcano the following morning. At 3 am I was woken by a knock on the door. A modest young man, in a woollen poncho, stood there meekly and said, 'I'm Udi, your guide. The sky is clear tonight with many stars, so it's a good view. Take a blanket. It's cold outside.'

The faint flicker from a torch was the only light as Udi led me across the Sea of Sand, the caldera of a past volcano, as we headed for the active crater of Mt. Bromo. Its name comes from Brahma, the Hindu god of creation, so this was a symbolic journey. If I could traverse the large plateau and climb to the top, to view the very core of an active volcano, then I was strong enough to let go of the past. The present was all I had, all there was to cling to.

There was no trace of the moon as we began our trek, and shivering in the bitter cold, I pulled the thick blanket tightly around me. As we crossed the plateau, chilled dew frosted my hair and ran down my cheeks in icy streams. Every breath I took hung suspended in space and an eerie mist shrouded our footsteps. One last flicker from the torch and then total darkness. It was only the crunching of gravel below our feet that kept us grounded.

An orange glow in the distance and the acrid smell of sulphur meant we were getting closer. When the plateau merged into hard rock, I climbed slowly up the steep stairs carved into its side. The first ones to reach the top, we sat on the ground and rested, watching the dim lights of horse riders crossing the plain towards us.

Staggering across the craggy ground to the rim of the active volcano, I peered into its raging belly, deep into its bleeding heart – to where the ground had cracked open and fed anger into its veins. It was like staring into the eye of a tiger. The volcano spewed fire and molten lava into the sky. Warnings were issued over the years as the volcano grumbled and groaned, hurling out rocks and other debris. Dangerous, it had even claimed lives but it spared mine.

It was time to let go of the anger so I headed for the calm of the ancient temple of Borobudur, the largest Buddhist temple in the world. Built from 760 CE to 840 CE during the Golden Age of the Salendra dynasty, a volcanic eruption buried the temple in ash. Mangled in jungle growth, Borobudur lay forgotten for hundreds of years. It was restored in a major project in the 1970s to expose its immense glory and was declared a World Heritage Site in 1991.

Ten terraces on three levels, representing a three-dimensional cosmic mandala, mirror the spiritual path one must follow to reach Nirvana. A masterpiece of history, over one thousand relief panels tell the story of Buddha's incarnation and his teachings. Carvings of nubile dancing girls, majestic elephants and processions of brave warrior kings line the walls, making it the largest and most complete collection of Buddhist reliefs in the world.

On the terrace roof is a profusion of stony Buddhas and bell-shaped stupas, each containing a seated Buddha protected by stone latticework. To reach in and touch the Buddha's foot is thought to bring good luck. I sat cross-legged beside a Buddha statue, one of over 500 statues that once lined its terraces, and gazed out over the green countryside smudged with red blossoms, just as they had for centuries. I was alone and in a state of peace.

In this place of pilgrimage, in the face of years of neglect and volatile natural forces, there was stillness. In a frenetic world consumed by progress, it exuded tranquillity and a sense of familiarity that hounded me throughout my travels in Java. Strangely, it felt like I was home and the strong feelings translated into a longing to be reunited with the past.

This connection intensified when I reached the regal city of Yogyakarta, the cultural capital of Java. The city lies at the centre of

Java's 'Realm of the Dead' surrounded by ancient ruins. It teems with the ghosts of past kings and rulers, sacred objects and revered spirits. Music and dance flourished here over the ages, along with performance and puppetry.

The Kraton palace, dating back to the 18th century, remains the residence of the ruling sultan. Walking barefoot across the marble floor, beneath the vaulted ceiling of the Glass Pavilion, I inhaled the rich scent of wood and aromatic blossoms. The smell triggered visions of the past – the wail of holy mantras and a royal procession, vibrant in peacock blue and batik. Then came the stylised movements of a dancer, her body wrapped in gold and her spirit encased in silk. It was all coming back. So very near, yet out of reach.

One of the eccentricities of travel is the people you meet along the way. Phoebe was a true Brit, the gung-ho type, who in lives gone by would have been wrapped in mosquito netting with smelling salts at the ready. She had no filter and talked incessantly. We shared a room in Yogyakarta where she paraded around virtually naked, chomping on tropical fruit while recounting useless historical data or a wild adventure of her imagination, which at least was very fertile. My patience was waning by the day but still, I persevered.

Enrolling in a batik class as a distraction, I dripped hot wax on my cloth to create a vivid scene of a volcano while Phoebe's tiger looked more like a dinosaur. At the class, we met Amy, a New York fashion designer, with fingers as adept as they were refined. Amy was the epitome of the American socialite, elegance personified, and I wasn't sure which one of them made me feel more out of sync with humanity but it was a delicate balance.

One day Phoebe whisked me away on a bicycle carriage to the site of a romantic tryst. 'To the Water Castle!' Phoebe blazed, the driver at her command. A single lily in the mossy pool was the only remnant of the past, the tiles chipped and faded. Perched at the edge of the pool, we climbed the stairs to the tower, the perfect vantage point for a king to gaze upon the ladies swimming below and make his choice. The king was said to throw a rose and whoever caught it, among his wives and concubines, was the 'chosen' one.

This place surely was a hotbed of jealousy. Or did these consorts simply accept their fate, part of an age-old tradition, and consider themselves fortunate to be one of the king's entourage? Was I wrong to demand an exclusive relationship with Remy for he was born into a different society and I was an intruder from another land? Love to me was all-consuming. Even the sultan had his favourite among the many but she too came from another realm.

Tucked away in a small alley was a secret marriage chamber. A private courtyard shielded the dark cave, the flickering flame of scattered candles casting silhouettes on the cave walls. Two rocky slabs, placed side by side, formed the bridal beds, and sprigs of white jasmine and pink rose petals softened their union. Crumpled notes and old coins, wedged in the rock crevices, were left by those who came in prayer for this was no ordinary couple.

This was the sacred pairing of a mighty king and an ocean goddess. It was during the reign of King Senopati in the 16th century, that this bond was forged. One day the king sat in meditation by the ocean, creating such a surge of energy that Mount Merapi shook, stirring the Goddess of the South Seas, Nyai Loro Kidul, to rise from her underwater kingdom.

Hers was a tragic tale. Once the daughter of the Sundanese king and queen, the king's other wives and concubines, in a jealous rage, cursed both women with leprosy, turning them into ugly crones. Forced out of the kingdom, the queen died in a forest. The princess wandered south to the ocean where she collapsed from despair at the edge of a cliff.

Woken by the sound of waves, a voice commanded her to jump into the ocean. Desperate, she plunged off the cliff and sank into the watery depths only to be transformed into a goddess, the ruler of a vast underwater realm. King Senopati, overwhelmed by the vision of her as she rose from the water, asked the goddess for her hand in marriage. She accepted his proposal, vowing to empower and protect the king. and all of his descendants.

Their union remains intact and each successive sultan pledges his allegiance to the goddess. Every year lavish offerings, along with clippings of the sultan's hair and nails, are taken to the ocean so the couple can renew their vows. During regal processions, the Ocean Goddess sits beside the sultan in the first carriage, while his earthly wife sits in the carriage behind to show due respect.

To neglect the goddess is dangerous. The surge of the seas around Java is mighty and despite the country's conversion to Islam long before, its heritage is steeped in mystical practices that are deeply ingrained in the culture. Hotels perched on the ocean in Bali and Java often set aside a special room to honour the Goddess of the South Seas. A gesture of respect and a spiritual insurance of sorts.

In the silence of the cave, her presence was obvious, her shadow captured in the sheen of the petrified glassy walls. When I closed my eyes, the soft lilt of a woman's breath grazed my cheek. The salty scent of the ocean flooded the cave, along with the distant sound of waves. The goddess *was* there. With every sigh, she breathed life into me. Once a mere mortal, she understood the pain of scarred emotions and the strength needed to rise again.

Dating back to the 17th century, Imogiri is the traditional burial place for the royalty of central Java. A steep staircase leads to the sacred tombs where the kings of Surakarta are buried on one side while the kings of Yogyakarta lie on the other. In the centre, in pride of place, is the tomb of the esteemed third king of the Islamic Mataram kingdom, Sultan Agung.

It was Amy's encouragement, Phoebe's galloping pace, and my desire to escape her historical rants that helped me scale the four hundred stairs. Traditional Javanese dress was required at the grave site, so behind a discreet screen an elderly man wrapped a batik sarong over my skirt and wound a bolt of batik cloth around my chest, leaving my arms bare as was the custom.

After removing my shoes, I wandered around the grave site of the ancient rulers and waited my turn to enter the revered tomb of Sultan Agung. Only one person was allowed into the tomb at a time and the anticipation was building until it was my turn.

Stooping to enter the crypt, I was struck by the perfume of a thousand rose petals – not only those newly scattered on the grave but also the accumulated fragrance of countless lifetimes. An old man, chanting beside the sultan's tomb, was lost in a cloud of sandalwood. Slowly the incense enveloped me too, and beams of light radiated onto the cave walls from the grave. A ghostly apparition slowly appeared, within the particles of light. Words were whispered, in a foreign tongue but I struggled to understand them.

When I emerged from the tomb, into the harsh light of day, it was hard to return to a normal state. Spread out, across a vast plain was the outline of Mt. Merapi, the volcanic domain of the Ocean Goddess, mistress of both fire and water. The fire was a measure of her anger, the ocean a symbol of her forgiveness. I sat down on a grassy verge where Phoebe was passed out. Amy was nowhere to be seen. Sitting quietly, a magnetic pull distracted me.

Among the crowd was a man with energy so powerful that he stood out amongst the rest. As if compelled, I walked up to him. He had the bearing of a Javanese aristocrat from his impeccable attire to the ruby ring he wore and was astute enough to realise that ours was not a chance meeting. After a brief talk, Soedano handed me his card and issued an invitation. 'There will be a ceremony in my home this evening for the Ocean Goddess. Please come as my guest.' As Amy flowed over to my side, he added, 'You are both welcome.'

The house was packed with guests by the time we arrived. Soedano, our gracious host, was elegant in a blue silk shirt and batik sarong with a matching Javanese headpiece. As we stepped into the living room, I admired the exquisite dagger on display in a glass cabinet. Its gold handle was studded with gemstones, and the iron blade was wavy and sharp. 'It's the family kris,' Soedano explained, 'handed down through the generations. It contains the collective power of all our ancestors. It's shaped that way to inflict maximum damage.'

Distracted by the arrival of more guests, Soedano left to welcome them as the house filled up with more than a hundred people. Traditional Javanese dress had been laid out on the bed for Amy and me so we could participate in the ceremony. Shuffling out of the room in our tight sarongs, and with a bolt of red batik wound around our chest, we followed the crowd into a large hall and took our place, standing at the back to be less conspicuous.

Soedano walked to the front, escorting an elderly woman, the trance medium, so the meditation could begin. After kneeling beside her on the rich Persian carpet, she soon fell into an altered state, her body an empty vessel for spirit. A few minutes later the woman slumped to the floor and a loud voice boomed through her. It was that of a man. Everyone in the room shuddered and as Soedano leaned over to brace her, she whispered in his ear.

Soedano rose to his feet, and passing all the gathered devotees, he scanned the room while making his way to the back. Everyone watched closely and moved out of his path. I was shocked when he stopped in front of me. 'Spirit has spoken,' Soedano said, staring at me. '*You* must lead the meditation. Come take your rightful place.'

Consumed by resistance, echoes of the past, of being singled out by spirit in England, surfaced. I followed Soedano and knelt beside the trance medium. All eyes were on me and there was not a sound, not the wisp of a breath or the crease of a smile.

Closing my eyes, subtle beams of blue light flickered all around and then an image appeared – the sultan bathed in golden shadows. His radiance swamped the room and my mind soared to a different level of consciousness. I had no idea how long I remained immersed in the sultan's grip, but it was only the rumbling of the crowd that jerked me back to a precarious reality.

Our long bus trip to the beach at Parangtritis remains a blur. Notorious for its wild waves and dangerous currents, it is the province of the Ocean Goddess, the entrance to her mythical kingdom. Standing on the ridge of a sandy dune, the howl of the wind tangling my hair, the sea was pure black velvet frosted with white peaks. It merged with the volcanic black sand until there was no dividing line, the myriad of stars the only light. A sketchy vision of the goddess flickered through the water; strands of seaweed studded with pearls.

A large silver tray, covered by a white sheet and flowers, was laid out on the sand as an offering to the goddess. In one graphic movement, the medium's gnarled fingers cast aside the cloth to reveal the severed head of a buffalo, its eyes parched of sight, bulging and glassy in the moonlight. The tray was hoisted up by several men and thrust into the ocean, a trail of flowers blazing a path behind it. Then everyone joined in, plunging into the fierce waves.

I too fell into the water, dragged along with the rest. The waves sucked me under but I was not to become part of the goddess's entourage because her preference was for men, especially those wearing her favourite emerald green, to become her consorts. Another wave crashed over me, and then another. The surf dragged me under as I gasped for breath. Then someone's hand grabbed mine, and I was lifted out of danger and pulled to the surface.

People all around me were struggling to catch their breath, while I crumpled in a wet heap. Meanwhile, the medium drew symbols in the sand, a garble of indecipherable script. Circles within circles, patterned with rocks and twigs. Everyone fell silent, as the drama built. Then came the prophecy. 'The Ocean Goddess is pleased,' the old lady announced. 'The next year will be a good one.' A collective sigh of relief as I looked up to the heavens for guidance. Shafts of light beamed down upon me, illuminating the night.

CHAPTER ELEVEN

FANTASTIC TALES

It was time to cast my fate to the wind once more. Deciding to fly around the islands of Indonesia, my first destination was Medan, in the north of the island of Sumatra. After a long delay, the plane landed in the city after midnight, the stars struggling to appear in the thick grey smog. To add to the desolate mood, the airport terminal was deserted with the only cab just leaving the rank. Luckily, the passenger motioned for the driver to stop.

Winding down his window, the stranger spoke with an American accent. 'I'm going into town, like a lift?' When I caught sight of his deep blue eyes and broad smile, I gladly accepted. 'I'm Matt, Matt Sloane,' he said, helping me into the car. A gentleman as well.

Stationed in Guam, Matt was a pilot in the US forces and was honed to perfection, in every sense of the word. Forcing myself to look away, I stared out at the bleak streets of the city, the houses and shops padlocked as a reminder that I should be more cautious.

When we arrived at the hotel, a bleary-eyed clerk at reception rustled through his guest list. 'Yes, Mr Sloane, you are registered.' When Matt asked for another room for me, the clerk shook his head. 'Sorry, we are booked out. There is a big conference in town.'

Tired, I collapsed onto a lounge. Matt came to my rescue once again. 'My room is a twin. You're welcome to share it. Don't worry, I'm harmless.' Craving the comfort of a warm embrace, he was far more at risk than me, so I accepted. The room was peach and spacious, decorated with paintings of exotic wildlife.

Matt jumped in the shower while I lay in bed, soothed by the sound of the running water. When Matt emerged, I pretended to be asleep. He was naked except for a towel and I groaned inwardly. His body merged into a delicious maze of curves and his skin glowed. No man had the right to be so intoxicating.

Matt slid into his bed and turned off the table lamp. I buried my head in the pillow and admonished myself for having indecent thoughts. In the still of the night, with a mellow light shining in from outside, I watched the rise of his chest and the gentle lilt of his breath. For a brief moment, Remy seemed a million miles away. A memory that did not belong to this lifetime but to eons before in another place and time, when I was far weaker and more vulnerable.

The following morning over breakfast, surrounded by brisk businessmen and the smell of cloves and stale cigarettes, I planned my next move. Matt had a car and driver waiting and was off to visit his friend in a nearby town, while Lake Toba was my destination. Heading in the same direction, he offered me a lift halfway.

When we reached his friend's town, Matt insisted on waiting with me for my bus so we sat on the side of the road, drinking cold Coke. As my bus approached, Matt heaved his bag over his shoulder and, after one last glorious smile, said goodbye.

It was ridiculous to feel his loss but his energy was contagious. One last reprieve and there was no mistaking that voice. 'Do you think there's space for one more on your bus?' I felt instant butterflies. Matt wore no rings and, unlike Remy, had the spirit of a man unencumbered by life. He was free and so was I. While he stretched his boundaries in a physical way, with martial arts, deep-sea diving and jumping out of planes, mine was a quest to go beyond any limitations and discover my truth. It would take us both a lifetime.

Shimmying down the crowded aisle, we sat at the back of the bus, wedged between a wrinkled lady and a squawking chicken in a basket. With a crunching of gears and a flurry of feathers, we were on our way. Besotted with Matt's blue eyes, the old lady reached out to stroke his blond hair. Matt knew how to please and when he winked at her, she erupted into laughter and began chatting away even though we clearly didn't understand a word. As a final gesture, she reached over and put Matt's hand on mine and then broke out in a smile. Matt, not one to disappoint, planted a kiss on my cheek.

The old lady had planted another seed but we both shrugged it off, as flashes of the countryside passed us by. After a long ride, we were met with a stunning sight. Spread out across a huge volcanic depression was Lake Toba, the largest lake in Southeast Asia. Taking a boat ride across it, the air rich with the scent of pine trees, we chose a small homestay that jutted out over a rocky point, overlooking the water. Styled in the traditional way of the Batak people, the huts were carved out of dark wood and patterned in red ochre.

That evening we sat among leafy blossoms, sipping drinks on the terrace of our hut, watching the sky transform from dusky pink to vibrant orange. 'Make a wish,' Matt said, as the first star appeared in the sky. Out of endless possibilities, Matt sensed what I longed for and taking my hand he led me inside the hut.

Matt's touch was electrifying and negated any sense of reason. As we fell onto the bed in a passionate embrace, a strong wind rustled the curtains even though the windows were shut tight, followed by a sudden drop in temperature. Then the sheets rippled as if stroked by a ghostly hand, and we were forcibly split apart. Matt was pinned down on the bed but jerked free, while I lay frozen in fear. Matt's grip broke the spell, and he pulled me out to the balcony.

We took sanctuary on a grassy verge near the lake, as he held me in his arms. 'What the hell just happened?' Matt exclaimed, beads of sweat forming on his forehead. 'I've never felt anything like it before.' Matt was trained to fight enemies on a physical level but supernatural forces were another matter, one in which I had greater experience. It didn't make it any less frightening.

Remy had always protected me from the dark side with his force field. Now that we weren't together, was I at risk of attack once again? Or did an evil entity preside over our room, one that resented us for invading its territory?

Another thought, even more sinister. Was Remy, the master of spells and the dark arts, the cause of the attack? Did he have enough power to cross seas, traverse islands and build psychic barriers to prevent me from being with another man? It was too terrifying to even contemplate so I cast the thought aside.

Years later, a similar incident took place while travelling with a friend, Michelle, to northern Thailand, to the mountain town of Chiang Rai. On our way from Bali, we passed through the Cameron highlands of Malaysia, marvelling at the brilliant butterflies and rich scenery. Overnight we stayed at a small hotel where I met a Thai paratrooper who was on a training mission. During the night as he moved closer to me, the same thing happened. A strong energetic force tore us apart and he made a quick exit, never to be seen again.

The following morning, Matt and I said our goodbyes. It was a mixed parting, regret tinged with nagging questions. Our union was not meant to be. As he boarded the boat to cross the lake, he blew me one last kiss. I waved to him until he was out of sight and then, unwilling to stay alone in this haunted place, I planned my next move. Anywhere would do.

With no reason not to, I headed north to the town of Bukittinggi, *tall hill*. The road was treacherous, weaving through a series of hairpin bends and rugged scenery. Mountain streams tumbled over stark volcanic valleys, earthly tremors creating a dramatic landscape. It was a gruelling trip and it took many hours to reach the town.

Horse carts, with red pompoms and jingling bells, cantered through the streets lined with flowers. Ladies, demure and veiled in chiffon, walked by, proud of their heritage. The Minangkabau people represent the world's largest matriarchal society. While Islam may favour men and boys, it is the women among these people who prevail. Ownership of all property is passed down from mother to daughter, through successive generations.

My hotel was pleasant and sunny, bordered by craggy peaks and forested valleys. After a few days of rest, I walked to a promontory overlooking the stunning Sianok Canyon. After admiring the view, I climbed down to the underground caverns. These caves had served as a wartime prison, tunnelled into the base of the mountain by the Japanese who occupied Sumatra during World War II,. They still echoed the cries of the people once trapped inside.

Further up the hill, there was a prison of another kind. It was a zoo where animals were stuck in small cages, shrieking in anguish. Most were mere shadows of their species. Three gibbons in separate cages were in varied states of distress. One was banging his head against a wall, another desperate to reach out and comfort him through a small crack in the concrete. The third one, autumn red, was sitting quietly in his cage, contemplating his fate.

To console him, I stood close to his cage and spoke. He loped over to me, happy to chat. His eyes lit up as he stared into mine. Then he poked his arm through the mesh wire, and his tiny palm beckoned to me. Passing him peanuts, he was not interested. Rather it was the comfort of contact that he craved. Taking his tiny palm in mine, I massaged it gently and then worked my way up his arm as he whimpered in pleasure. He passed me his other arm and then thrust his tummy against the wire. I tickled it and he began to giggle.

As a crowd gathered to watch, the little gibbon stretched out his arm, curled it gently around my neck and pulled my head close to his, while he crooned to me. We stood locked in an embrace for the longest time. When the zoo about to close, he screeched as I went to leave. He called out to me, one arm protruding through the wire. His tapered fingers waved me back while the other hand tapped on his chest, for his little heart was breaking. I pledged that he would never be truly alone again, for he was forever part of me.

The plight of animals in this country rocked me to my core and it took many years for their dire situation to be reversed. In the early days, a friend of mine in Bali, engaged to a rich local businessman, turned up at my hotel in a black Mercedes with a baby orangutan, in nappies, in the front seat. I was horrified. She, on the other hand, was delighted.

When riding on the back of Remy's motorbike one day, stopped in traffic in a small alleyway, my eyes were drawn to a gap below the gates of a house. It revealed an incredible sight. A lethargic tiger chained to a wall, lying on a slab of cement. I was outraged, broken-hearted and felt helpless. It needed to be reported, but to whom?

Over the years, wildlife bodies were formed and government authorities removed animals at risk. One friend had a baby gibbon as her pet, but it was taken by officials to be released. The Sumatran tiger, the only surviving tiger in the Sunda Islands of the Malay Archipelago, is critically endangered with logging and deforestation of its habitat major factors in its decline. A magnificent animal, its extinction would be a tragedy.

In the early years, domestic animals were doomed too. It was pitiful to see wounded and malnourished dogs wandering the streets, hanging on to life by a thread. The dog meat industry thrived, only recently banned. Cats were left to roam, unharmed, because I was told they embody the soul of a person. The arrival of foreigners, who kept animals as pets, created a shift and there is hope that there will soon be an end to their misery.

Travel is a curious mistress. It is the people or places you connect with, those who capture your heart, or your interest, which have the most impact. The connection may come from the past, a fleeting romance, the meeting of minds, or simply the result of a realisation that there is a different reality than the one you're used to. It can act as a source of wonder or a pathway to a greater understanding, but whatever the case you will never be the same.

On the final leg of my trip in Sumatra, travelling south to the city of Padang, past thick tropical vegetation and traditional longhouses, the bus arrived at a roadside café late at night. While devouring some chicken with rice, and passing up on the other questionable offal dishes, I watched as two local policemen walked in to check everyone's papers.

One of them demanded mine and then asked if I was travelling on my own. A Western woman, decades ago, on a remote highway in Sumatra, travelling alone in the dead of night, unheard of.

'You're a brave lady,' he said in Indonesian. *'Sangat berani.'*

For me, my life was unspectacular but to others it was unbelievable. It was all a matter of perspective. In years to come, the Balinese were shocked that I lived in a big house on my own. *A single woman in a big house alone.* Unheard of, until it's not.

There were more threads to my travels, more fantastic tales still to come. Kalimantan is the Indonesian territory in the south of Borneo, the third largest island in the world. The Malaysian states of Sabah and Sarawak, and the oil-rich kingdom of Brunei, lie in the north. The island of Borneo conjures up exotic and remote images but its dense jungles guard its secrets well. A whole new adventure was set to unfold, one of marvel and disbelief.

The coastal city of Balikpapan was dotted with tankers and the flare of distant oil rigs, as the plane flew over its murky harbour. Seated next to me was American businessman, Dan Rivers, jaded by constant trips to negotiate deals and oversee oil plants.

Waiting at the airport was his friend Big Red, a towering Texan, with a titian beard and a broad southern accent. Red gave me a bone-crunching hug when we met and then peeled off the ring of a can of beer with his teeth, before offering it to Dan. He was happy to drive me to my hotel, but first, he was eager to share some of the sights.

We stopped at a local pub for a delicious seafood platter while rock and roll hits pumped out from a tired old jukebox in the corner. A friendly game of darts was followed by some outlandish tales, and lots of laughs. These two men served as a reminder of the relief of the fleeting, and the times when the trivial is welcome.

After a few nights' rest, I headed north on a rickety bus that struggled to make it along the rough gravel road that cut through a forest of tall trees. Bands of monkeys stood alert on the roadside, waiting for any morsel flung from the bus. Lost in a maze of tangled roots and tropical plants, shafts of light and rainbow butterflies lent an otherworldly feel to the dense jungle. The warning cry of a bird, and the streak of others in flight, amplified the effect.

In a single moment, the kaleidoscope of colour dissolved into a stark void, my eyes struggling to adapt to the bright light. The heat became unbearable, and the only sound was the hollow buzz of insects. A picture of desolation, all around the lush rainforest lay barren. Large tree stumps, the only remnants of once magnificent trees, stood witness to the extreme loss. The spirits of the trees were exposed, the brutal bare earth calling out their names.

The bus trip ended in the seedy port town of Samarinda, on the Mahakam river. The stench of rotting vegetation and giant logs floating by in the water were a reminder of the graphic scene I had left behind. Trips upriver, in an array of unseaworthy vessels, to the lands of the Dayak tribes started from here. Once head-hunters, the Dayaks were a fascinating people but the thought of days spent on crowded decks in unbearable humidity through steaming jungles quickly lost its appeal. Adventurous I may be, but stupid I was not.

Instead, I flew south to the floating city of Banjarmasin, built on marshland and connected by a maze of canals and waterways. To best explore it, I hired a *klotok,* a motorised canoe, and skimmed past a stack of houses perched on stilts over the murky water. Families engaged in their daily activities squatted on wooden platforms that swayed on the water. The children swam happily among the debris, waving as the pale stranger passed by.

In the night I ventured into the marketplace among crowded laneways, inhaling the scent of the aromatic spices and a colourful display of fabrics, jewellery and other delights, many unfamiliar and rare. It was the gemstones that appealed the most, for Borneo was an island full of hidden treasures. One stone, among many, attracted me. Sapphire-blue and flecked with golden lights, it exuded a special energy that drew me under its spell.

Once back in my hotel room, I showered away the grime of the day and then tried to clear my mind as I sat on the bed. Clenching the stone in my hand, my meditation was marred by images, all vying for attention. Matt, and his clear blue eyes, paralleled the stone's colour, pulsating with clarity and confidence. Then came the dark penetration of Remy's gaze. It consumed the blue, as it probed deeper, as if Remy were tracing my every move.

I felt both strong and weak at the same time. Strong because I had ventured out alone on this amazing journey, and weak because I missed Remy. Forgiving him was out of the question, but disregarding my feelings felt even more pathetic. Then a terrible thought taunted me. Maybe our love was not as strong as I believed. What if Remy had stopped loving me? Suddenly I felt vulnerable and lost.

Turning on the radio on the bedside table only added to my despair. Words flowed from the music, 'Baby, I miss you', over and over, until I could resist no more. Slowly I picked up the phone and did what I vowed not to. I dialled *that* number. Above the pounding beat of music at the club, I heard Remy's voice and his pleas.

'I was wrong,' he said, begging me to return. 'I don't want to be without you. Please come back.'

Overcome with an instant sense of relief that Remy still loved me, and that our bond had not been shattered, now came the moment of decision. Go back to Bali, to a life in disarray and doubt, or keep on running. It was a difficult choice, one I was not ready to make.

CHAPTER TWELVE

SILENT SENTINELS

Some memories are like diamonds, sparking like shards of crystal in the chasms of your mind. Yet when reality bites, they melt into icy flakes that trickle through your fingers until they are lost forever. Loss of trust and betrayal forge your heart into ice, no longer supple or forgiving. Simply not ready to return to Bali, I boarded a flight heading for the island of Sulawesi and the far-off homeland of the Toraja people. Getting there was a challenge.

With its propellers whirring noisily, the small plane lurched into the air on its way to the closest point to Tana Toraja. Gazing over rugged granite cliffs and emerald valleys, I nibbled on some fried bean curd in the airline lunch box I found on the floor, next to my shoes. It wasn't long before a sudden draft of wind and a nasty jolt alerted the co-pilot we were nearing our destination. Dropping his newspaper, he grappled with the throttle as the plane ricocheted across the tarmac and came to an abrupt stop.

It was followed by the inevitable rush to be first off. Luckily, I stayed put in my seat, nearly impaled on an antique wooden spear wielded by a serious French traveller in khaki. He brushed past me clenching his prized relic, among other wrapped artefacts. The push to get off was pointless because we were all stuck in a small van for the trip to Toraja Land. Squeezed in the front seat next to the tour guide, Palo, it was a rough ride, very hot and humid. The landscape was otherworldly and lush, with jade ravines and erratic mountains cutting through the sky like jagged glass.

After a day of rest, I hired Palo as my guide to best experience the local culture. Our first trip was to an outlying village to witness the funeral ceremony of a prominent man in the community. The burial rites of the Toraja people, *Rambu Solo*, were deeply entrenched in their culture. This was one of the few societies in the world where death assumed more prominence than life.

Based on the belief that a dead person is merely sick, death is not final until all the appropriate rituals have been completed. Many pigs and buffalos are required as a sacrifice, the number a reflection of the standing of the deceased in the community.

Palo led the way and as we traipsed across the dry earth of a parched rice field, the heat became oppressive. Crossing over a narrow ridge, the traditional bamboo buildings of the village were visible, their sweeping curved roofs draped with bright red fabric. The dead man was Catholic so the railings on the veranda of the houses were painted with crosses. Despite this, the villagers retained the animistic roots of the old religion, *Aluk Todolo*, the way of the ancestors, respecting tribal lore and the history of their origins.

From one of the wooden balconies, a young woman, her dark hair swept back in a neat bun, gestured for us to join her. Dressed in apricot brocade, she wore a wide collar of coloured beads with a matching headband. Removing my shoes, I climbed up the ladder and crept across the rattan mat to offer my gift of a carton of cigarettes to a weathered old man puffing a pipe in the corner. His toothless grin was a sign of acceptance.

Joining Palo, seated on the floor, we were served sticky rice cakes and tea. The older women, weighed down by heavy black turbans, gossiped among themselves. Their lips reddened, they chewed on betel nut mixed with lime in Pippa leaves, and a wad of tobacco.

Distracted by shouting, a procession, in the dark colours of mourning, entered the compound, led by a man wielding a baton. Squealing black pigs, tied to bamboo poles and carried by four men, and buffalos nibbling on grass, followed unaware of their dire fate.

'A sacrifice is needed,' Palo explained, 'for the soul's journey to the afterlife.' Years ago, freshly severed human heads were required but now buffalo heads were acceptable. Animals follow their master to heaven to become part of his celestial herd. 'To be wealthy in *Puya*, the afterlife, is more important than prosperity here.'

When Palo gestured for me to climb a ladder up to the richly decorated death house, where the elaborate gold-painted coffin of the deceased lay, I declined, not wanting to intrude. Other guests, in ornate beads and bearing heavily laden silver platters, climbed up to pay their final respects while I stood beside a large solitary stone, placed upright in the ground. It represented the stature of the dead man, but his corpse needed to be carried to its final resting place, a grave high in the rock face with others of his clan.

'It is said that our ancestors descended from the stars, from the Pleiades, on a crescent moon. Only death opens up the portal to our eternal homeland and we must not arrive empty-handed.'

The next day we headed for Lemo, one of the most preserved grave sites. A labyrinth of small wooden doorways had been carved into the high cliff face which was streaked in bands of orange and black ochre. These guarded the ancient burial chambers. Overhanging vines cascading down the rock face, twisted roots, and poisonous trees of fragrant trumpet lilies, added a layer of protection. It took extreme perseverance to create these chambers, men perched on steep bamboo ladders using sharp flint hammers to carve each grave.

'The earth is the giver of life,' Palo replied when asked why bodies were not buried. 'It cannot be polluted by death. Up high the graves are safe from plunder.' It was an eerie sight. Crumbling balconies in the cliff face, stuffed with lifeless wooden statues, *tau-tau*, represented each of the dead whose spirit made the perilous journey to the far-off 'Land of the Souls'. Like silent sentinels, their eyes vacant and longing, they looked down over those they left behind.

Palo led me to the entrance of a cave, an ancient burial site. Inside the air was stale, sucked dry by the passage of time. I stumbled over some scattered rocks, while my eyes slowly adjusted, and I backed away. Skulls with sunken eye sockets peered at me from deep within the rocky crevices, forming a ghostly lineup, an eerie reminder of the inevitable passage from life to death. The desecrated coffins, in rotted hardwood, were a testament to the passing of time.

The last stop on our trip was as poignant as it was touching. 'Come with me,' Palo said, leading me down some stone steps into a leafy grove. The forest floor was dappled with sunlight and clumps of bamboo. A majestic tree stood in the centre, with small, thatched doors carved into its bark. 'These spaces have been hollowed in the tree trunks to place the bodies of babies who have died.'

'Babies cannot be placed in the family rock graves because, before the age of two, the child still needs to be nurtured. So, trees with white sap substitute for the mother's milk.' The strong vines twisted around the tree trunk served as a trap to deter any intruder, the tree nurturing the baby's journey into the afterlife. The soulful presence in this sacred place, the natural site of the primordial mother, was overwhelming. It was impossible not to be moved.

'Do you want to spend the night in a traditional Toraja longhouse?' Palo asked, aware that I was worn out. The offer was tempting, as it was a long drive back to the hotel. 'It's on the top of a mountain and the view is spectacular, but it can get cold up there.'

Palo hadn't mentioned just *how* cold and as we drove up the bumpy road, the smattering of stars was the only light to be seen. Palo did not brighten the mood. 'The people here are superstitious. Anyone suspected of sorcery was tried in the past by plunging their hand into hot pitch. If it burnt, they were guilty and beheaded.'

'That's a no-win,' I sighed, reflecting on the toll of those accused of witchcraft. This fear of the dark side was universal.

'During the war, there were many sightings of the walking dead,' Palo added, 'and the Japanese occupiers were so frightened they did not mess with the local villagers.' I didn't doubt it, judging by the feeling of dread driving along this isolated stretch of road.

The guesthouse was shrouded in thick fog. A bowl of hot vegetable soup was welcome as we warmed by the fire in the dining room, listening to a crackly radio. Tired, I followed Palo up a steep bamboo ladder to the sleeping hut, ducking through the solid wooden doors and the carved buffalo head that guarded the entrance. Inside the longhouse it was even colder, the open room large enough for ten mattresses. When Palo suggested cuddling for body heat, I threw a hard pillow at him and relegated him to the furthest corner.

I froze during the night, no matter how many blankets I piled on top of me. The smoke from the mosquito coil sent me into a coughing fit and as I reached for my bottle of water it fell down a wooden slat into oblivion. That was it. *I had enough.* The thought of

Bali suddenly seemed very appealing, as did the warmth of Remy's embrace. My nose was losing all feeling, and my soul was in danger of following it. Looking at Palo, curled up in a comfortable ball, his loud snoring sent me further into a downward spiral. I was a desperate woman. Desperate for the familiar, for love lost, and more than anything, a sense of belonging. For me, that was Bali.

CHAPTER THIRTEEN

IN THE SPOTLIGHT

It was a tense return to Bali but Remy was genuinely sorry for all the hurt he had caused. It was his explanation, rather than his excuses, which sealed the deal, allowing me to see the world from his perspective. Life is not black and white but rather all shades of the spectrum. The expectations placed on Remy from an early age, in a society steeped in tradition were heavy enough to make even the strongest soul buckle under pressure. Many mistakes were made, and many transgressions, but no one can claim to be perfect.

From childhood, Remy was groomed to be the chosen link in a priestly chain, one steeped in magical prowess. But Remy was just a man. He was not a demigod, he was *just a man*. The power of Mars in the mystical sign of Scorpio when he was born, gained him access to a deeper reality, into the hidden secrets of life. They were fraught with danger.

This pairing also endowed Remy with a strong sex drive, one that catapulted him into a series of miscalculated affairs for which he would rarely pay. His ego was tied up in power, and every encounter, every secret liaison, fed his Scorpio desire for intrigue. With Venus in Scorpio, I was in no place to judge Remy, rather enjoying my forays into forbidden territory over the years. A primal driving force powered these strong Scorpio urges.

'Just one more chance,' Remy said, holding my hand. 'I was sure I'd lose you if you knew the truth.' For the first time, tears welled up in Remy's eyes and he showed a trace of emotion, a vulnerability not permitted in a man of his stature. 'Please, forgive me.'

While forgiveness might come in time, it was far harder to forget. Remy's letters begging me to come back to Bali tore apart my relationship with Brad and left him broken-hearted. He hated me with all the force of a good man betrayed, with even more ferocity than he had ever loved me. Bali was my destiny but it left many victims in its wake. Remy's family was distraught too but there proved to be a method in madness and a cosmic purpose.

'My second marriage is dissolved,' Remy said. Theirs was a religious union, so only a temple ceremony was needed to end it. 'Divorce is not so easy for my first wife for she is the mother of my children. She would return to her village, humiliated and alone.'

On the brief occasions I met his 'aunt', Remy's wife appeared drained and lacklustre, the radiance of her youth sacrificed to the demands of life. She had no sense of identity, the Balinese of the Sudra caste referred to by birth order. Her name, Made, meant number two, and there was little doubt that she felt overlooked.

'She is my cousin,' Remy explained. 'My marriage to her was arranged when I was young, as is tradition, and I never questioned the choice. The second wedding was to legitimise my son. You are the only woman I ever loved,' Remy pleaded. 'The only woman I have *chosen* to be with.

'My grandfather's spiritual gifts were passed down to me,' Remy stressed. 'One day I will quit my job and concentrate on my life purpose. You're from a different culture and cannot make the offerings needed for the temple ceremonies and special days in the Balinese calendar. These demands will increase as my spiritual path expands and only my wife can prepare them.' It was the position she aspired to, for she gained status as the wife of a future priest.

The only gain Remy and I had was *love*, for unlike many foreigners employed on the island, I was floundering. Sponsors for work visas were rare and difficult to obtain. As for Remy's wife, she had suffered enough. She deserved better and I did not wish to add to her misery. Married to Remy was her only role in the community.

In years to come, that respect was afforded to me. Whenever I strolled down the beach, I heard the muffled whispers of the local ladies huddled in a group, *'Mangku Istri.'* 'Wife of the priest'. This title afforded me protection from the harassment many Westerners faced. As the partner to a holy man, it was presumed that you were endowed with certain mystical gifts of your own. With an ingrained fear of all things magical, they were wise to keep a distance.

Remy's family had no problem accepting me, smiling whenever I entered their compound because I was seen as a saviour of sorts. The second wife caused upheaval in their home for many years. At one time, Remy and his two wives even shared a bed. So despised was she that the family conspired to remove her but their efforts failed. My presence tipped the scales and the second wife was sent packing, much to their relief.

In the end, I agreed to stay with Remy as long as he only slept in my house. On that, I would not compromise. The passion between Remy and his first wife had faded long ago, and there was no way I would put up with any playboy antics. Remy agreed to my terms but old habits can be hard to shake, and it would be a true test for him.

To begin our lives with a clean slate, Remy insisted on a purification ceremony. So on the chosen day, we stood side by side on the beach as a sinewy old priest, dressed in white robes, hovered above us on a craggy rock. The holy water he trickled on our heads from a woven palm frond, ran down our bodies in a cold stream.

In the distance, the lights of fishing boats twinkled over the horizon as the crescent moon rose in the sky. With waves crashing down upon the shore, we waded into the ocean for the final cleansing. The force was so strong that I was sucked under but Remy dragged me out, and we collapsed onto the sand.

The priest looked down at us from his imperious height and with his bony finger, laden with a cluster of signet rings, he pointed at the sliver of the moon. If only one wave of his hand could undo all the damage or heartache, or guarantee the future, but such things are not yet defined. Nor is it in the lap of the gods because only a person can *shape* their destiny and create the dimensions of life.

So marked the beginning of a new chapter. Remy lived with me in my small rented house and was free to return home to his family during the day, and even more crucially to pray in his temple twice daily because that was vital to his existence. To cope with the demands of life in Bali, I employed a nice lass, Ketut, from a nearby village to help. She drew water from the well in my backyard for I was incapable of winching up a bucket of water. Showering was tricky, as I flung buckets of water over my head. There was nothing worse than shivering with cold, only to close the bathroom door to be stared down by a huge beady-eyed gecko.

With only a small television, and most shows either Chinese kung fu or Indonesian soap opera, I felt isolated. Telephones were virtually non-existent and with no taxis at the time, most nights I'd hop on the back of Remy's motorbike and go to the club, staying till the early hours of the morning so we could drive home together. Luckily, I loved to dance and as disco music had made a comeback, it was a cross between funk and disco inferno.

After a year together, it was time to lay down stronger roots, as our relationship entered a new phase. The challenge of doing it rough was losing its appeal and it was time to invest in the future. Using my share of the sale of the house in Sydney, I bought a unit there as a home base and then leased a large block of Remy's land in Bali, for 20 years, the maximum allowed a foreigner. Sheltered by towering bamboo, the plot was ideal.

With pencil in hand, I imagined my dream home, drew the plan, and handed it over to an architect. With Remy by my side, we watched the house take shape and supervised the planting of a beautiful garden, with towering palm trees, lush ferns and a rainbow assortment of bougainvillea. With an automatic water pump, a bath with hot water, and basking in the air conditioning, I was in heaven.

I employed a Javanese lady as a helper and cook, and a Balinese gardener who cut the newly planted lawn and climbed the trees for coconuts. It was ideal. A masseuse came to the house twice a week, to gently massage away any stress, and a monthly facial and the occasional cream bath for my hair completed the beauty routine.

While it was great catching up with friends for lunch on the beach, I needed more. A purpose, to challenge me and fuel my ambition. Remy was off most days doing his thing, so I needed to discover my own. Fate stepped in to define the next phase of my life.

Invited to attend a formal event at an exclusive hotel in Bali, on this island of petite women, I had a dress made. Rather than fade from sight, I designed a flashy hand-painted black dress, sequined with a silver spider's web. It caused quite a stir on the night.

When several people asked to take my photo, the boutique owner at the hotel was impressed enough to ask me to make a dozen for the shop. They sold out quickly, so Remy rented a small shop and stocked it with dresses I designed and clothes bought from the markets, decorated with sequins and silver studs to be more stylish.

A restaurant nearby held fashion shows once a week, amateur at best. One night one of the staff rushed into the shop asking if we could fill in because the clothing for the show hadn't arrived. It became a weekly thing, and my brand expanded with each show.

One night, the Entertainment Manager for the Hyatt was dining at the restaurant and impressed, he asked if I was interested in a contract to provide fashion shows at the hotel each week. *Absolutely.* Dragging Remy along to keep it legitimate, the shows were a great success, and the guests were fighting over the clothes.

Sensibly, I hired a professional modelling agency and each show was choreographed under my direction. Soon the agency implored me to do shows at other five-star hotels in Nusa Dua, the upmarket tourist location. One show was held around the swimming pool, sequins sparkling in the hot sun. Haughty models and palm trees, just as I once imagined. All those sketches at high school and university of glamorous fashion shows were a premonition.

Another hotel featured my shows in their nightclub. At times, there were scuffles after the show as the clothes were fought over. One night, an Englishman asked me to reserve an outfit for his girlfriend, but by the end, Claudia from Naples had snuck into the changing room, ripped the dress off the model and was wearing it.

When Nigel protested, I said, 'If you can get it off her it's yours.' Luckily, I managed to get another one to him the next day.

Staff from the nightclub came out to witness the scene after the show and were left shaking their heads. One summed it up best, 'When other people do fashion shows, they're bankrupt. When you do it, *money falls from heaven.*' In the ultimate compliment, a stylish French man came over to me one evening when the show ended.

'I have seen parades in Milan and Paris' he declared, 'but yours is better.' My ego soared, bolstered by success. I was nearing 40 and this was my time to shine and stand in the spotlight.

It didn't end there. One day the manager of the nightclub turned up at my house to ask me to do the fashion show for the ultimate event, the PATA travel convention. 'You're the best on the island,' he pleaded. It turned out to be a grand night with a massive audience.

When the DJ announced that I was the top fashion designer in Bali, to the sound of loud applause, my mind did a backflip. To all those years as a frustrated teenager, forced to make my clothes, and to a world that failed to recognise the diversity of sizes. I wanted to paint the world beautiful, full of people who walked proud and felt fabulous. It was time to allow everyone a moment to shine.

Remy was used to being in the spotlight, with people flocking to his bar to watch his crazy antics. Then one night, the unthinkable happened. The club went up in flames. All that was left in the morning were charred glasses and broken bottles. Remy's world fell apart. With his identity challenged, Remy was forced into his life purpose.

He stepped into his new role as *pemangku* priest without any fanfare, for many years of practice had led up to this moment. Every month, on the night of the dark moon, he made a pilgrimage by small boat to the haunted island of Nusa Penida, in his quest to defeat the dark forces. Challenging the evil spirits in the bat cave, he indulged in a delicate power play between good and evil. I wondered how much of his spirit was contaminated in the process.

Remy dare not offend the dark deity that inhabited the island because he truly believed this evil god saved his life. Remy shared the story of how a curse from a rival family caused the death of his sister, after she collapsed one day riding home from school on her bicycle. Next youngest in the family, the curse transferred to Remy and he fell gravely ill.

'I could feel the life force leaving me,' Remy confided. 'Then came a vision of the demon ruler of Nusa Penida island. He promised to save me if I built a temple in his honour and made offerings to him for the rest of my life.' It was a precarious alliance. 'Only an evil god with great power,' Remy argued, 'could break the spell.'

It was a different take on light conquering darkness because Remy was convinced that only a darker god with greater deadly power could take on its weaker rival. Remy was in a position now to help others who fell victim to these forces. When people turned up at our door, most desperate for relief from a magic spell, Remy felt obliged to help them.

The more Remy was drawn into his mystical world, the more he increasingly became immersed in conversations with unknown spectres. These interludes increased in frequency and intensity until he appeared to be in an altered state. Remy often called out in his sleep, in a strange voice that was not his, waking me in fright. I was floundering in a twilight world, worried about what eerie entity may be lurking nearby. It was my worst fear come to life.

Each day Remy rose before sunrise, bathed, and after prayer, he was off. All that was left behind were the fallen blossoms on his pillow. He became more religiously extreme, angered when I hung my dress up on a hook. Nothing worn on the lower part of the body could be higher than the head which was deemed holy. He even burnt our pillows after some friends leaned against them on the sofa.

The man I had fallen in love with was vanishing. Remy was becoming dangerous too, as he fell into a state of trance without warning. One day, while skirting around a curvy road that clung to the side of a cliff, Remy lost control of his motorbike. Engaged in a private conversation with spirit he was far, far away. I jerked his arm upright, just in time to save us from plunging into the valley below.

Even his family were worried. One day his daughters came to the house asking me to attend an 'exorcism' ceremony to purify their father. We developed a good relationship over the years, the girls visiting my house when they needed guidance or a Western perspective. Now we united in a common cause, in a bid to save their father.

The ceremony to cleanse Remy was frightening, and his younger daughter held my hand throughout. It was clear that Remy's soul was being shredded by an entity that made him unrecognisable. His eyes were hollow and after the priest performed the ceremony and doused him with holy water, Remy slumped to the ground.

As I watched Remy's spirit dissolve into pieces, I was conflicted, torn between love and dread. Remy had become the epitome of what I had tried to escape by coming to Bali, a dark force with the power to damage and destroy me. In many ways, our roles had reversed and it was now my turn to rescue him. It seemed fate had other plans, leading me to a far-off land and another incredible episode from the past. It seemed it was up to Remy to save himself.

CHAPTER FOURTEEN

LOVE IN THE JUNGLE

'The road to your destiny leads from Bombay in India,' the old fortune teller said, peering at the lines that crossed my palm. The setting was perfect for such an illustrious declaration. Perched on a staircase within the Grand Palace of Bangkok, the golden pagodas shone in the afternoon sun, adding weight to the humidity. I was on one of my unending visa trips out of Bali, but India was not on my list to visit as it seemed so far off and out of reach.

Still, it was a tempting destination, so I asked the universe for a sign. Its roots were planted several years before while I was having lunch with my friend Emily, who worked for a tour company in Bali. When an acquaintance mentioned that a new Australian Consul was coming to the island, Emily's eyes lit up. 'Is he single?' she asked. It seemed an odd question, not usually the first thing to pop into your mind, but she seemed hopeful.

It proved rather prophetic because soon after we met the new Australian Consul, John, at a nightclub. There was an instant connection and, at the end of the night, as unlikely as it seemed, we three walked arm-in-arm up the road as if we were old friends. The relationship between Emily and John grew and, as fate decreed, ended in wedding bells within a year. Theirs was a perfect match and I was honoured to be their bridesmaid on their special day.

Over the next two years, I enjoyed invitations to attend consul dinners and other social functions, and it felt good to share in their happiness. They were the enchanted couple, living in the luxury enjoyed by those expats who attained an elevated position on the island. With a good salary, a high rank and a spacious house, theirs was a comfortable life. Mine was a lot more precarious.

Time flew by and we lost contact until one day, by 'chance', I was on an escalator at a department store in Denpasar when I passed John going in the other direction. 'I've been trying to contact you,' John said, when we met up, 'to invite you to our farewell dinner.'

Two years had passed and John's term of office in Bali was up. Previously, he had told me that they would be returning to Canberra after his overseas service, for a mandatory break between postings.

'So back home?' I asked, amazed at how fast time had passed.

'No,' he replied. 'It was unexpected but I've been promoted to Australian Consul-General for Bombay in India.' I was stunned. Sharing the recent prophecy in Bangkok, John had no hesitation in inviting me to visit the city and stay with them. It all fell into place.

The stars shone brightly when I turned up on their doorstep in Bombay months later, the city's name changed to Mumbai a few years later, in 1995. I was their first visitor, and Emily and John were still settling in. It was good to bask in the comfort of their home and relive some of our memories. Emily knew of the issues with my Balinese priest, but I didn't want to share just how bad the situation had become. Their lives seemed so easy until Emily confided how hard it was for her to be continually sociable, being a natural recluse.

A whirlwind of social events followed, Emily often bowing out on some pretext. She was glad to have me as a 'substitute' and so I found myself, in a turquoise sari decorated in gold, in the back of a black limousine alongside John, with the flags of my country blazing at the front. Street children's faces pressed against the glass as they peered into the darkened windows, hoping to catch a glimpse of the passengers. I never expected to be in this position, especially to be saluted by uniformed guards when I got out of the car.

Posh parties at swish venues followed. The Irish Consul put on a wonderful soiree on the terrace of the Taj Mahal Palace Hotel overlooking the Gateway of India. Lots of bubbly and interesting company made the night special. Soon after, there was an evening at the Canadian Consul's home and a lovely dinner as guests of a Parsi family, with so much to learn about their culture. It was wonderful but an irresistible force was prompting me to move on.

After two weeks, it was time to head off wherever fate led me. A cavalcade of places and people flashed by, both breathtaking and confronting, as I headed south on the bus to the palmed beaches of Kerala on the Arabian shoreline. It was hard to take in all the frantic sights, smells and colours of India as I headed north.

All the dramatic contrasts – regal palace hotels, beggars and cows wandering the streets and bearded holy men dusted with flames of orange, looking as if they just stepped out of a cosmic inferno. The sight of the Taj Mahal and vivid Rajasthan was inspiring, but there was still no connection. Kathmandu in Nepal was the last stop on my trip. Was it the final piece of the puzzle?

Arrival in Kathmandu was fraught with tension. There was trouble in the air and an evening curfew had been imposed. One of the oldest inhabited cities in the world, it was a maze of alleys, holy

Buddhist temples with painted eyes and mystical bells, and a treasure of statues, shrines and stupas. With unrest brewing, the man at the desk at my small hotel told me to leave the city for a few days and head down south to the wildlife reserve of Chitwan.

The arduous journey to get there, in a rickety bus, was along one of the most treacherous roads in the world that curled around the Himalayas, vehicles and buses scattered in the river far below a reminder of the peril. After five gruelling hours, we reached a small dusty village on the edge of the wildlife park.

I nervously waited on the side of the road for someone to appear. And they did – three men in khaki, the driver a standout. Not another attractive man in a uniform, on a jeep in the middle of nowhere! Switch the desert for the jungle and this had the making of another classic adventure. I couldn't be so lucky twice in a lifetime.

After a bumpy jeep ride along an overgrown track, we reached the ranger station at the entrance to the park. It was patrolled by two men brandishing rifles, a staunch attempt to curb the dreadful practice of rhino poaching for their valuable horns.

Often thought to be confined to Africa, it was the Indian one-horned rhinoceros that roamed free in Chitwan National Park in Nepal. Protected, this species of rhinos was brought back from the brink of extinction, and now more than 4000 rhinos roam the plains of Nepal and northeastern India.

The wildlife park was also one of the last sanctuaries for the Royal Bengal tigers but the chance of spotting one was rare. Known for their stealth, the tigers in the park, presently numbering more than 120, hide in thick vegetation, preferring to remain unseen and feed on the plentiful spotted deer. Their orange coat and brown-black stripes distinguish the Bengal tiger from other tiger species. In this rare, isolated part of the world, leopards, sloth bears, and an array of reptiles and bird species are also found in the park.

Several lodges are scattered throughout the park but when the man at my hotel in Kathmandu showed me the brochure for *this* lodge and came back with a booking for another one, I insisted on the first. I had no idea why but I was adamant. It was only a matter of time before the truth emerged but, with only two nights at the lodge, fate needed to intervene, and fast.

It was not long before the jeep reached a ring of thatched huts in the middle of a clearing. Once I'd settled into mine, one of the guides suggested a supervised walk in the reserve, along with a pretty Danish lass, Nell, who had arrived earlier. We headed down a scrub path, dodging thorny bushes and the odd foraging wild pig.

With only the guide's wooden stick for protection, I didn't feel safe. My instincts were sound because the next minute the ground rumbled like a subterranean earthquake and I heard a mighty clash. I stood rooted to the spot while the guide started to sweat, creeping his way through the leaves for a closer look.

The earth was vibrating and I was worried that it was about to open up and swallow us whole. Then came a mighty thud, and another. Nell did a disappearing act into the distance while the ranger ran back over to my side and muttered, 'Two rhinos fighting. Quick, run and hide behind a tree!' The only trees scattered around me were saplings. There was no way my body would be concealed behind one, or an entire grove. It was time to panic.

Suddenly a major jolt and a rampaging rhino thundered past me, missing me by a hair's breadth. I was petrified, cast in stone. When the danger passed, the guide led me back to the camp trying to calm my fears. 'The next time you see a charging rhino,' he advised, 'run zigzag. A rhino's head is so heavy it can't turn its neck fast enough to keep track of you.'

Surely the guide was jesting. I was about to lock myself in my cabin and not come out for the next two days. The smell of toasting marshmallows at the campfire that evening induced me to emerge. Nell was already there, along with three guides. Four other guests, a Dutch couple and two lean Swiss backpackers who had just climbed Everest, were singing a questionable version of a John Denver song, appropriate for a night in the forest.

I joined in for a while but feeling tired after a long day, I got up to leave. That's when *he* walked into the circle – the camp's striking manager in his jungle greens – the hunky man in the jeep. My attention was captured and I wasn't going anywhere.

When he turned to face me, the fire sparked. With his eyes fixated on mine, he strummed the guitar and softly sang 'Waiting For a Girl Like You,' as my soul swooned just a little. There was magic all around as rays of moonlight filtered through the canopy of leaves. This was the setting of enchanted forests and erotic dreams.

As the group disbanded, Nell ran her fingers through her wavy brown hair and smiled at the manager, Jud, with a seductive glance but he seemed not to notice. When I stood up to say my goodbyes, Jud reached over to touch me, and an electric impulse charged up my arm and then catapulted headlong into my nether regions.

Jud leaned over and whispered, 'Wait for me over there, by the elephant stand in the clearing.' The waft of his words settled on my cheek and his scent was intoxicating – tropical vines mixed with tiger's breath. If there was an aftershave called *Safari Escape*, or *Jungle Sensation*, he was wearing it.

A single shaft of light beamed down upon me, as I stood waiting in the wooded glade. I was less swept away and more worried that a lethal boa constrictor would slide out from the bushes to crush my body into sawdust, or worse still, that the rhino would return to finish me off. Then came the sound of footsteps.

Jud appeared out of the shadows and strode towards me, every perfect inch of him, and my heart started thumping with every step. Without a word, he swept me into his arms and kissed me. I wanted the moment to freeze. Just the two of us under a star-filled night that frosted the sky with sherbet. This was pure fantasy come to life.

No novel could capture the romance of that night, and few moments matched its intensity. Nor could they match the setting or the absolute absurdity, and splendour, of it all. It was the *True Confessions* of my childhood, lifted from the page to come to life. Surely the years had dragged any last trace of desire away. This was the confession I had dreamt of, and it deserved my full attention.

Another special man, in the most unlikely of places, a supernova among the rest. These exceptional men were the catalysts that defined my destiny, powerful magnets to a fated interlude in my life. The fact that this man was attracted to me made *me* feel extraordinary too and in the mystique of the jungle, a restless past life whispered to be heard. It was both exciting and unsettling.

The magic grew when Jud led me down a stony path to the elephant stable. There we sat, hand in hand, watching the antics of these incredible animals. Under a silvery moon, they danced. They sang and threw hay until they had stacks piled on their head, behind their ears, or strewn around their stomach like a hula skirt. Together they swayed and played. When I suppressed a giggle, the elephants stopped and stared at me. Jud warned me not to offend an elephant because they are sensitive creatures, with feelings easily hurt.

After a night of magic, I awoke to the sound of the elephants heralding the start of a brand-new day. There were six Asian elephants in the stables, and they trumpeted at the crack of dawn.

The elephants rejoiced in life and when I brought down an apple to make amends, we became friends. That afternoon I went down to the creek to cavort alongside them, splashing away in the water with the herd. Baby Apu loved to squirt water from her trunk, so I kept out of range but could not help being swept away by her joy.

The following day my mood soared when I found Jud had carved my initials into a tree, alongside his, in a love heart. We were even immortalised in the railing of the elephant stand. A dark cloud began to lift as I felt valued once more. It was a brief liaison up to now but our attraction had deep roots, anchored in the past. I was unsure what I'd been up to in my past lives, but at least they appeared wildly diverse and incredibly interesting.

As a treat, Jud rowed me down the Rapti River the next day, in a dugout canoe, past thick forest growth and a medley of bird calls. This was a million miles from my reality and I knew I was blessed to be there. At a clearing on the riverbank, an elephant waited to take us back to the lodge. It was Ana, the gentlest of the herd.

With no elephant stand here, Ana had to kneel so I could climb onto her back. I refused to step on her leg, for she seemed fragile and precious. Her keeper encouraged me to get up but in the end, it was Ana who gave me permission. She looked me in the eye with her long, sumptuous lashes and smiled. The meaning was unmistakable and she trumpeted happily as we returned to the lodge.

That night was restless, racked by so many conflicting thoughts that I couldn't sleep. Just as I was about to run from my hut to the toilet block, there was a loud snort. A rhino was munching on the grass outside, and its hot breath was seeping through the hut's log walls. Now I was trapped. Falling eventually into a light sleep, I was woken by a knock on the door. Groggily I got up to open it, only to find Jud standing there. He took me in his arms and said, 'Don't leave. *Please don't go.*' I hugged him back.

CHAPTER FIFTEEN

MOUNTAIN MAGIC

An invisible thread connects those who are destined to meet. Regardless of time, place and circumstance the thread may stretch or tangle. But it will never break. Chinese Proverb

Nepal was an elusive land, humble yet monumental and lost in time. As a country it was nuanced and its people spoke gently, the tenor of their words mirroring their soft character. Pure Pisces. On the surface. Theirs was a history steeped in conquest, the glare of the adjoining sign Aries alluding to bloodshed, rivalry, weapons and battle. The struggle for control dates back centuries and extended into the recent past, and the cost was great.

Nepal and Bali seemed light years apart, yet there was a striking similarity. Both places, one landlocked, and the other an island, possessed an aura of fascination. Both were exotic lands that evoked vivid images, with trails of incense clouding the air to entice the gods. More crucially, they represented the last two remaining Hindu kingdoms in the world, with an overlay of Buddhism. Despite the pressure to conform to modern ways, Nepal held on tight to its isolated position and Bali remained steeped in superstition.

The similarity did not end there. Remy and Jud were attractive men, with dark piercing eyes and carefully groomed black hair. They both possessed charisma and a distinctive aura which was compelling and made them stand out among the rest. People were irresistibly drawn to them, both men of authority who commanded respect in their own special way.

Despite their likeness, they were markedly different in character. One evening at the lodge I overheard two American ladies comment when Jud made his usual spectacular entrance, 'These jungle men sure are pretty.' Not one hair on Jud's head moved. Remy on the other hand would have revelled in the glory, enjoying the attention. Jud remained indifferent.

With my decision to stay with Jud at the lodge, I swapped the beach for the jungle, the tropical heat of Bali and earthquakes for the risk of monsoons and the wet season. While the monkeys of Bali boldly appeared on a clifftop or side of the road, to hold you at ransom as they snatched your sunglasses, or car keys, the creatures in the wildlife park were far more elusive. On one of my walks with a ranger, a sleepy leopard sauntered across our path but it remained haughty, allowing us only a brief glimpse. Thus its appearance was rare and highly valued, the majestic tiger even more so. In all my time at the lodge, I never sighted one.

Although the elephants were a joy, there were times of danger. I felt a bond with the herd but the drivers kept me at a safe distance, to avoid any potential incident. Few things are more frightening than a bull elephant on the rampage, usually when its testosterone spikes in a period known as musth. During that time, the one male elephant in the stable became so aggressive that he pulled the tail of the elephant ahead of him on its walk, letting out a mighty roar. That night, while pegged close together, the bull yanked at her trunk until it was hanging on by a thread. After the injured elephant was treated, the bull was sent to India to live out the rest of his days.

It was almost time for me to go away too but I didn't want to leave. I had stayed longer than I intended, thanks to Jud, for every night at the lodge was expensive. Over the course of my stay, our feelings grew and when it came time to leave Nepal, Jud decided to fly to Thailand with me, as Bangkok was my stopover. We spent a few days enjoying the sights, holy temples, royal palaces rich in gold, and pools swarming with koi fish, symbols of love.

The thought of returning to Bali was fraught with anxiety so when Jud asked me to come back to Nepal I was tempted. Remy was minding the house in Bali, but we had parted ways after eight years together. His playboy ways had not ceased and too many rumours about possible affairs, and a minefield of innuendo, left me drained.

Staying in Nepal was not easy. The country had a closed-door policy for foreigners, to minimise outside influence. Tourists at the time were not permitted to remain in the country for more than two months in a year and having turned my life around for a man once, I was hesitant to do the same again. Still, it was hard to erase the feelings we shared.

Pulling a great number of strings, Jud arranged for me to return to the wildlife park as 'guest relations'. Greeting new arrivals each day was a wonderful opportunity to feel like I belonged and not just passing through, and meeting people from all over the world was a bonus. Most were incredulous that I had such an opportunity and never a day went by without me being grateful for the chance to stay in Nepal. There was an increasing bond with every passing day.

Even though I had my own hut, most nights I stayed with Jud, safe in his arms in the comfort of his bed. Ours was a powerful attraction, powered by the need to touch and remain close to each other. In the morning as I lay alone in bed after Jud left on patrol, there were knocks on the door. The door would tentatively open and then slam shut when the staff caught a glimpse of me. It was somewhat risky but our secret remained hidden.

No stranger could enter the park, and the only one that managed to was a small tabby cat hiding in the back of the jeep. It was one brave and very stupid cat, as it hung out at the elephant camp and enjoyed running rings through their legs. When it took on Ana, she peered down at the cat and although she could have stomped on it, she gathered up a stack of hay in her trunk and dumped it onto the cat. The cat was on the next jeep heading back to town.

When the confines of the lodge became claustrophobic, Jud and I headed off for a break for a day or two. With Jud at the wheel, on a clear day, the view was magic. As soon as the jeep pulled onto the main road, the peaks of the Himalayas, smudged with snow, stretched far along the horizon. Only then did I realise the breadth of what I was surrounded by, outside the enclosed circle of huts in the jungle and the dark canopy of leaves.

Throughout our travels, Jud remained impeccable, his image as smooth as silk. He even ironed his clothes, and my scarves, so we looked the part. There was a clear aura about him and he was so sophisticated that I felt a little jaded beside him, not up to his high standards. Jud never made me feel that way and remained besotted.

Our travels took us along daring roads that appeared to lead into the side of a mountain and vanish into the abyss. When another vehicle approached, I held my breath as if that tiny gap would grant us safety but Jud never flinched. Our first visit was to the sacred area of Lumbini, on the Terai plains of southern Nepal, the birthplace of the Lord Buddha in 623 BCE. A most revered Buddhist site, the gardens are a place of peace and pilgrimage.

In Pokhara, we basked in the beautiful scenery and took time to relax. Jud hired a canoe to row us across the still waters of the lake, to enjoy the tranquillity and inhale the pristine mountain air. It was wonderful to have Jud all to myself, away from the demands of the lodge. Our relationship blossomed in the quiet beauty.

Pokhara is the gateway to trekking the Annapurna Circuit, with many backpackers resting here before an arduous climb through picturesque forests of flowers, waterfalls and terraced farmlands.

I never understood the need to conquer, to reduce everything to man's level. Why not be content to sit back in wonder and gaze at the moon, the stars and mountains, as part of a greater creation? Collecting chunks of earth, and landing on sacred ground, confines them to the physical plane and reduces them to bits of rock and dust.

There were ways to appreciate the earth without leaving an unwelcome trace behind, trekkers littering the mountains with debris and scattered remnants of their presence. The worst reminder was the remains of those climbers who never reached the top, whose frozen bodies never got to scale the heights or realise their dreams. Those who reached the peak took their triumph to the afterlife, savouring a split second of glory frozen in their subconscious. Their souls merged with the mountain, in the ultimate sacrifice.

Jud and I shared a respect for nature, and one of the things that endeared me to him was my affinity with animals. It was not only the elephants that took a shine to me, but I was a favourite with stray dogs, particularly white ones. That bond began in Bali because dogs

have an inbuilt radar when it comes to character. The first time was while meditating on the beach at Kuta when a white dog jumped onto my lap and curled up to bask in the positive energy.
On Sanur beach, I was displaced from my deckchair one day when a white dog jumped up behind me and refused to budge. Another time, sitting on the sand at dusk, a dog wandered over, nudged my arm upright so he could lean his head onto mine and we watched the sunset together. During a rabies outbreak, I was lying on the beach when a white dog ran up and slobbered a kiss onto my face. Would I be the first person to be killed off by a canine kiss?

In Nepal, it was the same. When Jud and I sat on a bench beside the river, a dog came and sat next to my feet. Others followed until I had a whole group beneath me. In the streets of Kathmandu, a pack of dogs followed me, and when Jud tried to divert their attention, after all, he was the wildlife manager, they only had eyes for me.

Love makes you do crazy things, and along with power and greed, is the greatest motivator of carnage in history. From dazzling to deranged, love plunges people into madness or inspires them to greatness. Stunning temples stand in its name, like the Taj Mahal in India, built by Shah Jahan in memory of his favourite wife, Mumtaz Mahal. Love propels men to scale balconies, like Romeo for his precious Juliet, and it led to both of their deaths by suicide. Even queens are not immune. Cleopatra resorted to the deadly bite of an asp so she could be buried in the same tomb as her lover, Marc Anthony. This homage to love is the stuff of legends.

Love can lead to murder too. In Nepal, this manifested on 1 June 2001, when a massacre took place at the royal palace. Thwarted in his love for a woman he was not permitted to marry, the Crown

Prince of Nepal allegedly opened fire at a family gathering, killing nine members of his family, including his father, King Birendra, before turning the gun on himself. In one horrific night, almost the entire Nepalese royal family was wiped out.

Crown Prince Dipendra was torn between love and his craving for power. Why didn't the prince just walk away to wed, and relinquish his entitlement to the royal crown? Others had. King Edward VIII opted for love, forsaking the British crown, to marry American divorcee, Wallis Simpson. It appeared that the Nepalese prince aspired to be the next king. Despite being a suspected murderer, Dipendra, in a coma, was king of Nepal for three days until declared brain dead. His moment of glory was brief and drenched in blood.

As much as I loved the wildlife park, the small perimeter of huts in the safe zone barred me from walking any further unescorted. It also ensured that the animals' natural habitat was not disturbed. When Jud had to make an unexpected business trip for a few days, I took the opportunity to follow a dream. My desire was not to scale Everest but to bask in its mighty shadow. I was far too close to the mountain to ignore its presence and it was only a matter of time.

On the treacherous bus ride around the Himalayas, I held my breath as the driver conquered the curves. From Kathmandu, it was time to face the divinity of the highest mountain on earth, and I opted to fly to its base and stay overnight at a small lodge there. It was a refuge for climbers who wanted to rest, before or after their attempt to scale Everest.

It was a perilous flight. There was only a brief period in the morning when a light plane could fly through the thick clouds and floating mist that enveloped the mountain range, erasing it from sight. While it was dangerous, it was a risk worth taking. So at the crack of dawn, on a clear morning, I clambered onto a small plane, and took my seat beside the pilot, watching as a box of oranges was offloaded from the plane to lessen its load.

Several small aircraft had been lost over the years in these mountains, where the slightest shift or gust of wind could be lethal. In 1992, a Pakistan International flight crashed on approach to Kathmandu and all 167 people on board perished. I remember the reaction at the time, the inevitable grief that such loss engenders. Close to 70 aviation accidents have occurred in Nepal since 1955, over 40 of which have been fatal. My descent into Kathmandu airport had been death-defying too, with the pilot struggling to safely land the plane, with the strong air currents among the peaks.

High terrain, unstable weather, and lack of modern equipment and technology were all determining factors, a reminder of the perils of a mountainous land. Adding to the danger was the possibility of altitude sickness if you ascended, or descended, quickly. A sudden rise or fall was more than the body was equipped to deal with. Difficulty adjusting to lower oxygen pressure at high altitudes could lead to headache, nausea, shortness of breath, and even death. These were risks many were prepared to take in search of their dream.

Few words can describe the feeling as you fly through a gap in the clouds, only to be swallowed up by mountain peaks iced with snow. In the front seat next to the pilot, I peered through a magical-looking glass, as the plane flew past rocky pinnacles, craggy ravines and hidden valleys, to appreciate the absolute grandeur of the earth.

Skidding over a flattened green landing strip tucked among the mountains, the plane came to a sudden halt. Three Japanese seated in the back of the plane remained silent, contemplating the challenge of the climb they were soon to undertake, perhaps nervous with anticipation or questioning their choices. Over 330 people have died trying to reach the summit of Mount Everest, looming highest in the world, at close to 9,000 metres. The toll is greater now with its growing popularity and climate change.

A guide was waiting to lead me to the lodge while the hikers were led in another direction, towards base camp. I was the only guest at the lodge and after a hot bowl of soup that evening I sat alone in the viewing area, beneath a glass dome. From there I looked out to the majesty of Mount Everest, so spectacular that it took my breath away. The full moon added to the mystical feel, as it inched across the sky and lit up Everest in a single stoic ray.

Adding to the sheer beauty was the significance of the date. It was Buddha's birthday, celebrated on the first full moon in May. Known as *Buddha Jayanti* in Nepal, it celebrates the day Buddha was born, his Enlightenment, and his death and entrance into nirvana. It is celebrated at numerous holy sites around Kathmandu valley, and in religious processions. The vibration of the beating heart of the mountain was audible and profound.

The fading glow of the stars reminded me it was time to sleep. Struck by the extreme cold, I tried to light the coal burner in my room but there was a warning not to use it without keeping the door open to provide oxygen. So it defeated its own purpose. When I finally drifted off, shivering under a pile of doonas, I was struck by the strangest vision.

A stream of Buddhist monks, dressed in maroon robes and yellow-crested hats, stood around my bed. Streams of incense curled up to the heights, as the sound of chanting filled the room. There was a sense of calm as one of the monks took my palm in his hand

and drew an intricate mandala on it. With no clue to its meaning, it felt like a protective seal.

Traditionally, a mandala is used to guide people along the path to enlightenment and signifies the universe in its ideal form, transforming a world of suffering into one of joy. Maybe spirit knew more than me, about my past, or the future, and what I was still to face. It felt more like a blessing, less a guide to perfection but a way of healing to achieve peace.

The next morning, I nibbled on a bowl of porridge as a camera crew from Germany made a loud entry carrying their equipment. They had come by plane, and it was ready to take off, back to Kathmandu. With altitude sickness taking its toll, I just made it on board, dizzy and disorientated. On the way to the landing strip, the guide took a photo of me in front of the peak of Everest. Later, it revealed a ray of light beaming down from the heavens and expanding around my body and within that light was the distinct image of an angel.

Needing to talk about my experience on the sacred mountain, I visited Jud's sister, Alisha, in Kathmandu. An intelligent and educated woman, she possessed a gentleness of spirit which she shared with her husband, Tashi, a Sherpa guide, and their sweet teenage daughter, Tara. Alisha was intrigued by my 'encounter' with the Buddhist monks. The mandala was of great interest but I couldn't recall its form so its meaning was lost.

I was grateful that Jud's family accepted me into their fold, relieved that Jud had found a woman they deemed 'worthy' of his love. Even years later they wrote me warm letters to retain this special bond. All were excited that Jud was due to join us in a few days, a promise he made to me to ease my feeling of desertion. He rarely visited his family in Kathmandu these days because the demands of the wildlife park came first.

When Jud arrived he was relieved to see me after the challenge of dealing with pressing business issues. A special glow lit up his eyes when he looked at me, as if his soul were smiling. If love was visible, glimmers of light would be radiating around us. His family sensed it too, Alisha confiding that her elder brother rarely showed such emotion.

With one of their relatives soon to be married, there was a party to attend that evening. When we arrived at the festivities, I met Jud's extended family who were most welcoming. Jud's parents were expressive and kind, and I danced with his cousins and friends. Jud released some of his self-control, and after a few drams of whiskey, he became the life of the party. It was good to see him not so guarded, and more spontaneous.

When Jud's teenage son, Raj, arrived, he was ecstatic to see his father, especially having such a good time. Jud's wife had tragically died many years before and Raj lived with his grandparents in a town some distance from the lodge so they rarely saw each other.

When Raj spotted me, he strode straight over and hugged me. We had met once before and he was much more reserved, but it was clear he'd snuck some nips of whiskey under the table. Happy, his mood was contagious, with everyone having a good time.

'Mum,' he shouted, clearly relegating me above my rank. "Mum, thank you so much.'

'Why?' I replied, enjoying the unexpected show of affection.

'Because you gave me back my father!' he exclaimed, kissing me on the cheek. His words meant so much to me.

Once again I had fallen in love not only with a man but also with his family, and the land he belonged to. A family to which he was almost lost. The look of joy on Raj's face as he danced on top of the table with his father was priceless. Even though his favourite Auntie Rohandra's lace tablecloth was trampled in the process.

A further blessing came with a love of a different kind. I was soon to inherit a family amongst the staff at the wildlife lodge. As the only woman working there, I was treated with respect and kindness. It was reciprocal as each one held an important place in my heart. A special day on the Nepalese calendar was set to solidify that bond. The festival of lights, Diwali, celebrates the victory of light over darkness, and good over evil. It lasts for five days, and Bhai Tika, the final day, celebrates the bond between brothers and sisters.

On this day, sisters express gratitude to their brothers and pray for their well-being and success. A brother respects his sister by bowing down at her feet and giving her a small gift, or modest sum of money. In return, she puts a garland around his neck and places a 'tika', or red dot, on her brother's forehead, symbolic of their bond.

I was honoured when three park rangers, one Indian and two Nepalese, asked if I would become their sister by ceremony. It was acceptable for close friends to seal their bond in such a way. I had no brother to protect or look after me so it deeply moved me.

They came, one by one, and after placing a colourful cloth garland around their neck, I dabbed the tika on their forehead. In return, each of my 'brothers' handed me a gift with great solemnity. Deeply touched by this act of respect, these men were special to me.

The men at the lodge could not return home for the festival, and as the only woman there, I offered to conduct the ceremony for any man who would like to become my brother. Six came forward, and my adopted family, and band of brothers, grew.

When one of the elephant drivers asked if I would bless my favourite elephant, Ana, and paint a tika on her forehead, I did not hesitate. Ana's beautiful eyes and long lashes were moist with tears as she knelt on the ground, and I painted a large coloured tika on her forehead. That's how I ended up with nine brothers and an elephant sister in such a far-off land. In Hindu mythology, the elephant is considered an incarnation of the god, Ganesha. The god of wisdom, Ganesha is the patron of writers and authors. As my 'sister' spirit, I remain inspired by the elephant's intelligence, wit and gentle spirit.

During the funeral procession of Crown Prince Dipendra, the alleged assassin of the royal family, a woman in a village along the way, hoping for a blessing for her child to be a son, crawled between the front legs of an elephant. The startled elephant tossed her aside with its trunk, killing her. When the priest mounted the elephant to cross the river it trumpeted, turning to chase the dignitaries back up the narrow path as they scattered in panic. An elephant is a very discerning animal, sensitive to the energy of those around it.

It was inevitable that my time would run out in Nepal. When the lodge owner heard an untrue rumour that Jud, his prize investment, was about to elope with me, he ordered me out of the wildlife park. Jud refused to send me away and he walked off the lodge with me. Nor would any of my 'brothers' betray our bond. However, when chaos broke out at the lodge after Jud left, I insisted that he return, refusing to be the cause of my brothers' grief.

When it came to the final parting, with my bags in the jeep for the start of the long trek home, a special ceremony was conducted to ensure I would be safe. Jud, hiding his emotions, emphasised that no one had been honoured in such a way before. Bright red powder was splashed around me, along with a tika drawn on my forehead. As I hugged each of my brothers, I knew this was not goodbye. Our link would span lifetimes. In the distance, I heard an elephant trumpet and knew Ana was saying her final goodbye.

Jud flew to Kathmandu with me and made sure I boarded the plane safely. One final embrace, prolonged and flooded with emotion, made our parting even more difficult. Once on the plane, I opened the letter Jud handed to me before he turned to walk away. He wrote professing his profound love and promised that we would be together eternally. To this day he still comes to me in my dreams. And so, Jud kept his promise to remain by my side.

CHAPTER SIXTEEN

STAIRWAY TO THE STARS

To keep an ancient promise, fate led me back to the enchanted island of Bali. My house was intact but empty, drained of positive energy, and the only modification was the iron bars Remy put on the windows. He was still chasing imaginary foes and it was a shock to see he kept a sickle under the bed. We did not get back together, there was too much history between us. I heard he had fathered another child, a Balinese son, someone to pass on his 'gifts'.

Although I was not certain of my next step, of one thing I was sure. I was no man's wife. That was already written in the stars long before I was born. Living alone was a difficult adjustment, but writing kept me inspired while my cat Abby grounded me. A white Persian, Abby was a true gem on this island of strays. She was gentle and clever, and together we went on supervised walks in the garden.

Languishing most days under the air conditioner, she leapt up whenever the masseuse came to visit. Then she would jump onto the bed and lay on her back so that I could massage her at the same time. We both appreciated pampering and the finer things in life.

I wrote about my life in Bali, hoping to find meaning in my journey and inspire others. My house was the perfect place for reflection, although my mind drifted off at times as I gazed out the window at my lush garden adorned with Buddha statues. Abby napped on my desk as I wrote, her favourite pillow the dictionary.

The only interruption was the occasional earthquake tremor, when the ceiling rocked and we both darted for cover under the desk, or the shout from the gardener when he encountered a deadly green snake slithering through the foliage before he made a run for it.

There was plenty to write about in Bali, my spiritual escapades just getting started. One day while walking along the beach at Sanur, I stopped at the Bali Beach Hotel to learn more about the hotel's 'special' guests. After making enquiries, I was fortunate to be granted access to the two private rooms in the hotel reserved for spirits. First, was a bungalow on the beach set aside for the exclusive use of Nyai Loro Kidul, the Ocean Goddess.

My encounter with the goddess in Java whetted my appetite and I was intrigued by the gravity with which she was treated. In 1966, at the opening of the Samudra Beach Hotel in Java, an old man advised the Sultan, who was a guest there, of his vision that offerings be made to the Ocean Goddess. His request was declined. Shortly after, there was a mighty roar, followed by a huge tidal wave. It rose from the calm ocean, drenching the guests and deluging the hotel grounds. It proved that it was not wise to ignore the Ocean Goddess.

At the Bali Beach Hotel, her bungalow, 2401, was set beneath swaying palm trees, with a view of the ocean. Inside it was decked out in her favourite emerald green, from bedspread to curtains, with a portrait of the goddess hanging above the bed. Scented blossoms were floating in the bathtub and scattered on the bed, immersing the room in sweet perfume. While there, an attendant in ceremonial dress entered the room carrying a tray of flowers and fruit, daily offerings for the goddess which he carefully placed on the table.

A culture that took its spiritual elements so seriously was to be respected. This devotion was even more pronounced when I visited a room in the main tower of the hotel, room 327. Originally devoted to the Ocean Goddess, it was now the spiritual abode of the first president of Indonesia, President Sukarno. Although the president never visited the hotel, he suggested its building as part of a war reparation program from the Japanese.

The president's private sanctuary was locked in time. A compelling leader, Sukarno became Indonesia's first president, ruling from 1949 to 1966, after declaring independence from the Dutch. His patriotic zeal was reflected in the furled-up flag of Indonesia laid out on the bed, next to the president's suit. It was displayed only on special occasions. Two pilgrims knelt in front of an altar in the room, praying for blessings from the past leader.

The energy in the room was eerie, but proof of its spiritual presence was vividly illustrated on 20 January 1993, when the ten-storey Bali Beach Hotel, the only hotel in Bali allowed to be higher than a coconut tree, burned down. Remarkably the president's room, on the third floor between two adjoining wings, remained intact, guarded by its dynamic psychic force. The bungalow of the Ocean Goddess was protected too and stood firm.

The day after the fire, with Mt. Agung looming on the horizon, I walked down the beach and stared in disbelief at the smouldering ruins of the hotel, with nothing left but blackened ash and twisted metal. It was inconceivable that anything survived the blaze, but in room 327 there was no hint of the huge fire that had engulfed it, just a burnt tinge on the plastic around the bottles of water. It defied reason but many things in Bali remain a mystery.

My house was not immune to the presence of spirit. The back of my yard bordered on an empty plot of land and across the road was a site where effigies of the sacred bull, all black and gold and glittering glass, stood ready to carry the deceased soul on its celestial journey. It seemed a few errant spirits strayed over to my house.

An angel picture that hung beside my bed as protection invariably fell to the ground each night and woke me up, no matter my efforts to secure it. Then one day, while reading on my bed, the angel picture flew across the room as if propelled by a ghostly hand.

A few nights later, Abby jumped into an alert position on the bed hissing, her back arched as her eyes scanned an 'apparition' up and down. Time to activate my crystals to form a cosmic shield. It was Abby and me against a world of wayward spirits.

Abby's name was short for Abraxas, chosen because of its mystic significance to ward off bad energy and my cat lived up to her name. It was just one in a series of inexplicable events but spirit was just getting started and there was a lot more to come. It could be very scary but I tried to remain calm and centred.

There were so many stories about magic and mayhem on the island – mystical spells, age-old curses, an irresistible smile, potions to make the object of your affection fall in love with you – so many that they became commonplace. Many things defied belief and I struggled to make sense of them. One of the most bizarre episodes happened one night at a club in Kuta, with my zany friend, Roxanne, by my side. It was an unlikely setting for what was to follow.

With many stories to share and lots of laughs, without a doubt, Roxy was my belly dancing pal in a Middle Eastern harem in a previous lifetime or a fellow monk in a Buddhist monastery on some distant mountain in Bhutan. Roxy was the one who breached the code of silence as we bent over in laughter, recounting stories about a wayward buzzard or how Brother Usher's flatulence interrupted a profound meditation. Just one look at the twinkle in her eye, those green Irish eyes, sent me into fits of giggles. Roxy was vivacious, bold and brazen, and a much-needed antidote to my loneliness.

As we sat in the club that night, swapping stories and sipping our drinks, a well-groomed man approached. 'Someone is waiting to meet you,' he said, his gaze focused on me, 'in Malang in central Java.' Roxy sat open-mouthed, unable to speak for the first time. 'Malik is a powerful healer' he added, 'and he wants to meet *you*.'

'If you agree,' Lawrence said, introducing himself, 'I'll arrange a plane ticket to Surabaya and a car will be waiting at the airport.' Unable to process his words, it would be crazy to accept such a proposition. None of it made sense but when Lawrence spoke more he appeared quite sane, a professional man with a sound reputation.

Roxy kicked me under the table when I refused his offer, but after a discussion, Lawrence agreed to accompany me on the trip. There were no warning bells or signs of danger, and to avoid Roxy's chunky shoes, I relented. It was too inviting a proposition to refuse and this strange offer smacked of a higher purpose.

Two days later Lawrence picked me up in the early morning for our flight to Java. It was a restless night, woken at 3:33 am when the alarm unexpectedly went off and the clock stopped. After we landed, the drive to a town near Malang took over an hour by car, with Lawrence at the wheel. The conversation turned to the history of the area, once part of the Mataram kingdom, and we stopped to view some stony remains along the way. Once again, it all felt so familiar.

When we arrived at the healer's home many people were waiting to see him. All the chairs were taken and the veranda was full.

As soon as we entered the living room a powerful man strode over to me and grasped my hand. 'You came,' Malik exclaimed, his grip tightening. 'I knew you'd come when the clock stopped at 3:33.'

None of this made sense, but Malik's stance was strong and assertive. Dark and moustached, his stature was that of a bodybuilder and his projected aura added to his bulk. 'Follow me,' he said, leading the way. Arguments were futile at this stage.

Led into a back room, Malik sat opposite me as he performed a healing. 'We must undo the damage of the evil spirits that have attacked you.' Taking my right arm, he ran his fingers along the path of an old injury, a remnant of the night when a louvre windowpane in my first house in Bali exploded in my hand. With his touch, my arm, already tender, started to throb and my head swirled. To my amazement, drops of blood oozed from my skin.

Malik closed his eyes and entered a meditative state, holding my hands in his. After what seemed an eternity, he exclaimed, 'You must learn to protect yourself from the dark spirits! Yours is a powerful journey for the light and so evil will try to attack you. Many people will benefit from your truth for you have been tasked with preserving the history of this land in your writing.'

Malik motioned for me to follow him as he moved his chair and pulled aside a rug in the middle of the room. Then he opened a trapdoor on the floor. Inside were steps leading to a small, dark room with only a dim lightbulb dangling on a wire to emit light. Malik motioned for me to follow him down the stairs, and even though I hesitated, I had come this far so there was no turning back.

When we were both sitting cross-legged on the rug, facing a small altar, Malik pulled the door shut. In the half-light, there was the eeriest presence of lost spirits. A young woman, draped in a shawl, was crouched in the corner. Her wail in an unknown tongue made me shudder. Malik spoke to her gently and she faded from sight. Then came the spectre of an old man, lost in his fears, but Malik reassured him with a string of soothing unknown words.

Then Malik turned to me, his eyes piercing the darkness. 'You must stay here,' he commanded, 'to learn the mystic ways. Only then will you be able to defeat your enemies. After several weeks you will be able to walk through walls and perform other feats.'

With thanks, I declined his offer. Why walk through walls when I could simply open the door? My protection came from a higher source, along with an inherent trust. Still, what ancient pledge had brought me here and empowered me to walk down steps into a dark cellar with a mysterious stranger? The next step led me upwards.

Not surprisingly, it was Roxy who set the gears in motion. Weeks after my return to Bali, she rang to tell me of an exhibition at Nusa Dua of rare artefacts from the Majapahit Empire. She knew that I was researching the mystical practices of this ancient Javanese kingdom and was keen to encourage my forays into the supernatural.

We caught a taxi there and then inevitably got lost. Rescued by two security guards, we hopped onto their motorbikes as they drove us to the venue. The small shopfront stood among others that were deserted. There was a strange, powerful energy as I walked through the door into a room that was laid out with glass cabinets packed with valuable antiques from the 14th century kingdom.

As I browsed through the display of carved figurines, daggers and other prized objects, it took a few minutes to realise that Roxy was not behind me. In fact, apart from the custodian of the collection, I was the only one there. I looked at Roxy through the glass pane where she stood outside, but she just shrugged.

It appeared that she was barred from entry, and when she tried to come through the door an invisible force field pushed her back. She was both shocked and disappointed, but it was beyond her control. Only those people who spirit condoned were granted access to this mystical prism and from the look on the elderly custodian's face, it was a rare privilege.

Standing transfixed at the bottom of the stairs in the corner of the room, I looked up to the floor above. This was a prohibited area, separate from the rest of the exhibition. With no idea of the 'treasure' it held, I felt compelled to climb the stairs – as if summoned.

A series of open doors had led to this special moment, the culmination of lifetimes of searching. The custodian watched as I took the first step upwards, then stood aside, allowing me access. Only spirit decided who was worthy of this special honour.

This realm was reserved for those who had passed the test of lifetimes. When I reached the top, I took a deep breath and entered the forbidden room. In the centre, in pride of place, was a glass cabinet, with flickers of light radiating from it. It held the most sacred of objects – the kris dagger of Gajah Mada, the renowned military general of the Javanese Majapahit Empire of the 14th century.

A famed warrior, he conquered the Southeast Asian archipelago of Nusantara, now Indonesia, to unite the land and bring the country to its peak of glory. Like all heirlooms, the kris embodied its owner's power and the accumulated force of their ancestors. It was a great honour to look upon this dagger, its blade visibly pulsating with beams of energetic light shooting from the metal.

This was another step in uncovering the wealth of knowledge and rich legacy of the Javanese kingdom. Even more intriguing was my bond with these ancient precincts and the force that led me back from previous lifetimes to trigger my life purpose. Some things are written in the heavens and this was a stairway to the stars.

Meanwhile, Roxy remained on Middle Earth, her pathway leading in another direction. We each have our road less travelled.

CHAPTER SEVENTEEN

FLOATING ON THE MOON

It's all about the kiss. That kiss, this kiss. It's subliminal, erotic and all at once breathtaking. I have been kissed hard against the smoking funnel of a cruise ship and softly in the silver moonlight. An ardent kiss on a beach in Bali from a near stranger, as we gazed at the stars, was spontaneous and unexpected. With our attraction too hard to resist, fireworks flew up into the air as our lips locked, as if arranged by a mischievous cupid in the sky.

Dancing with Roxy at a full moon party on the trendy beach in Legian, our eyes shut to groove to the music, I felt the urgent pull of someone's hand sweeping me away from the dance floor. My eyes flickered open to see a sexy guy guiding me towards the bungee jump tower. Was he mad? I was not about to jump off a high tower with only an elastic band to bounce me back up! Without a word, he whisked me up in the lift to the top of the tower.

As the full moon emerged from behind a cloud and lit up the waves rolling to shore, it consumed us and we danced like we were floating on the moon and would never seek solid ground again. The spell was broken by a distant shriek as Roxy spotted us from down below. Searching for her missing friend, she was told I was seen going up to great heights. She refused to believe it but one look at the hunky guy from afar and she understood.

Then there was the *almost* kiss, nearly as romantic as the real thing. After a hectic night at the bar of a deluxe hotel in Sanur, which Roxy dragged me to because she lusted after a long-haired Javanese guitarist she'd seen the week before, we watched European couples attempt the tango badly. Then with the first twang of Santana, Roxy and I began our belly dancing medley on the dance floor which seemed to stir the guys in the band to great heights.

When it came time to leave, Roxy decided to stay a while and chat with a man she fancied at the bar while I made a beeline for the exit and waited outside for a taxi to arrive. Then *he* walked out, the long-haired guitarist who was the object of Roxy's desire. The men from these parts, with their striking good looks and high cheekbones, were reminiscent of the Native Americans and had a special aura. Krishna sat beside me on the bench and asked if he could drive me home on his motorbike, obviously holding his guitar.

It was a good offer but I declined. I was on a man 'fast', cleansing any trace of them from my psyche. So, in consolation, he removed his guitar from its case and began to strum and sing "Unchained Melody". A balmy tropical evening, a shimmering moon and a hot guy who hungers for your kiss. He stares into your eyes, rolling his tongue around the sensual lyrics. Too much for the average person to bear but the taxi saved the day. Unbeknown to me a man was waiting for me at home, and I had just averted a disaster.

Who was this mystery man, the man skulking in the shadows? It all began innocently enough in 1996 when I attended an art gallery opening in Bali with my friend Trish. Living on the island since the

1960s, Trish had met her Balinese prince at the university she attended in New Zealand and was a walking encyclopaedia on the modern history of Indonesia, having endured much of it personally. Steadfast and a good Christian, with a lively sense of humour, Trish was my rock during the hard times while Roxy was my diversion.

After we meandered through the crowd at the gallery admiring the unique artwork and dodging the trendy ex-pats adorned in flowing caftans and dangling earrings, their hair invariably twirled on their heads in a loose bun, we headed for the appetisers. Trish slowly drank her glass of white wine while I had a few tentative sips, having never acquired a taste for alcohol, even in all my years spent at a nightclub. Southern Comfort drenched in Coke and ice was the closest I got to looking worldly but it was still hard to swallow.

At the end of the evening, I settled into the car as Trish drove us home. We didn't make it far before I yelled, 'Trish, turn the car around,' startling her. 'We have to go to Mojos in Kuta!' It was not one of the finest discos so Trish was confused. So was I. Strangely, she didn't object and we made it through the traffic in record time.

'Why?' was the only thing Trish said, as we dodged dangling wires to enter the club. The place was packed with drunken Aussies and brave locals, all pumping away to a bit of hard rock. Seeking sanctuary on the upper floor, we gazed down at the crowd from a safe distance. There was a chance for a chat up here but I was mute having just dragged a nice Christian lady to what looked like the devil's den of inequity. She appeared to be having a good time, or else was praying for redemption for the souls of all those below.

Lost in thought, as to the meaning of life, I suddenly felt a magnetic pull. It was dragging me backwards until I bumped straight into a man standing in the crowd. We now stood back-to-back, almost attached. He was talking to another woman but the thud shook them apart. He turned and stalked off but I chased him across the dance floor and tapped him on the shoulder. His face was not visible until now but when he turned around, I gasped.

He was drop-dead gorgeous and seemed so familiar, so mesmerising, that my body shook. It was the only time I had actively pursued a man since my rock star days, a welcome change from the usual urge of men to grab hold of my arm and alter the course of my destiny. When he asked for my number I scribbled it down and as our hands touched, an electric charge shot through us both.

Then without warning, he kissed me as the heavens melted into mulch. *Skyrockets in flight, an absolute delight. I wanted to kiss him all over. Hold me, thrill me, kiss me, kill me.* And he almost did, in a battle that would last the better part of seven years.

All the songs I had ever heard about the power of love or the lure of one last kiss, were meaningless in the face of such a magnetic pull. Agus was 20 years younger than me but it made no difference. In my mid-40s, the passing decades may have added layers of maturity and experience but my spirit remained forever young. When fate is involved, age is measured in lifetimes not years as past issues seek resolution or recognition.

Agus, an astute Aquarian, was an independent soul who was well-read and up to date with current affairs unlike many on the island who were stuck in the past. With a Balinese mother to pass on tradition and a Chinese father who impressed on him the value of learning, Agus lived on his terms since he was a child. As a teenager, he hopped onto the back of a truck and headed off to Jakarta, 1000 kilometres away. His family were frantic with worry but Agus was not one to consider the consequences, only the benefits.

Agus was like a tiger emerging from a golden cage and the world was his for the taking. Like his favourite song, he was the strange enchanted boy who wandered far in search of meaning. Much wiser than his years, but also extremely selfish, Agus believed he could have it all, no matter the cost. It was never going to be easy but neither of us could resist. So began a tumultuous episode of life.

Agus was one of the missing pieces in my zodiac set. I had been waiting for an Aquarian all my life, and while I had one female Aquarian friend, the male water bearer eluded me. The toll of carrying heavy water vessels cursed them with weak ankles and a strong desire to break free from bondage and discover their true purpose in life. Aquarians are eccentric, independent and worldly. I loved the challenge of trying to connect and learn what motivated them.

Astrology is both an ancient science and a gracious art. Through the looking glass of the cosmos, there are clues to be deciphered and much wisdom to be gained. Unlike Bali, where star gazing is restricted to moon phases to determine auspicious days, astrology is inherent to Indian culture where birth charts are compared for an arranged marriage to determine a 'good match.' The predictions of the Royal Astrologer of Nepal were highly valued and remained private, with their potential to compromise the monarchy.

Viewed through the lens of astrology, relationships take on a deeper meaning. Air signs are astute and intelligent, and rarely satisfied. My jungle man, Jud, was a Gemini, literate and educated at only the best schools because his father was in a high command position in the British Army. He was polished and sophisticated as was Erik, my Swedish love in London who was also a Gemini.

While Erik was calm and measured, Jud had the edgy vitality of a Mercury-ruled sign, unable to sit or concentrate on one matter for long. Like a tightly coiled spring, he became distracted and jumped up to deal with yet another urgent issue that had arisen.

The second air sign, Aquarius, searches for answers beyond the bounds of the accepted. I looked forward to exploring the universe through the mind of Agus and seeing where I landed. A Libra, the third air sign, I was attracted to Agus on a physical level and we were certain to stimulate each other's minds. Remy was a Libra too, his sense of identity was tied up with his appeal and giant ego.

My ex-husband, Luke, was the opposite sign to Gemini, fiery Sagittarius, the eternal wanderer. Learning through experience and averse to responsibility and commitment, they were always searching. Global travellers, there is no pot of gold at the end of the rainbow but that never stops their mission to find one.

Libra is best suited with fiery Aries, its opposite sign. Fire and air signs are a good match, fuelling each other's desires. Aries men flashed in and out of my life but were too high-powered to stay in one place for long and too fast to catch. No doubt a stormy liaison, I would be left standing at the starting gate while they raced off in their latest sports car or worse still, falling off the back of a jet ski, close to drowning before they even noticed.

The final fire sign, Leo, proved a flirtatious fling. Most were too loud and ambitious for my sensibilities and tended to unsettle my scales. They were better suited to the theatre or the military but there was the occasional timid one, like the lion in The Wizard of Oz, whose goal was to find courage in this lifetime.

As one of the gentle water signs, my partner, Brad, was a serene Pisces who faced life through a soft veil of music and make-believe.

Vulnerable, sensitive and otherworldly, he found dealing with reality demanding. I avoided jealous Scorpio, far too sexually driven and secretive. The third water sign, Cancer, came later in a dalliance with a Latin American with a gentle soul and a kind heart. It was like riding through life on the wings of a dove.

Capricorn, the earthy goat tends to be serious, and conservative to a fault while virgin Virgo is both practical and obsessive. With my moon in the third earth sign of Taurus, it appeared that I was sufficiently grounded not to need anything to weigh me down. Or maybe a rampant bull was still to come. Earth goes best with water, far too heavy and demanding for fire and air signs.

Many factors must be considered in a birth chart when doing character analysis, plotting progressions or assessing a good match. Signs, houses, planetary lines and angles all come into play, and it is a complex process. From the moment of birth, the movement of the planets sets the stage, triggering episodes that become life lessons. How we face, and deal with each one, determines our growth.

While Sun signs may be compatible, the Moon's placement signifies emotions so if they are at odds, it's a no-go. A delicate Moon in Pisces would be crushed by an emotionally distant partner like a freedom-loving Sagittarius. Mercury is communication so a chatty lass would not be a good match with a reclusive Cancer. Venus and Mars indicate physical attraction and the vital spark between two people, Jupiter brings happiness and optimism and even Saturn has a role to play so that when the going gets tough, they'll stay around.

Many planetary lines bound me to Agus and we were fiercely attracted. Together, we forged a physical bombshell and an emotional minefield, so we were in for a bumpy ride. Uranus in the picture sparked electricity between us but also guaranteed that ours was an erratic match, with many highs and lows. Neptune joined in too to form a deep spiritual bond and love of music, while a strong Pluto tie spoke of a karmic past-life connection.

Agus had used his good looks to his advantage, having travelled abroad sponsored by some besotted lover. Still, there was a softer side to Agus, a transparency that was authentic. Sitting in a club, with a string of girls giving him the eye, he turned to tell me how lucky he was to be with a woman like me, and how beautiful I was.

Whether walking along a road in Sydney or on an isolated beach in Bali, he did not hesitate to tell me how much he loved me, with the warmest hug. On my birthday he turned up on his motorbike balancing a cake, a bunch of flowers and a small puppy dog. How could you fail to love such a man? Until the dark side emerged, smothering you in doubt as you walked on broken glass.

Agus was a man of contrasts, a man with incredible potential, whose hidden self was lost in the shadows. We laughed so much when we were together but any argument would see him retreat and lock down to an unreachable place in his soul. No amount of pleading could wrench him from his inner sanctum and much to my frustration, he closed off and rigidly refused to speak.

Still, when he was his buoyant self, the mere sight of him was enough to make my spirit soar. Each afternoon when I met up with friends for drinks, the sound of his motorbike as he approached the café raised my spirits, even more when he leaned over to kiss my cheek. Men on the island did not usually express their affection in public but Agus had no qualms. There was an expansive quality to his spirit and our union broke many barriers.

Agus had his own house in Denpasar but spent most nights with me in Sanur. Whether dining at restaurants, beach cafés, local dumpling trolleys or cheap markets for delicious chicken satay, we enjoyed each other's company. On the back of his motorbike, we headed off to explore the lush rice paddies in Ubud or far-off valleys.

Dancing at Hard Rock Café to great rock bands on a Saturday night was fun but the intimacy of the drive home on the motorbike, along the highway after midnight, was best. Clutching onto his firm chest, with the breeze brushing my cheek, I leaned against him to the sound of silence, repelling any stray ghost lost in the night.

A Jupiter connection tied us to adventure. Agus was the original wandering spirit and I was the eternal stargazer. So we headed off, into the horizon for a far-off destination, wherever the urge took us.

We travelled east across the islands of Indonesia to Lombok, then across to Sumba and Sumbawa, where we were awoken in the early morning by people fishing under our bungalow. Looking through the gaps in the floorboards, I spotted a whole family hauling in their catch. They were quite loud expressing their joy.

The most memorable island was without a doubt, Komodo, with its fearful dragons. A guide with a stick was all we had to fend off large Neanderthal lizards with teeth as sharp as razor blades and a hearty appetite for unwelcome strangers. Plump ones were no doubt favoured, so I was at risk. It was not a place for a solitary stroll along a grassy verge or watching a sunset on a remote beach.

Staying on the island for the night, we got into an argument. Agus sulked on the porch of our hut while I strode off. There was nowhere to go. The stairs led to the domain of the dragon so I opted for bed. As soon as I lay on the grotty mattress on the floor there was a thud and a giant rat scampered down the wall and ran right past me. Grabbing my sarong, I hid under it and imagined I was in a luxury bungalow in Tahiti, with fancy soap and scented hand lotion. And definitely room service on a silver tray.

On the island of Flores, we passed beaches speckled with smooth teal and pink rocks, as our mad driver sped around hairpin bends to the pulsing beat of 'Deliverance'. We rose at dawn and climbed into the back of an old truck to view Kelimutu, the three-coloured lakes clustered together within a volcanic crater.

It was a spectacular sight. The large turquoise-blue lake was the resting place of good souls who had passed over. Separated only by a crater wall, the dark red lake was reserved for the ill and infirm while the black lake held those souls who had done wrong.

In life, turquoise represents the good times, those filled with sunshine and happiness. Then comes the dark red sunsets when you are forced to draw on your will to survive and emerge victorious. Facing the darkness of transition you are reborn to view the world, and your place in it, in a different, more advanced way.

Such is life and on that fateful night, years later, Agus was the man standing in the shadows. He was the shadow of my past and a glimmer of my future, and it was up to me to decide which one.

Writing became my outlet. It never registered that my life was extraordinary until I began to write it down. There are two kinds of writers. Those who are compelled to write when they are young, penning essays or poems because it is part of their being, or authors who write because they have something to say. I fell into the second category. Driven by a lifetime, or an event that needs expression, they long to share their story as a source of inspiration for others.

My first book, *Bali Moon,* flowed from the heart. A compilation of my life in Bali, the words just tumbled onto the page, releasing me from the debris of the past. After I shared my experiences, I received emails from readers who loved the descriptions or could relate to my story, as it mirrored certain aspects of theirs.

Little can compare to holding the first copy of your book in your hands for you have created a piece of yourself out of a vacuum, from the void of creation. Getting an agent can be harrowing so I decided on self-publishing which came with the challenge of getting my book placed in bookshops. Many writer's conferences advised it was not possible but I was determined to prove them wrong.

It was the late 1990s and I was out to break barriers. While back in Sydney, I gave talks about my spiritual journey at the Theosophical Society. After speaking about my experiences with magic, a forlorn woman came forward to express how important it was for me to acknowledge the existence of evil, having faced it for herself.

My talks provided an open door into the society's bookstore, the Adyar, but how to get my book noticed? When the manager asked in which genre the book should be placed – autobiography, travel, self-help or spiritual, I replied, 'On the best seller stand.' It worked and in the limelight, soon all copies of my book were sold.

Time to aim bigger. Stalking a large bookstore, Dymocks, I hid among the bookshelves when an attendant crept up behind me. 'Can I help you?' she asked. Caught out, I rambled something about my book, thinking I had no hope of having it placed here.

'Let me see if the buyer is available'. Len was in the office and asked if I had a copy of my book with me. Flustered, I promised to bring it in the next day. I turned up with few expectations.

'Yep, it looks pretty good,' Len said, flicking through the pages. 'We'll order 30 copies.' Just then, the store manager walked in and picked up the book.

'This would be perfect for a book launch,' he commented. After catching my breath, I told him that I had a Balinese dancer friend who could perform on the occasion.

'Well, that's settled', he replied. 'We'll hold an in-store event and arrange the publicity.' The evening was a great success and it was my first taste of recognition as an author.

After meeting a romance novelist at a writers' conference a few weeks later, she arranged an introduction to her literary agent who convinced a book distributor, new to the publishing field, to take *Bali Moon* on as their first title. I was on my way to success.

At the Maui Writers Conference in Hawaii, my pitch to the US agents engendered interest. Magic was a trendy topic and after a session with a Hollywood agent, she remarked my life was less a movie and more a series. She followed me around the conference, waiting for a pitch for a TV script but I had yet to write one.

With my book published in Australia, I returned to Bali where Agus encouraged me to pursue my dream. So on my next visa trip to Singapore, I took a taxi and visited the office of a publishing company, with the only English-speaking bookstores in Indonesia.

Shown to the manager, he looked at the book and considered my sales in Australia and then said, 'We'll go ahead and publish the book or else buy up all the copies and transport them to Jakarta.'

Like a set of dominoes, it all fell into place. When the first shipment of my book *Bali Moon* arrived in Bali, a media conference took place in their central bookstore, with Agus by my side. It was a wonderful moment, to see an entire wall covered with copies of my book. Journalists interviewed me and a camera crew from the local TV station asked questions for their audience. Fans and friends were there too, in my moment of glory.

It was followed later that evening with a book launch at a major hotel in Kuta, thanks to their generous British manager, Jock, who provided the food and a great venue. To draw people to the event I approached different sponsors to provide prizes for a raffle to be held on the night. As if by magic, they all agreed. Walking into the Ansett airline office, it took only one request, and airline tickets to Australia were provided as the main prize.

I was even gifted a flowing lace dress for both occasions from an elite boutique so I felt like Cinderella doused with fairy dust who had stumbled her way into the ball, with Prince Charming by her side. Not expecting him to accept the invitation, I was delighted when the Australian Consul arrived to give a speech to a room packed with guests. Fantasy had transformed into reality and for that one special night, I was enchanted. Yes, enchanted.

CHAPTER EIGHTEEN

THE KING AND I

Bali Moon was a strange phenomenon, and although I had no intention of writing a sequel, there were interesting subjects I still wanted to research, ones that raised my curiosity and would make good articles. One story was particularly intriguing, a collection of sacred mystical masks that a royal family in Bali had under its protection.

Organising an interview at the palace was difficult but Agus was the key. His elder sister was married to the nephew of the King of Blahbatuh, one of the eight regencies in Bali. It was his ancestral family that had the 21 sacred masks in their possession. Her husband arranged a meeting at the palace to discuss these precious antiques, handed down over centuries, and I had the honour to be granted an audience with a member of the royal family.

At the scheduled time, Agus brought along a friend who was more familiar with the heightened dialect required to speak with Balinese royals. In the Bali caste system, the highest caste are the priests, the Brahmanas, with the title Ida Bagus or Ida Ayu for a woman. Kings, nobles and warriors rank second, as Ksatrya caste, with the names Agung or Agus. Third are the Wesya, the merchants and officials, usually called Gusti, Ngurah or Dewa. Most people in Bali are Sudras, the workers and farmers, and their names, typically in birth order, are Wayan, Made, Nyoman and Ketut, a sequence repeated with more children.

Shown into a courtyard to await our meeting, I took shelter from the sun under a thatched *bale* hut. Soon I was joined by an elderly gentleman in a batik sarong and tunic, and we started a conversation in broken English. Shock followed when Agus and his friend entered the compound. 'This is the King of Blahbatuh,' Agus's friend said, introducing us, 'Gusde I Gusti Ngurah Djelantik.' I was mortified because I was sitting opposite the king.

It was a forbidden practice as a king must sit higher than a 'commoner'. The king calmed my fears with a smile, 'No problem,' he said, as I apologised. After learning a little about the history of the kingdom, the talk turned to the sacred masks, each with mystical power. None was more revered than the mask of Gajah Mada, the great military hero of the 15th century. I already had the privilege of viewing his kris dagger and wanted to learn more.

After a long and informative discussion, the king graciously issued an invitation to join him the following week for an important ceremony. Held once a year in the palace temple, the masks are unwrapped and cleansed by the Hindu priest who watches over them in a sealed chamber in the temple compound. The whole village is obliged to attend the temple and unite in prayer on this special day.

As I entered the temple for the ceremony, dressed in a purple brocade sarong and lace kebaya, Agus stood beside me in a white tunic buttoned in gold, crimson sarong and white headpiece, his Balinese heritage shining through. The scent of frangipani blossoms tucked behind our ears, and the gong of the gamelan orchestra, made it otherworldly. I had trespassed on a world so alien to my own but strangely it felt as if I belonged. That I had taken my rightful place.

The entire village was crammed into the large courtyard, watching silently as the temple priest stooped over the king sitting cross-legged on a mat at the front. The priest blessed the king with holy water while uttering secret mantras. It was impossible to look away because the scene was mesmerising, a page out of time.

After the ceremony, the king stood up, swamped by the villagers seated around him. Then he turned around slowly, scanning through the crowd. When his eyes fell upon me, and then Agus, the king motioned for us to follow him into the sacred chamber of the holy masks. What followed was enacted in slow motion.

It was accompanied by a collective murmur in Balinese, among the villagers, when they saw me summoned by the king. 'Who's that *bule?* That foreigner. Who's that girl?'

Stepping over the threshold, into the inner sanctum, the king ushered us into the small dark chamber that held the masks. I stood between the king and Agus, hardly drawing a breath for I did not want to disturb the sanctity of this hallowed place.

The chamber had been sealed for so long that the air was deathly still, but now the masks stirred as they were woken from their slumber. I was swept back to a history of regal kings and brave generals, to an era that defined the country. This moment defied belief and was so obscure, it demanded to be frozen in time.

Laid out on a table were the 21 sacred masks, free from their cloth shrouds and displayed in all their glory. Ancient voices echoed in my ears, cries of victory and the scent of glory. Each mask depicted a prominent figure of the Majapahit Empire of Java, dating back between 1325 and 1650, and characters from Balinese mythology. This was a treasure trove of history and custom.

Amid the display, the mask of the military general, Gajah Mada, stood out. Supposedly an actual cast of his face, the mask emitted a coppery sheen, the bulging eyes and fierce countenance were an expression of his might. The mask shone as if newly carved and not moulded centuries before. It radiated a special power, one that was as desirable as it was elusive. Touching was not permitted.

'Several years ago, a high caste man came here,' the king said, 'and insisted on trying on the mask. The priest could not refuse because of his rank, bending to his demands. As soon as the man put the mask on, he collapsed and died.' Each mask possessed the power of the figure it imitated, all far too volatile to tamper with.

Only people of high status, presidents and sultans, had access to view the masks. President Suharto, who immersed himself in a mystical realm as part of his quest to boost his power, demanded to borrow the mask of Gajah Mada. The king could not refuse.

On the bumpy flight from Bali to Jakarta, the mask was said to have spoken, guiding the pilot through the severe storms. Once there, it hung on the wall of the presidential palace in Jakarta until the day Suharto stepped down as president when it rattled and disappeared before miraculously returning to its private vault in Bali.

No one questioned the authenticity of such claims because belief in the metaphysical was inherent to Bali's mystical past. It was a true honour that the king had bestowed upon me and Agus, allowing us to be in his presence and view his priceless collection.

A link in a lengthy royal ancestral chain of Bali, the king understood that his collection must be preserved, in words, so that their legacy was recorded for posterity and could never be lost.

The next stage in my journey was triggered when I attended the Bali Travel Mart some months later. Held in one of the five-star resorts in Nusa Dua, it was a plush event to promote tourism. As guests entered the lobby, stunning Balinese dancers, wrapped in gold satin, cast flower petals at their feet as they walked along the welcome carpet, to the jarring sound of the gamelan orchestra.

On the first evening, I attended the launch of a new travel magazine, chatting with two writers undertaking their first business venture on the island. I also had the opportunity to talk with several Balinese dignitaries and heads of the tourist trade, who were very interested in my spiritual encounters. It was a subject inherent to Balinese belief but an area rarely entrusted to a foreigner.

The following day, at afternoon tea, I sat at a table with several journalists, one from Japan and the others from South Korea. With few words spoken, I drank my tea and indulged in the cakes. I had yet to realise the repercussions of this pivotal moment in Indonesia's history, for it happened suddenly with little time to register.

President Suharto, leader of the country for 32 years, resigned on 21 May 1998, with little warning. There was much conjecture as to who would take his place with fears that the country could descend into chaos or become unstable after his long term of rule.

In a dramatic entrance, several dignitaries walked into the large function room, trailed by reporters, who were warned not to come close to the guest of honour. That would have to wait for the media conference. Surrounded by Balinese VIPs was an esteemed guest, Amien Rais, head of one of the biggest Muslim parties in the country and one of the leaders of the reform movement that led to the president's resignation. Rais later became Speaker of the People's Consultative Assembly of the Republic of Indonesia.

Taking their place at a table in the centre of the room, the group were soon engaged in deep conversation. Ten minutes later, while sipping on my tea, someone took hold of my arm. 'Come with me,' a voice said. '*They* want to talk to you.' Almost choking on my cake, I wiped crumbs off my lips as I was hauled to the centre table.

Everyone, including the media, was now staring at me as I stood in front of the table of the VIPs. One of them, the head of the tourism sector, was the man I had spoken to the previous night about my book, at the magazine launch. In the background, I heard the mutterings of the press and gathered guests as they watched in awe.

'*Siapa dia?* Who is she?'

'Please,' I was asked by the men at the table, 'tell Mr Rais why Bali is important to the world. You are a writer from abroad who has lived here for many years and written about our special island.'

Despite the pressure, and after some hesitation, I spoke my truth and hoped I did myself, and the island, proud. I explained why the spiritual values and allure of the enchanted island made it unique and prized in the world. Once I got started there was no holding me back and all the men looked satisfied with my response.

Afterwards, I went onto the terrace for some fresh air. A distinguished man emerged from the room and walked over to me. 'My name is Gusde,' he said, shaking my hand. 'I'm interested to learn why spirits singled you out, a foreigner, to meet our special guest. No one else was invited to speak to him so it is most intriguing.

'Next week' he continued, 'a meditation will be held on the beach near Nusa Dua on the night of the lunar eclipse. Please attend as my guest.' So began a series of mystical encounters and an enduring bond with a man who was destined to become my mentor.

Before attending the meditation on the beach, Gusde asked me to his office to be 'screened', no doubt to see if I was worthy of being part of this mystical clan. Gusde was a hotel manager in Tuban, near the airport, and his office was overlaid with the trappings of a devoted man. As I took my seat, the strong scent of cempaka blossoms and rich incense rose from the Hindu altar in the corner of the room.

To prove my place in the heightened sphere of spirit, Gusde called in one of his staff, who acted as a medium, to come into the room. The medium soon fell silent and then his eyes flickered as he went into a deep trance. After a few minutes, he roused and grabbed a pen, writing down a message from spirit. Gusde smiled as he read it, nodding his head as if agreeing with his own judgment.

'This lady was once younger sister to the advisor of the royal court of the Majapahit Empire of Java,' Gusde read. 'She has returned now, centuries later to fulfil a promise to record the history of the kingdom so it can be preserved forever.' Gusde then revealed my name in that lifetime, an honorary title relegated only to those of high standing in the court. It was to be a message repeated often.

It seemed inconceivable that centuries ago I was part of a Hindu-Buddhist kingdom that survived the country's transformation to Islam. Yet my planetary soul line – Sun, Mercury and Neptune, passed through these islands, confirming a powerful attachment. Beyond that, I felt such a strong bond with the place and the people.

A connection to the Javanese royal court seemed unreal but it meshed with my ancestral line, although the setting was oceans apart. My father's ancestors were once valued advisors in the court of the Spanish royals. It seemed my past was not tied to Europe but rather to an ancient distant Hindu kingdom many light-years away.

Ripples of rainbows flowed across the wet sand – ebb and flow, forward and back, timeless and lost in time. It was the night of the lunar eclipse and waves crashed onto the shore. There was no sound, just the waves caught up in a hypnotic trance. Beside me on the woven mat was Gusde, circled by men in white, all chosen as the moon's champions to ensure she would awaken from her hazy dream. Slowly the full moon was swallowed up by the earth's shadow as darkness consumed the light and the sound of the waves intensified.

Whispered mantras caressed the moon, slowly seducing her light to return once more. The flickers of light turned to silver and a glassy shimmer lit up the ocean. The wail of an old woman, the trance medium, disturbed the stillness of the night. Pleas, ancient pleas, rocked her to her feet and she stumbled towards the water. Several men ran after her, dragging her back from the ocean but the old woman resisted, the call of the mystic impossible to ignore.

This was not only an eclipse in the night sky but also an eclipse of my soul. I was wavering on the edge of reality, facing a new plane of existence. A heightened plane where things defy human logic and lie outside the parameters of what is known. An evolved world that required a belief in the unbelievable and an enormous leap of faith.

The first hurdle to overcome was to be accepted by a band of men who had no great love of foreigners. Gusde had few misgivings as he led me into the darkened courtyard of a house in Denpasar, in the centre of the city. Under a thatched wooden hut was a coffin laid out in state, a large framed photo of the deceased – an older man, not yet past his prime, in pride of place.

The mood was sombre, but the silence was broken when a young man strode out from one of the rooms. 'What is *she* doing here?' he barked. He had recently replaced his deceased father as head of this clandestine group and possessed the arrogance of youth. 'A woman, and a foreigner! She should not be here.'

Other men emerged and uttered their agreement.

Gusde interjected. 'She has been chosen among many for a great honour so we cannot deny what is destined. Only spirit can decide so we must reach out to them for the answer.'

Finally, all in agreement, I was ushered into a large room to await the verdict of spirit. A medium was called in, a woman who was heavily pregnant, and the whole scene seemed so ambiguous. With the lights dimmed she began her transition.

I remained silent, for words seemed inappropriate in the face of what followed. It shook me to my very core. After a few minutes, a voice boomed out from the medium's body, a male voice so deep that it caused a tremor in space. A collective buzz in the room was followed by silence as they listened to the spirit's words.

'It is the spirit of Gajah Mada,' Gusde muttered, as all the men responded in awe to the presence of the country's esteemed hero, who had never manifested before. This was extraordinary.

The atmosphere in the room became hot and clammy, as rings of stale cigarette smoke drifted up to the ceiling. Words followed until there could be little dispute as to his presence. In an ancient tongue, the words were lost on me but they mesmerised the rest.

'We are honoured,' the leader said to the spirit, '*you* are here.' The young man turned to me, his tone more gracious than before.

'Our great hero says that we must protect you as you have been chosen to record the history of this glorious country.'

I was surprised when all the men moved their chairs in a circle around me. These men, *The Sons of the Heroes of Indonesia*, had formed, hoping to shape the future of their country. With their arms outstretched, they projected an energy shield encircling me with protection. Closing my eyes I felt a tingle and then a mighty jolt rock my body. It was followed by a surge of power and an overwhelming awareness. This *was* my rightful place, and my time had come. It was yet another amazing interlude in the journey of my life.

From this and mystic interludes to follow, came my second book, *Bali Magic – Reflections of a Reluctant Psychic*, rising above the personal to a higher mystical level. The book deserved its debut in Bali, the island that inspired it, and once again it all fell into place.

One day while enjoying tea with my Javanese friend Lily at plush new villas in Sanur, the manager offered to show us around the property. Each villa was named after a zodiac sign so when I mentioned I was an astrologer who'd written a second book on Bali, the manager insisted that the launch of *Bali Magic* be held there, a great public relations move for a new venue.

The date was set and the invitations printed. Lily and I set out to deliver them. The first went to the palace at Blahbatuh to honour the king, the 24th descendant of the dynasty, and his wife, in gratitude for the wonderful opportunities he afforded me. There was no expectation that he would come as we only managed to get the invitation to the palace gates. I remained optimistic, hoping that he might make a rare appearance.

The next stop was the Australian Consulate and several honorary consuls. Friends and acquaintances were added to the list until all that was left was to see who would turn up on the night.

The scene was set at the villas, with lotus flowers and candles floating in the pool on a balmy evening. Many people arrived and while I was signing the books, the manager broke through the line. 'The king and queen are here,' he said, rather frantically.

Their arrival made quite an impression with the locals, driving down the narrow street leading to the villas in a regal old black Mercedes once said to belong to President Suharto. After the appropriate greetings, I presented the royal couple with a gift-wrapped book. Around the pool, surrounded by people eager to talk to him, the king looked delighted. He whispered to me, 'It's my birthday today,' He smiled, obviously enjoying the attention, pleased to celebrate his special day with nice company.

The next to arrive was the Australian Consul-General, then came the Czech, Brazilian and Hungarian Honorary Consuls, followed by a string of expats and friends. Beside a vase of pink roses, I signed books till there were no more left. It is a book launch I will always remember and it couldn't have been more perfect.

There was one more moment of glory for *Bali Magic*. The reluctant psychic was about to be exposed to the limelight. My book distributor, arranging flights and hotels, flew me to Jakarta for a media conference. Held at one of their bookstores, I was advised that many journalists may not turn up because of the atrocious traffic on a Friday afternoon. They all came, however, eager to interview the foreign woman with such an interesting path in Indonesia.

Over the next few days, articles flooded the media. A two-page piece and graphic illustration appeared in the *Jakarta Globe* newspaper with the headline, 'Island of Mystical Adventure.' It read, 'An Australian writer has penned a second volume of her unusual life in Bali.' Travel magazines followed, including the *Garuda Indonesia Inflight Magazine*. It was a thrill to read about myself when I was high in the sky on my return to Sydney.

Stories with headlines like, 'Into the Mystic', 'A Knight's Tale' and *Hello Bali*'s 'The Clairvoyant Wordsmith', with the welcome words, 'It appears the writer from down under has more than a talent for just writing.' One of my favourite quotes came from a journalist at *Tempo* magazine. She wrote, 'Ms Knight is of Greek/Italian background, cultures with strong women, so it comes as no surprise that she is a strong woman on an island of strong men.'

I was reminded of these words years later, flying from Tel Aviv in Israel to my birthplace of Salonica in northern Greece. It was 3 am and a driver was waiting at the airport to take me to my hotel, amazed that a mature lady on her own, with a walking stick, came from such a place at such a time. The walking stick had become necessary after spinal surgery but it did not hinder me. When the driver asked about my connection with the city, I opened up.

Recounting my father's story, I told of how he escaped a death march at the end of World War II by jumping off a bridge into a deep river below to reach safety. So he avoided the dire fate of the majority of Jews of Salonica who met a gruesome death at the hands of the Nazis. The young driver looked at me and said, 'You have inherited your father's courage.' His words resonated with me.

Just like my father, I refused to be defeated.

CHAPTER NINETEEN

MIND GAMES

The hardest thing in life to surmount, despite all my attempts to deny its severity, is physical pain. Many people suffer in silence with conditions too hard to diagnose and symptoms dismissed because they are too difficult to assess, cast off as quirks of the imagination.

For many years I was plagued with pain but no doctor could provide any answers. After my earlier surgery, it was a different type of pain that racked my body. My muscles alternated between spasms and numbness, and touch became almost impossible because my skin was tingling and on edge. My sensitivity to light increased and loud noise, especially high frequency, became unbearable.

Going from one specialist to another I felt like a human ping-pong ball, bouncing from one rejection, and set of raised eyebrows, to the next. My doctor warned me, 'No one will believe you're unwell because you look good.' Such was the depth of the human condition and the stigma attached to 'bunging it on.'

Fortunately, my doctor was like the brother I never had and was a Pisces to boot. That ensured some level of compassion and he stuck by me while others scoffed, branding my symptoms as the rantings of a bored, lonely woman. With a long history of problems,

I was a person in urgent need of medical care and a far-sighted doctor to unearth the cause.

The only conclusion was 'that it was all in my head'. If only they knew just how close they were. One visit to a top immunologist, who I later learned had a fraught reputation, was the final slap in the face. With no objection to me reading my medical reports, my doctor warned me against it. When I read, 'This poor depressed woman will probably convince someone else to cut her open,' I was outraged. I tore the report into shreds and threw them in the bin.

Then came the psychiatrist my doctor referred me to, as some form of support. The psychiatrist was the conservative type who looked down at you through the eyes of judgment. His wrinkled suit and highbrow attitude were signs of a man sadly in search of a personality. The conversation was banal at first but when he asked whether I ever slept with a man on the first meeting, it seemed crude. 'Should I wait till he buys me dinner?' I asked. Was this a sign of a weak moral compass or was I a depraved woman?

Flustered, he got out of his chair and showed me to the door after only 30 minutes, with the words, 'Don't come back until you learn to control your anger!' The vein in his throat was throbbing, desperate to escape the noose of his tie and years of subversive thinking. Wasn't he the one who was supposed to guide me through my non-existent anger? How could a man with so many serious issues end up in a position to harm so many patients in his care?

My doctor never sent anyone else to the psychiatrist's office after that and he never gave up on me. His receptionist made it quite clear that she thought I was pulling some sort of scam, to get some benefit or other. The unwelcome pout, the snide remark, and the condescension. As the human filter to the doctor, she appeared to possess special powers that allowed her to discern the truly ill and infirm from the sly and degenerate trying to pull a swifty, so I could live on a tropical island with a maid. Forget about the isolation, the gross humidity, the nasty neighbours, deadly mosquitoes, Bali belly, the constant noise and a severe case of dengue fever.

There I was in Bali, drenched in sweat and unable to get up. I was living alone at the time and tests confirmed that it was dengue fever, both chronic and acute, proving that I had the dreaded disease once before, its diagnosis lost among a batch of other catastrophes.

My housekeeper had gone to Java without letting me know, and the inept gardener came into the house and tried to make a cup of tea. Having no idea how to work the stove, he turned on all the gas knobs without lighting them, left them on, and then went home.

If not for my cat, Abby, who raised the warning, we would not have made it through the night. I staggered from my bedroom into the kitchen just in time. The gardener had unlocked the front gate before he left so that the doctor and ambulance could enter and take me to the hospital, as organised. They never turned up. With no telephone, I hoped that my body had the strength to pull through. It did, but not without a raging fever and a great deal of suffering.

When I bumped into the doctor several weeks later, I asked why he hadn't come as promised. My soul bristled when he replied, '*I forgot.*' More likely he was up at a temple praying which is what I should have been doing but I pulled through, nonetheless. Be it for the grace of God, my cat, Abby, and a profound inner strength.

Back in Sydney, I went from one specialist to another as I was dissected and diagnosed with female issues, dodgy kidneys, a peculiar gall bladder, food allergies and fibromyalgia. Extreme sensitivity to light, noise and touch turned me from a person deserving of sympathy into a nuisance. Frustration added to my humiliation as few friends wanted to go out with me because I always complained about something. As the nerve pain worsened, I had to find a wall to brace myself on if I sneezed to prevent an electric shock down my arm.

Then I saw a brilliant professor of rheumatology at St. Vincent's Hospital who refused to abandon me. 'Fibromyalgia is a label of convenience. Let's see what's *really* going on!' At long last, I had a champion who believed in me, one willing to go the extra mile to uncover the root of the problem. One who didn't think I was delusional, suffering from Munchausen syndrome, trying to self-harm, or otherwise destroy my body before the medics had a chance to.

It was at this stage that the great Almighty had someone invent the MRI machine on His behalf. One that would terrify you, thrust you into a metal tube and bombard you with a cacophony of noise, a heady mix of jackhammers and machine guns, to distract you from the horrific pain you're already experiencing. Then by some miracle, you may have earned the right to know what's potentially killing you. And if you've been especially good or still have a long way to go in the evolution stakes, you might get to live longer so you can share your gifts, and tales of woe, with the rest of society.

After the results came back from the MRI, my neurologist, top of his field at the same hospital, called me. A personal call. That can't be good. An icy sheath descended over my body to protect me from the news. *Chiari Malformation.* It wasn't my imagination after all, but it did come down to my brain. I was born, they believed, with an enlarged brain which caused a build-up of fluid in my skull. My brain herniated, blocking the spinal cord which was filling up with fluid. One sneeze could snap it, they said, the cord was so thin. Without surgery, I would slowly lose every muscle in my body.

Devastated by the news, I was unsure what to do. The neurologist sent me straight to the neurosurgeon who suggested I could afford to wait a while, weighing up the risks involved. That gave me time to seek a second opinion. A few weeks later I sat with my anxious mother in a neurologist's office at another hospital. She took one look at the X-rays and then charged down the hall, exclaiming to the other medics, 'Look at this syrinx, it's a beauty!'

I'm glad she was impressed by the influx of fluid in my spinal cord, but it did nothing to allay my fears or calm my mother who was on the verge of a breakdown. It raised my status from a crazed hypochondriac to a patient of substance, one worthy of respect.

When the muscles in my right arm began to deteriorate, and my breathing became laboured, I decided to fly to London to consult a specialist who was using a different, less intrusive, technique to enlarge the skull. It was my life that I was dealing with, and I was scared. It was 1998 and I was just about to turn 50. There were still so many years left but an even more frightening scenario was that I would become *less* than I was, a thought I couldn't bear.

In need of support, I phoned Agus in Bali. He rose to the occasion and despite all the hurdles I asked him to meet me in Denmark after my London medical appointment. Good friends offered to have us stay with them in Copenhagen for a well-needed break. I left it up to Agus to arrange visas and then I flew to London.

After a prolonged discussion with the specialist there, he advised that the best option was surgery in Sydney as my neurosurgeon was one of the best in the world. So, emphasising there was no immediate rush in case I died in the process, I chose to wait a while and enjoy life just in case. I went to Denmark to meet my friends and Agus arrived two days later. After a lovely catch-up for a week, we decided to see a little of Europe while we could.

Agus had an issue with visas, as all had to be applied for before leaving Indonesia. No consul in Copenhagen would give him a visa until our very last try. We approached the Honorary Consul for Hungary, two lovely ladies in their home. After a chat about my mother's birthplace, it didn't take too much persuasion, and we were off.

It was my first time in Hungary but there was not enough time to travel to my mother's town in Transylvania. Only sad memories remained there in any case, with her childhood home gone. Instead, we went to Budapest and were stunned by the grandeur and classic beauty of the city, poised grandly on both sides of the Danube River.

Strolling along the charming city streets, we ventured into one of the healing spas and baths. It was separated into the men's and women's sections but when massive masseuse Boglarka opened the heavy door for me to enter, and turn me into a human pretzel, I was out of there. Agus was on the run too, having escaped Lazlo on the other side. Agus made quite a splash when he entered the pool. With his tanned, perfect body, among the old flabby men who had eaten too many pastries, there were many admiring glances.

We also had to make a run for it from the sports stadium that evening. Agus was a soccer fanatic but had only got to watch major events on TV. Now he was in the thick of it and he cheered loudly when the Swedish side scored a goal. Alas, we were seated in the Hungarian home side section and everyone turned around and glared at him. Looking oddly out of place on this continent he was forgiven and we made a quick exit.

The trip to the countryside by train was picturesque but Agus slept through most of it. It gave me time to ponder my mother's sad memories, of her family being torn from their home during WWII, in what the British Prime Minister, Winston Churchill, described as one of the most horrible crimes in history. Over the course of several months, from May to July 1944, around 440,000 Hungarian Jews were cruelly rounded up and sent to Auschwitz-Birkenau concentration camp, where most were immediately gassed to death.

In the reflection of the glass window on the train, I saw my mother's face as a shy, innocent girl. Then came the grandmother I never knew, her eyes moist with tears as she held the hand of her son, just seven years old. This sweet boy was forced to stare into the eyes of the devil, the infamous Dr Mengele, who held the power over life and death in Auschwitz. *'Which one do you choose?'* he barked, demanding my grandmother decide between her children.

The young boy's fate, and that of the rest of her family, was sealed when stripped bare and terrified, gas poured out of the showerheads. It was a horrific end to their last moments on earth. Only my mother survived, although much of the time she wished she didn't, consumed by dreadful memories that ate away at her.

In her greatest moments of despair in years to come, I begged my mother to seek help but deep down I knew that no counsellor could penetrate the sacred wound in her soul. Nor could they ever understand the depth of its source. Beyond that, the memory, as horrid as it was, was all she had to cling to. It was the last vestige of a family that was otherwise lost to her, the last time she saw their faces clearly or the tortured sound of their final despair.

That evening Agus and I relaxed in a quaint Hungarian town. I never confided my family's past to Agus but he was sensitive to my feelings and as we walked along a grassy verge he handed me a freshly plucked dandelion and told me to make a wish.

Life, that was my wish. We sat at an outdoor restaurant enjoying the food, the ambience and the music. On many street corners, musicians played the violin, and more, with sensitivity and skill, and it reminded me of a time when man was kind, creative, and inspired. Very soon it would be my time to face the music because an enlarged brain cannot wait forever, and the planets had aligned.

It was a risky operation and the surgeon advised that a permanent shunt, from my head to my chest, would be installed to drain away the excess fluid. This needed to be replaced every few years. The thought was mortifying and so I turned to the wisdom of astrology.

Saturn, the planet that brings stress and illness, had moved to a critical point in my progressed chart, triggering this episode with my health. Meanwhile, Jupiter, the planet of good fortune, with its 9-12-year cycle was set to aspect Saturn in a positive angle. That was the time for the best outcome, so I set the date for the surgery.

Without asking why, the neurosurgeon operated on that day. I sat in the chapel in the hospital before the surgery, next to my trembling mother, and prayed for a positive outcome, not just for me but also for her, because she had suffered enough.

God was listening because the surgeon rushed into my room after the surgery, with a broad smile, to tell me how perfectly the operation went. There was no need for a shunt, he exclaimed, because the fluid had expunged itself. I had staked my life on astrology, and with the grace of God, my belief was validated.

The surgeon had sewn a patch of fabric into the back of my skull, to expand its size, and give the brain room to move. The right side of my face and the back of my head would alternate between numb and painful for the rest of my life but at least I was alive.

In a strange cosmic set-up, months later, while waiting to cross the road, I started a conversation with the lady beside me. We ended up at a café for a cup of tea and a chat. It was not chance or mere coincidence that brought us together. She was a nun who also had brain surgery for a similar condition, but she did not escape the need for a shunt, and her life had been dictated by ongoing surgery and pain to replace it every few years. Hers was a life of uncertainty and made me appreciate just how fortunate I had been.

After my return to Bali, when people asked what was wrong with me, I replied, 'My brain was too big, so the doctor had to make my head bigger so it could fit.' They looked confused for a minute but after some thought, invariably replied, 'You must be very clever to have such a big brain.' It afforded me some notoriety.

A newspaper article appeared years later, with the caption, 'Size does matter', with a photo of Einstein's brain. It was found on examination to be larger than the average brain. It followed that I was very clever too. In any case, I had gone from a person with imaginings of pain to a patient of magnitude, with a unique story.

My neurologist, a renowned professor, very staid and formal, always had a student by his side. 'Here comes this very interesting lady,' he said, impressing on the student that one could have a serious condition but still lead a rich, fulfilling life travelling, writing books, and inspiring others. What a marked change of perspective.

It was Agus who saw me through the surgery. My parents came to the hospital every day but they were elderly and were in no position to look after me, nor would I expect them to. The few other family members were preoccupied with their own lives, and I was no longer in contact with any friends in Sydney after many years abroad.

Agus flew out to Australia to care for me after going through a process with the Consul to prove his intention. What a massive shift it was for him. Despite his instinct to shirk all responsibility and be carefree, he helped me take my first tentative steps down the hospital corridor, tenderly taking my hand and leading the way.

Agus travelled across Sydney each day, staying alone in my apartment until it was time for me to come home. Recovery after the surgery was slow and painstaking, the severe pain easing over time but the damage remained. Agus stayed by my side and was my rock.

Then came a huge blow – a phone call that changed everything. Agus's father had fallen gravely ill and his family urged Agus to come home. I told him to go back to Bali, not wishing to add to his burden, despite my deep need for him to stay. He was conflicted.

Agus's father had gone through his own version of hell in the 1960s when a purge of suspected Communists in Indonesia claimed 500,000 lives. Java and Bali were some of the worst hit, with many Chinese marked for death. Agus's father was thrust onto the back of a truck heading to an isolated beach to be shot and dumped into an unmarked mass grave, along with countless other victims.

A reprieve came when one of the officials recognised him as a loyal party member. To test his allegiance, he was given a list of names and a sword and told to execute them. He went through the motions but instead hid those marked for death in the ceiling of his home till they were safe. His father had strong moral fibre, the seed of which had been planted in his son. It needed time to mature.

There was no way Agus could stay with me while his mind was on his family, but when the taxi door slammed to take him to the airport I felt devastated and helpless. We kept in touch by phone almost daily as his father slowly recovered. More bitter news came six weeks later, ironically on Christmas Day. It was a mighty blow.

Agus's younger brother found out that his girlfriend was pregnant and they had no choice but to marry. It was the custom on the island. The ceremony could not go ahead until his older brother, Agus, was married first. I was certainly not the family's desired daughter-in-law, nor did I aspire to be. Older, Western, divorced and unable to have children. No way.

With no other choice acceptable to his culture, Agus did what he swore never to do, he complied with tradition. He went ahead and married his cousin and rang me in tears the day before to say that it would be my name he would utter in his marriage vows, such was the depth of our love. It tore me apart and him even more so.

Deep down I knew a child was waiting to be born to him. I had seen it in his birth chart, and there was no denying destiny. Two strong cultures, Balinese and Chinese, had come together, with an ethic that demanded a child and an heir. There was no contest.

A year after his marriage, a daughter was born and as a token of his love, Agus named her after me, despite his wife's objections. The closeness between Agus and I never diminished and months later when I returned to Bali, as much as we tried, we could not stay apart. We were not proud of the deception but love is a potent thing.

Over time it became clear that there was no link between Agus and his wife, except for their child. Even she knew it in the end. Although he spent most nights with me, Agus looked after his daughter well and loved her greatly. It was an uneasy situation for all concerned. Agus arranged for me to meet his wife and child, to see if we could work out a solution but it was a disaster.

Theirs seemed such an unlikely match. Agus was an attractive, charismatic man and she was plain and surly. An arrangement was never going to happen. Agus wanted to make the pieces of his life come together, however difficult, but she refused outright. Nor was I prepared to compromise ever again. My life was precious, and not one day could be wasted waiting and stressing for a man with so many obligations. Still, ours would remain a lifetime bond.

CHAPTER TWENTY

HAWAII BLUE

There are places in the world where one feels an intrinsic bond. Planetary lines, plotted on a world map at the time of a person's birth, indicate where these soul alignments lie. This process is called Astrocartography. Each planet has a meaning and soul dynamic.

Venus brings love, Mercury, a chance to learn, while the Moon lends a tender or dreamy texture. Mars promises energy or a warning of danger. Jupiter tends towards opportunity, while Saturn ensures restrictions. Uranus indicates excitement and sudden change, Neptune may lead to spiritual enlightenment, while Pluto, in a harsh aspect, delivers a heavy dose of karma and is life changing.

We all have our special places. A scene from a movie may trigger a memory or a vision of the future, a song can resonate with the past or a promise of things to come. The film *South Pacific*, with its lush tropical setting and the song 'Bali Hai', mesmerised me from an early age. Filmed on the north shore of the Hawaiian island of Kauai, the words seemed to echo through the chambers of a shell, filtered through the ocean tide. Bali was my special island.

Many movies were filmed on Hawaii's shores, with the jagged jade mountains, crystal blue waters and deep valleys forming a stunning backdrop. They were ripe with romance and mystery. In

Hawaiian folklore, Pele, the goddess of creation and destruction, reigns over the island chain. Her domain is one of volcanoes and fire, her rage erupting in streams of lava, destroying everything in its path.

My first visit to Hawaii was to Waikiki, the tourist haven on the island of Oahu. From the balcony of my hotel room, I looked out over clear azure waters, with Diamondhead in the distance. The peaks behind me were studded with rainbows and stardust, and it was love at first sight. I shared a special bond with the island – with the people, the music and the sigh of the breeze. Every ripple that rolled to shore from the sea whispered my name and the white doves on the sandy beach outshone the grey pigeons I left behind.

On a world map, the strong Sun and Neptune connection at my birth rose in Greece, where I was born. It peaked in Bali, a tiny dot on the earth's surface. A sacred place, it was integral to my spiritual passage. The planetary line set through Hawaii, where my heart felt full and my soul found peace. Three beautiful locations in the world, that I loved the most, tied together by the pull of destiny.

An undercurrent of romance existed in both Bali and Hawaii. Perhaps there was magic in the air, or I fitted in more with their ideal of beauty with my long dark hair and brown eyes. My stay in Hawaii began with a stunning parade through the streets of Waikiki.

A stream of powerful women, decked out in a colour to represent their island home, rode by on horses decorated with matching flowers. Vivid blues, pink, green, yellow and purple, in a stunning cavalcade fit for a rainbow. These islands were steeped in splendour.

My connection with the people proved rather humorous at times. One evening on a crowded bus heading to a major shopping centre, I asked the driver where to wait for the bus to return. He got out of his seat and stood on the pavement telling me in detail, 'Don't use that stop because it's too dark, and ...' Meanwhile, the bus passengers were getting agitated. One irate guy got off the bus, muttering as he passed, 'I want what *she's* got!'

It was a surprise when men held doors open for me, or simply smiled. Evenings were spent at the nightclub at the Sheraton Hotel, with a stunning view over Diamondhead, talking to people from all over the world. The band there was great, and the virgin cocktails, sublime. There was a good vibe and lots of good conversation.

A courteous gent from Japan chatted away and then sent me postcards to keep in touch. A gregarious policeman from Chicago invited me to go for a drive to Diamondhead. A true gentleman, he walked close to the pavement, opening the car door for me. When we stood at the peak of Diamondhead and gazed down over the lights of Waikiki, it was exquisite. Waves rolled in, in harmony with the vibration of the moon, and I felt attuned to the cosmos.

With the island's evolved vibes, I visited a spiritual church near Diamondhead, referring to the calcite crystals found on a beach close to its volcanic core. I met some nice folk at the church, for theirs was an amalgam of faiths and their prime goal was to raise the spiritual frequency of the world. I shared many of their beliefs.

The people in Hawaii were more open, for the islands had a relaxed vibe. Men approached for a chat, happy for the company. When I exited the elevator of my hotel in Waikiki, my neighbour came out and introduced himself. Soon after, a note was slipped under my door, a drawing of me and an invitation to go on a picnic addressed to 'the lady from down under' and signed with Claude's name and phone number. I didn't take him up on the offer.

The next day I was approached at the most romantic of venues, McDonalds, and the opening line was a classic. 'Are the sundaes still a dollar?' Before I had a chance to reply, the stranger sat down. He lived in a condo near my hotel, and I accepted an invitation to visit him that evening. He was a musician who held concerts all over the US. Taking out his guitar, he entertained me with a private concert. It was refreshing to have male friends because they rarely approached me, on that level, in other parts of the world.

On my second stay in Hawaii, I chose a hotel on the beach next to the famed pink Royal Hawaiian Hotel. My room had a stunning ocean view, and I was soothed by the sound of waves from my balcony. The twang of guitars and the band playing Hawaiian melodies set the mood for afternoon drinks and it was bliss.

The concierge who greeted me when I arrived was charming. After shopping in the evening, I stopped at his desk to ask about his island heritage. Then after buying some treats from the hotel shop, I retired to my room for an evening of movies. Just as I had nearly drifted off to sleep, a message on my phone jolted me awake.

It was from the cute concierge. OMG. I jerked to attention for the message was mildly provocative. I responded, but after a few more explicit messages, it was time to stop the conversation.

The next day I tried to dodge the concierge desk but it was clear from the look on the staff's faces, and the subtle innuendos, that the news had leaked. When I waved at the concierge in passing, a woman ran out from a shop, grabbed my phone and insisted on taking a picture of us. Was it about to be splashed over the newspaper, or even worse a repeat of Bali? It was time to take my leave. I was here for a spiritual upgrade, so no more intrigue.

Finding a back exit, I walked along a path that wound around the beach, stopping to marvel at the outline of the turtles shimmering in the clear night waters. The moon cast its lustre over Diamondhead and the ocean, weaving its spell. Feelings stirred within me each time I visited Hawaii, so it became my annual chosen retreat.

Real magic tied me to these islands, but my trip to Hawaii the following year started badly. Worn out from the flight, it was not the time to be singled out to have my baggage checked. When the customs man put on his gloves, I knew I was in for the long haul. The guy next to me had his luggage splayed out on the counter and I dreaded them going through the contents of my suitcase. The sound of a zip opening and my life was about to be spread out before me.

'What island do you like most?' the custom man asked. 'Maui, Kauai or the big island of Hawaii?'

'No,' I countered. 'Here, in Oahu.'

'Why?' he asked. 'Waikiki, and the nightlife?'

'No,' I replied honestly, 'because the mountains sing to me.'

He looked into my eyes and then zipped up my suitcase.

'You can go,' he said, waving me through.

In any other place in the world, I would have been certifiable and had every item in my luggage scrutinised while the alert beagle, having lost interest, would have headed for the suspicious felon with an unsavoury crotch. In Hawaii they understood.

On this trip, I met vivacious Carly one night at a club. We clicked from the start. With a broad smile and outgoing personality, she loved to dance and have a good time. Her husband was a US naval man and they lived on the military base. Hoping to explore more of the island, I asked Carly if she would drive us around the next day if I paid for a car. She happily agreed.

My request was specific. It *had* to be a red sports convertible. A few days later, Carly called me from a rental car lot. At Avis, 'they only have a blue one.' Next, 'silver'. At the very last lot, they were unloading a brand-new red convertible, never been driven.

So off we went on our adventure. I was not sure why I insisted on red until I recalled a favourite movie *Blue Hawaii*, where Elvis drove around the island in his red sports car. I wanted to copy his moves and relive the tingle I felt as he sang the 'Hawaiian Wedding Song' against a backdrop of lush valleys and mystical mountains.

Flooded with the elation of freedom, we drove around the cliffs, heading for the north shore of Oahu. It was another dream come true. Carly's dream was different. She had a crush on an artist, helping when he painted one of his giant oceanic murals on the side of a building. Wyland was an artist of great repute, and Carly knew he was currently at his home on the north shore.

She called him and was ecstatic when he invited us to stop by so he could meet the clairvoyant Aussie friend she'd been raving about. When we reached the gated community, we were buzzed in.

Wyland was standing outside when our red sports car made its grand entrance. Welcoming us, he invited us into his home on the ocean. He had another guest, Rod, a friend from California, and we enjoyed drinks on the patio. Wyland's genius was evident as he showed me around his studio, with all his colourful sketches and paintings. This was the space of a man who was clearly inspired.

Wyland was a prodigious artist, environmentalist and visionary who painted massive murals of whales and dolphins in many countries around the world, to emphasise the need for protection of the ocean. Now they adorn more than 100 skyscrapers and public buildings, large marine images to promote his conservation program.

Wyland's passion was obvious but he also had a cool, mellow aspect. In the kitchen, getting drinks with Carly, he proposed setting me up with Rod who had just been through a nasty breakup. Carly had seen a picture of Agus, bronze and bare-chested in his sarong, and told Wyland about my hunky Balinese lover, 20 years my junior. Wyland was impressed and abandoned his plan. Instead, he ordered pizza and as we sat outside, he blurted out, *'You must be one hell of a woman if you can attract a hot young island guy.'*

I spilled my Coke while the others looked both shocked and amused. This was a man who spoke his truth without any filters.

Afterwards, I walked down the beach with Rod as the waves lapped at our feet. We sat on a smooth rock and talked about the stages of life, but just like the phases of the moon, each passed as quickly as they had come. Like a careless whisper, they left their mark and just as the moon separated night from day, that was life.

Before I left, Wyland gave me a giant hug and gifted me a copy of his book, complete with prints of his fabulous works of marine life. Only after I got home, did I see the dedication he'd written on the front page, 'To my favourite psycho', the word crossed out to read *psychic*. I laughed, for it was a compliment from a man who had touched the spiritual realm and made it his mission to dedicate his life to it. That is the promise that awaits us all.

Our connection did not end there. A year later I returned to Hawaii and took the circle bus to the north shore. At the Hilton, I was delighted to see a work in progress from the great man himself, a giant mural on the side of the hotel. Wyland was on top of a cherry picker, putting the final touches to another of his 'whaling walls'.

He looked down from his bird's eye view and yelled, 'Hey Aussie!' making a speedy descent from the heights to greet me. It was a brief reunion but remains 'one of the best'. It was good to be recognised by a man of distinction with a wicked twinkle in his eye.

That evening I caught up with Carly who got two tickets for the Ricky Martin concert, *Livin' la Vida Loca*, a week later. On the night, we relived the joy of music, as Ricky zoomed onto the stage on the hood of a Ford Mustang in his fitted leather pants. When he shook 'it' like he meant it, all the girls and guys in the arena swooned. He ended the concert with his hit, 'The Cup of Life', and as his final gesture, his hands touched his lips in prayer.

We returned to the hotel in a somewhat euphoric state. I turned to see Carly collar Ricky's manager and assorted personnel in the lobby and she was leading them down to the nightclub. For me, without the star it was nothing. My life-long quest was to shoot for the brightest star, and I never regretted it. Yes, Ricky. I will definitely live 'La Vida Loca' in pursuit of the crazy life.

Chasing stars.

CHAPTER TWENTY-ONE

DREAM WEAVER

Neptune rained its droplets down upon me the day I was born, drenching me in love of a higher kind, and the blessing of dreams. Dreams *can* come true. Like leaves on a lucky clover, or bristles of gossamer blown from a dandelion, each of my wishes came to pass. Was this a reward for past good deeds or fine actions still to come?

It scarcely mattered. My first attempt as a dream weaver happened unwittingly, as I gazed at a cruise liner in Sydney Harbour when I was 16. From the sleek white hull to the scent of foreign ports, I was hooked. My first cruise came soon after, with my father, a generous gift to mark my graduation from high school. My mother and sister stayed behind, busy with work and other matters.

Standing on the porch of a small church in American Samoa, I met a Polynesian island boy and he was the first ever to write me a love letter. It was penned in beautiful script, from the heart of a poet. I was his 'pale yellow', an island flower. For a teenage girl, it was *dizzying*. The fact that my father spotted it first in the post and hid it in a drawer where I found it weeks later, proved it was *forbidden*. Jimmy included photos of himself, one dressed like Elvis and the other, in native gear wielding a club, and I keep them till today.

More letters followed, many from Chris, the nice British lad I met at Sydney Harbour, crew off one of the ships. Our longing was lived out through our letters as he cruised the world. What an intoxicating mix – lust, forbidden fruit, exotic lands, and waiting lips. Yet there was something more to it – the call of destiny, an inkling of what was yet to come, and the passage to a place far more fascinating than the mundane world I refused to get used to.

That first cruise in the '60s was on P&O's *Arcadia* followed by many others, as I traversed the ocean in search of adventure. The Russian cruise ship, *Belorussia,* was fun with high-voltage music and dance but it did not light up my world. The Italian Sitmar and Greek Chandris lines carried me to open seas, as did NCL, Holland America, Celebrity and Royal Caribbean years later. Princess lived up to its name as the 'Love Boat'.

A friend from college, Cathy, a refined redhead, joined me on a cruise on the *Sea Princess*. It was a relaxing holiday, and our dining companions on an adjacent table were two gay guys who were charming company. Then, laid out on my side of the table one night, was a blue 'floragram' and a long-stemmed red rose.

I blushed when I read the note. 'To the dark beauty with long hair, I will be wearing the same. Can we make a date for later tonight? PS I love your body and your smile.' Apart from being a fabulous ego boost, the night was exciting as I searched for the mysterious man with the rose in his lapel. And find him, I did.

On a later cruise in the 1990s on the *Fairstar*, at a function in the Zodiac lounge, I entered into a discussion on astrology with the ship's captain, recalling some of the mystical encounters during my time in Bali. The captain was intrigued and invited me to his private enclave to talk more. Our discussion lasted for more than an hour.

He jotted down my details when I expressed my desire to become a guest speaker on a ship. The timing wasn't yet right but the evening ended on a perfect note and left a lasting impression.

After disembarking, while unpacking in my apartment, the phone rang. To my surprise, it was a man with a broad Italian accent. 'Hello,' he said, cheerily. 'It's Captain … I'm sailing the ship through Sydney Heads and wanted to say goodbye. I hope all your dreams come true.' One dream already had with the sound of his voice and his kind wishes, adding whimsy to my life purpose.

To stave off the boredom of life back in Sydney, I did volunteer work and many opportunities were available. These included several weeks at the Maritime Museum at Darling Harbour, then onto their sailing yacht with other avid boaters. Carrying cups of tea up steep steps on a rocking boat proved too much so it was short-lived.

There were stints at the Opera House, art installations and other cultural events. One of my favourites was acting as secretary to judges at the Sydney Eisteddfod, jotting down scores while watching an array of young talent in the song and dance competition. There were so many budding young stars and on one occasion I got on so well with the judge, a talented pianist, that we went for tea and became friends. It mirrored my ongoing respect for musicians.

Volunteering for a charity ball, in the grand ballroom of a luxury hotel in Sydney, my role was raffle ticket seller. We each had our allocated aisles and chatting away with the guests, I was often asked to sit down and join the table. Money kept pouring in, so I hurried off to hand in my stash, before running back with more tickets. It was exasperating when the volunteer leader intonated that the reason my sales were so high was because of my low-cut top.

I was incensed but if my 'assets' raised money for charity, they were worth their weight in gold. At the end of the night, the golfing men, many of whom were bald, gave me their complimentary hair products and a lovely arrangement of flowers. I struggled to jam them into the taxi while the nasty miss went home empty-handed. There is always a benefit to smiling, no matter your chest size and sarcasm has no place at a charity event, or elsewhere.

Earlier, during a break with the other volunteers, I yelled, 'Does anyone want to come on a cruise with me?' A timid voice replied, 'I will.' A receptionist for solicitors in the city, the young lady agreed to go whenever she could get time off. So, we set the date, packed our bags and embarked on *Pacific Jewel* a few months later. Little did I know that the planets had aligned – Venus, Mars and Jupiter in harmony, to open the door to my future.

Once on board, my cabin mate headed off each day to the gym at 7 am while I slept in. With the date for the planetary conjunction approaching, I requested that Guest Services contact the bridge to find out the best place and time to view it. They got back to me with exact instructions: '4 am, starboard side, at position 3 on a clock dial.' Planetary connections hold great meaning if we take notice of the implications and these three formed a strong combination.

Jupiter is beneficial and aligned with Venus and Mars, positive things are bound to happen if they form good aspects with your birth planets. As I stared at this beautiful pattern in the sky, I was in awe, the sparkling lights blazing bright were omens of good fortune.

The next day I was informed of a stargazer's meeting. There were only five other passengers there, along with Emma, the lovely lass from Entertainment 'I don't know anything about the stars,' she announced, rather desperately. 'Does anyone?'

It was my cue to step in. People listened intently as I spoke, even more so young Emma who was intrigued as to why she kept seeing the numbers 11:11 repeated. Explaining the significance, 11:11 along with 22:22 and 33:33, were prime numbers, major steps for those on a spiritual path. Emma was so enthusiastic she asked the cruise director if I could give a talk on astrology.

It was only a few days before the cruise ended that I was scheduled to give a talk in the Casbah lounge. Many people turned up and were so impressed, they complained why I was not on the program earlier. As they lined up to talk to me, I asked someone to take a photo. A great move and it engendered the response I'd hoped for.

After the cruise, I sent the photo to P&O Australia and expressed an interest in becoming a guest speaker. A reply came asking if I would like to speak on a cruise to the Pacific in May of the following year. Ecstatic, I quickly wrote back to accept. Deep down I felt I would be cruising sooner, off to New Zealand.

Heeding my inner voice, I emailed again, offering my services if they needed someone at short notice. I was free. No partner, no children, no mortgage, no job and not even a cat. Soon after, I was offered a cruise in several weeks to New Zealand. Just like that!

So began a wonderful period of my life with more than 35 cruises as a guest speaker, spanning 15 years. These 'golden' years began later in life, at age 50, proving that age is no barrier. On board an array of cruise ships I met many people, each with their own story. My talks on Bali, on the island and my unique experiences there, were well received, providing a deeper insight into an island that many had visited before, as well as for those who had never been.

It was the astrology talks that had the power to change lives. Many people were interested, some already on the path to spiritual learning. Others were initially averse to the subject but were open-minded enough to attend and were soon converted because the proof was compelling. Men were the most reluctant but soon became interested. They took the next tentative step on the path by acknowledging that there is something more to life than the obvious.

Harsh sceptics could not be convinced, less disbelief in the subject than the concept. How could a cosmic force dictate our character or the course of our life? These forces do not dictate but rather *reflect* who we are and the lessons we need to learn to advance.

Scientific Aquarians often don't believe in anything that can't be physically proven and argue the point. Aries are self-determined while strict Capricorns are sceptical. The other earth signs, Virgo and Taurus, are pedantic but may possess enough zest to lighten the load. Those people with a dogmatic belief in religion often refuse to tread an uncertain path beyond the strict guidelines of their faith.

While the forces behind astrology may be difficult to understand, there is no question of its accuracy. The metaphysical *cannot* be reduced to physical terms but neither can the most important elements in life. Love, trust, faith, and other infinite spiritual forces can't be measured but they govern our lives in greater measure than the length of a string or a complex scientific formula.

The tangible is not nearly as comforting as those unseen forces that shape us and lead us in the right direction for personal growth. It is rewarding to touch someone profoundly and to provide sudden clarity on a subject that has vexed or eluded them in the past.

Little can be more satisfying than standing on the stage of a large theatre and *deserving* the spotlight because you have ignited the spark in your audience. Or holding people enthralled in a more intimate setting where you can hear their personal story until a common thread weaves humanity into a splendid tapestry.

A touch of humour helps. Had the Virgos organised their cabin and put in their dietary requirements, or how many Capricorn men had goatee beards like their symbol goat? 'Pisces rules the feet' I joked, 'because they were fish in a past life and had none,'

A mother rushed up after my talk to tell me that her two Pisces children were born with webbed feet, and another that hers was a talented ballerina. One Gemini mother confirmed that she had lung issues, her Aquarian son had weak ankles and her Capricorn husband had knee problems. Astrology never failed to prove itself.

In one exercise, I divided the room into groups of star signs to uncover similar traits among them. It spoke volumes when the Scorpio mob descended into dirty tactics. 'He wasn't our leader,' one man fumed, 'but he pushed the other guy out of the way.'

Libra had descended into a love fest while Cancer was moved to tears. When the groups were joined with their opposite sign, each one was asked to choose their perfect match. Of the outcomes most true to their sign, the Aquarians triumphed. With their 'community' mentality, when it came to choosing their soul mate, they all stood up and embraced each other in one giant group hug.

On a deeper level, there were true breakthroughs. For the father, whose son passed in the Bali bombing at the age of 27, the talk about the significance of the 27-to-29-year Saturn cycle, and the passing of so many gifted people at that age, held true meaning.

Musicians like Kurt Cobain, Jimi Hendrix, Janis Joplin, Jim Morrison, Amy Winehouse and actors Brandon Lee and Heath Ledger, all died at that age – on earth for one life cycle only so they could face their dark side. Now, his son's last words suddenly made sense, his son was plagued with bad dreams and a sense of finality. It didn't make it any less devastating but it provided some comfort.

Birth charts provide insight into the past, a road map to the future and the hope needed to get through a difficult time, for it too would pass. People at crossroads, some even suicidal, chose a different path when presented with an understanding that there was a higher purpose to their life, one that required great courage.

One of the most touching comments on my talks was written by an elderly lady. After thanking me, she wrote, 'Now, I will just accept what happens as part of my destiny, the good and the bad. Thank you for your wisdom. I will remember you till my dying day.' There were so many stories of transformation, gratitude and insight.

Then came the frown on a young girl's face. Just 14 years old, she looked glum when she approached me. 'I'm a Virgo,' she said, 'but I'm not. I *know* I'm a Libra.' She was born on the cusp of the two signs, so after talking to her mum, I checked the planetary positions for the moment of her birth. Amazingly at 10 pm on the day, the exact time of her birth, the sun just moved into Libra.

When I told her she was indeed a Libra, a broad smile swept over her face, 'I *am*!' she was ecstatic. She could not relate to Virgo, and in fact, had three planets in Libra amplifying her beautiful Venus energy. At last, she could reclaim her identity.

When planning talks on board, the cruise director allocates the time and place. At times, the venues were not the best – a crowded bar with lots of noise while some were scheduled during lunch but I learnt to go with the flow. When I brought up this issue with one cruise director, his response was a backhanded compliment. 'I could put you in a dark corner,' he said, gesturing to a niche in the passageway, 'and you'd still attract a huge audience.'

I rarely do birth charts on board a ship because of the sheer volume of people who request one. However, there are exceptions. That was the case with a British captain, a Scorpio, with a profound interest in the metaphysical. At the Officer's cocktail party, I was talking to some passengers when the captain walked by. 'Astrology is the oldest science known to mankind' he remarked. It meant so much that he acknowledged the depth of the subject.

The captain was astute enough to compile his own birth chart but wanted a deeper reading. In his private den, I considered his planetary placements. The moon, one's emotions, was in Capricorn, a stoic position but perfect for a captain to remain detached, to leave home at the age of 16 to join the merchant navy and never look back. This was the placement too in the chart of a reporter for a Sydney newspaper who came to interview me, with a need to stay impartial, and a surgeon whose profession required dispassion and objectivity.

One of my cruises coincided with a lunar eclipse, on the night of the full moon party. I went up on deck to get a good vantage point. Everyone was dancing to the music, with others standing on the top deck watching them. In the sky behind them, the shadow of the earth was edging over the moon. Everyone was facing in the wrong direction. Flustered, I yelled out, 'Turn around!' and most did just in time to see the moon darken; they gasped at the sight. I inherited a group of young stargazers who were entranced from that time on.

One of the most graphic examples of the power of the universe came when I read the birth chart of a cruise director, Mark. He was another Scorpio, like many who worked on ships due to their affinity with the ocean. The sign of Sagittarius came a close second, with a passion for travel and life experience. From the position of the transiting planets, it was clear that a major change was coming for Mark. It would be a sudden one as unstable Uranus was set to join Mark's natal Sun on January 19 of the following year, after 83 years.

Some months later, I was asked to come into the Sydney office by my contact Laura, to discuss some future cruises. While there, she asked if I could look at her chart. Laura was a lovely lass and I was pleased that a major transit was about to trigger her natal Venus.

'Next week,' I said, 'you're going to fall in love.' Oh my, that was a tall order. Laura was incredulous, arguing that she'd be at a baby shower with no men around. I couldn't take my words back but I was hoping for a minor miracle, and the support of the universe.

The following week, I received a phone call from Laura, breathless and excited. 'You'll never guess, I've met someone. I think it's love. My plans changed and I was asked to check out the entertainment on one of our three-day cruises. That's where we met. It happened so quickly,' she added, 'and when we were lying in each other's arms, Mark jumped up and asked what date it was!'

Unbelievably, it was January 19. My prophecy came true, for both of *them*. Two people from separate readings, months apart, one on land and the other at sea, came together by divine intervention.

Laura invited me to a surprise party when Mark moved to Sydney and, to add to the mystery, his mother, a spiritual artist, flew in from interstate. As a token of appreciation for his reading, Mark gifted me a card of one of his mother's paintings. I was amazed – it was the same picture I had hanging over my bed in Bali for years.

It was all so incredible, and their relationship blossomed. It wasn't long before Laura and Mark married and they remain happily together, eight years later. What I did not tell them until after their wedding, not wanting to influence the outcome, was that when I left Laura's office on that fateful day, a spirit message came through.

'Laura would make a perfect partner for Mark.' I dismissed it, so out of reach. ever doubt the universe for it can weave magic.

An article appeared in a magazine about their fated meeting, ordained by the stars, with the headline, 'That's creepy!' Not really. It's just another day for spirit and they never fail to impress.

CHAPTER TWENTY-TWO

THE LOST CONTINENT

It was distracting to be at an island's beck and call but also mesmerising. After completing my second book, *Bali Magic*, I thought I was done with Bali - with nothing left to say. I was very much mistaken. All the ferry trips across Sydney harbour could not erase thoughts of a musky pink sunset on a tropical island, and the memories I had left behind. They were embedded deep within my psyche.

One day, while sitting on a bench on the side of a highway waiting for the bus, as cars and trucks sped by, I spotted a weed desperate to grow in a crack of cement on the median strip that separated the lanes of traffic. It was my epiphany. I was an orchid in need of a hothouse and instead, I was wilting on an asphalt highway, smothered in fumes and dust. Bali had been my hothouse but its heat had become intolerable, burning my soul.

Each time memories of Bali surfaced, I pushed them to the back of my mind, until the day they became impossible to ignore. Much to my surprise, an article popped up on my computer screen about my book *Bali Moon* and it was reproduced increasingly on other sites. After I had the article translated from Indonesian, I desperately wanted to meet the writer, especially after learning he was a spiritual guru who had written over 100 books.

On reading *Bali Moon*, the guru issued a rebuke to the island. 'It was like a slap on the face,' he wrote 'both to the left and right cheek. On the left, the subjective side, as an Indonesian and on the right, more globally, determining one's identity as a human being. The author's time in Bali, with all its trials and disappointments, opened up her inner consciousness. But when these trials are linked with Bali it is challenging for us all.

'While polygamy may be accepted by Balinese, it is unacceptable for foreign women who find themselves in this situation through a series of lies and deceit. There are wider repercussions and Bali is being challenged. It is our responsibility to be better.'

This moral reprimand on the practices taking place in Bali added to my compulsion to write a final book because there were still things I had left to say. Motivated to return to Bali, this time it would only be a visit. The changes on the island, the overdevelopment and the heavy traffic were depressing and impacted the original fabric of the culture.

Once in Bali, I teamed up with my friend Lily to track down the guru. He was in Jakarta so instead we drove to his Bali ashram for a meditation session. A few people were sitting in a circle there, humming to the beat of an Indian drum. Buddha statues studded softly lit cavities in the wall and a display of religious symbols, cast in bronze, lined the front wall. The Muslim crescent moon and star, a Celtic Cross, the curved symbol of the Sikhs, a Hindu Ohm and the perfectly balanced Yin and Yang of Buddhism.

More surprisingly was a brilliant six-pointed Judaic Star of David, gratifying in its recognition. Judaism is not recognised as one of six official religions in Indonesia even though the Jewish faith is one of the world's oldest religions, dating back nearly 4,000 years.

Around 1000 BCE, under the rule of King Saul, Solomon and his son, King David, the land of Israel was a unified Jewish kingdom. Christianity was formed over 1,000 years later, in the mid-first century CE, based on the worship of Jesus, a Jew who never renounced his faith. The Muslim faith came much later, around 610 CE when the Prophet Muhammad first shared the words of Allah.

As I travelled around the mighty nation of Indonesia, I felt a strong affinity with the people, no matter their heritage or to what island or culture they belonged. Drawn by mutual respect and goodness, many would not have cared that I was Jewish. Most didn't know what that meant and I scarcely had much of a notion. Some chose to believe what they had been told but there was no real basis for a rift. Yet a *word* was enough to have a race persecuted over the centuries, a cause for hatred where only kindness and love existed.

On his return to Bali several weeks later, I met the guru in his Kuta centre. Wearing lime green robes, and a bracelet of green gemstones, the guru was a large man with a powerful presence. We spoke of the need for unity and peace, both expressing the hope that one day we could live in a world undivided by lines of separation. Imaginary lines were carved into the minds of those motivated by power and greed, their hearts corroded by envy and rage.

I told the guru of the unspeakable horror my family faced in the Second World War, along with millions of other Jewish people who were brutalised and murdered. *For absolutely no reason.* I had no idea why we were the innocent target of such hostility. Why all the resentment against the Jews when all they wanted was to read a book, or even better, to write one? Or compose music, cure a disease or invent something to make the world a better place.

'All those beautiful souls,' I said. 'Good people - kind, gentle, and intelligent, who harmed no one. They deserved a better fate.'

'I can't explain why evil exists in the world,' the guru replied, 'except to encourage man to do good. Darkness always tries to extinguish the light, for it works best in shadows.'

We spoke for the longest time about the vulnerability and complexity of the human condition. At the end of our meeting, the guru invited me to attend the Bali Arts Festival that evening, for a performance by his members as a show of unity and a testimony of peace.

The amphitheatre took on a strange yellow glow that night, the full moon hovering between the carved stone gateways that accented the stage. Flickering shadows cast silhouettes around the arena as the dancers streamed silently onto the stage. Performers representing a Muslim cleric in white and a priest in the cloth of Christianity were followed by a Buddhist monk in orange robes and the golden strut of a Hindu priest. I was the token Jew in the audience.

This was the ultimate mingling of religions and the chant of many faiths. The performers' voices merged into one, forming a circle of unity. The rumbling clouds echoed the music, like the voices of a celestial choir, sealing the sentiment of accord.

When the performance ended, the guru rose from his seat and spoke to the crowd. Then he walked over to me and thanked me for coming. 'Would you consider giving a talk at our centre,' he asked, 'on astrology. So that we can understand its part in the cosmic plan.' Even though Bali was steeped in mysticism, astrology was a subject not part of their spiritual heritage, the planets too distant and elusive.

On the night of my talk, I was surprised to see a row of buses parked outside the meditation centre. The hall was packed with devotees, excited for the presence of a VIP guest. People were squatting in the garden and even standing on the road, listening to a loudspeaker. My anxiety grew, as I was to be the opening act for a 'special' guest.

Hoping I could stir the crowd's interest in a subject unfamiliar to them, I was introduced to the young lady who would translate my talk into Indonesian. Taking a deep breath, I began. 'Astrology is a science that dates back many centuries, to the ancient civilization of Babylonia.' The words flowed as my enthusiasm for the subject took over and the audience listened intently. Many questions followed, delving into the deeper aspects of the subject. Then a young man raised his hand to ask about the birth chart of Indonesia.

'Indonesia's national day falls on August 17, as you know,' I replied, 'so it comes under the sign of Leo, the lion. Leo is ruled by the Sun, making it both radiant and powerful. Therefore Indonesia is a proud, strong nation with a great deal of influence.'

Much to my surprise, everyone suddenly rose up and after a burst of applause they all began to sing the national anthem. Such a rousing show of patriotism was unexpected but when a man in the back of the room stood up from the shadows and said, 'It's good to be proud but pride must be earned,' the room fell silent. With those few words, the spiritual guru had made his presence felt.

Towards the end of my talk, I was interrupted by the wail of police sirens. The door flung open and a stream of court attendants, in royal blue jackets and batik sarongs, filed into the room and sat on the floor around me. The room hushed as a small, regal woman in rich lace and batik walked in. She was both elegant and composed and it was clear she was a Javanese aristocrat. The guru rose to greet her and then introduced us. The VIP guest was Sukmawati, the daughter of the first president of Indonesia, the famed Sukarno.

She shook my hand in a rather vapid way, perhaps because of a lingering distrust of foreigners inherited from her father. Very conscious of her elevated status, Sukmawati sat on a chair at the front, which now took on the pompous bearing of a throne. When her turn came, she spoke about her ideals and hopes for the country. A candidate for the next presidential election, her sister Megawati Sukarnoputri had been elected president in 2001.

Throughout her talk she was a vision of elegance, her hands drifting through the air like delicate petals in the breeze. It was not so much what she had to say but rather the way she said it. It was less about who she was and more about where she came from. Her father, President Sukarno left his indelible mark on the nation.

Sukmawati was too engrossed in her private world to notice my presence or care. She smiled at the crowd and walked with the guru, as they disappeared into a private room. There was nothing to tie me to their clandestine world for even though we may have shared similar ideals and hopes for the future, we remained worlds apart.

In Bali, my third and final book about the enchanted island, *Bali Hai – A Woman's Journey*, was launched by my loyal book distributor, putting the final seal on 20 years of my life. Back in Sydney, fate stepped in once again. One night I was at my local leagues club Wests for a quick bite to eat. The bistro was good and when in need of some mindless therapy, I played the poker machines. It took my mind off the sense of alienation in a big city, lost among a crowd.

I needed a sign that night but there were no wins or shining lights. Instead, there were warning bells. Grabbing my handbag off the ledge next to the machine, and searching for my wallet, I realised it was missing. It dawned on me that it had been stolen, with all my cash and credit cards. It was Friday night and the banks were closed.

Notifying one of the staff, the Security manager was soon by my side. He couldn't have been nicer. Shown into one of the offices, I was given a hot cup of tea and a slice of apple pie, while phoning the credit card companies to cancel the cards. After reviewing the security footage and spotting the thief, I was escorted to the police station across the road to file a report.

Back in the club, I was advised to order whatever I liked at the restaurant, on the house. I was then told to return any time over the weekend, and my meals were on them. It was way beyond the expected, even more so when the Security manager handed me an envelope, with $100 inside. 'This is from me, personally,' he said, 'Just pay it back when you can.' He then instructed the club bus driver to take me home and escort me to the door.

I was overwhelmed by the kindness. As soon as the banks opened on Monday I went to repay my debt, with a thank you card to express my gratitude. When the manager learnt I was a writer, he offered to hold the launch for my latest book, *Bali Hai*, at the club, in their function room. This kind gesture and the events that followed restored my faith in the generosity of man. From a negative incident came a great outcome, so rare, but no doubt engineered by a higher source that continued to direct me along my life path.

My bid to stay away from Bali was the ultimate test of my resolve. Having fulfilled my karmic pledge, I vowed never to return. Even on cruises as guest speaker I was reluctant to go ashore in Bali, concerned I would awaken old wounds, run into one of my exes, or be exposed to the harsh light of day on an island much loved and so changed. Then came the day I had no choice.

A promotional video was being shot on board my cruise, and after my interview, I was told another entertainer was due to board in Bali and occupy my cabin. This had never happened before as I always stayed for the length of the cruise. Besides, Bali was not a disembarkation port and passengers who wanted to leave in Bali were not allowed. The fabled island had summoned me once more.

There I was, standing alone on the dock in Bali, with my suitcase. The only one. With immigration formalities already processed on board, I wandered through the arrival hall with my declaration form. 'Where is Customs?' I asked a local lady reclining on a bench. Her reply was typical. 'Probably gone to lunch,' she said, yawning. So I just walked out. Bali hadn't changed so much after all.

My good friend Claire came to see me at the hotel on the first day. A journalist at the launch of *Bali Moon*, we had become good friends. Claire was a special person, the epitome of kindness and logic. After lunch, she confided that she had been fighting a battle with cancer, and her time was limited. I was devastated. We spoke often by phone in the following months before she passed away. She left a lasting impression on so many. The universe had blessed me with a priceless opportunity to see, and hug, Claire one last time.

On the second day of my stay in Bali, I invited Gusde, my spiritual mentor, and his wife for lunch. They arrived elegant in their heightened position as high priest and priestess. Gusde now with the title Ida, arrived in a gold sarong and white tunic with his kris dagger tucked into his sash while his wife was serene in white lace. They had now redirected their lives to their priestly purpose, as evolved spiritual souls to guide others along the path.

The staff at the hotel bowed as they walked by, not only because of their heightened status but also because Gusde was once the hotel manager there. I booked this hotel believing there were no ties to the past. However, its name had been changed and this was the very hotel where Gusde had called me into his office for the first time and I learnt of my past life in Java from his trance medium.

After catching up on the events since we last met, we discussed many subjects over lunch and then retired to my hotel room for a meditation. Whispered mantras, splashes of holy water and a trail of scented incense lulled Gusde into a trance, his wife in her own state of meditation. I watched enthralled as Gusde spoke in an unknown tongue, communing with a spiritual force he alone was privy to. On returning to a normal state, he told his wife to hand me the crystal bracelet she wore. She took it off her wrist and placed it on mine.

Gusde had led me on a remarkable spiritual journey and now a calm sense of closure swept over me. Before leaving, Gusde handed me a small bottle of holy water and instructed that I do a cleansing on the beach, to remove any last trace of negative forces before leaving Bali. At dusk, I headed down to the ocean. Wading through the shallow waves, I splashed the holy water over my head and prayed. The sky changed from electric blue to liquid gold, as the sun set over my beloved island. Was this to be my very last goodbye?

My time with Gusde was brief but exceptional and this reunion held great meaning. There could be no denying the strong force that tied us together. Years before we lost touch after Gusde was transferred to Jakarta, as head of training for the hotel chain. I was living in Bali at the time and greatly missed our spiritual connection.

One day, while alone at home, an offer came up from Air Asia. It had opened up a new air route, linking Bali with Bandung in Java, and was giving away limited free tickets. Bandung was one hour from Jakarta, and as I had never been there before, I thought why not? It took a while, but I found the only dates when I could fly there and back for free. For some strange reason, most hotels were booked for those two nights, but I finally found one.

On the plane heading to Bandung, I stared out the window at the crescent moon searching for answers as to why I felt compelled to come to this city in the dead of night. By the time we landed, the moon was reduced to a sliver of light. The airport terminal was deserted and I waited in the shadows until the hotel minibus arrived.

As it pulled up, I noticed the hotel's name on the side of the bus and it dawned on me that it was part of the chain that Gusde worked for. When I checked in at reception, I asked the clerk if Gusde was still part of the company. I was surprised by his response.

'You are a friend of Mr Gusde!' Treated now with more interest, he confirmed that Gusde was a senior executive in Jakarta.

When I asked if I could get a message to him, he replied with a broad smile, 'No problem, madam. Mr. Gusde is at the hotel *now*, conducting a training course for the next two days. You're welcome to leave a note.' It was unbelievable. The cosmos had outdone itself.

The next morning I received a message from Gusde, inviting me to join him and his wife for breakfast for a long-overdue reunion.

'Let's see what spirit has in mind, by bringing us together,' Gusde said after we'd eaten. After a few turns in the corridor, we stood outside their room. *It was exactly opposite mine.* Out of a hotel of 100 rooms, our rooms were directly opposite each other. Spirit had got me this far to Bandung so why have me walk any further?

Sitting around the coffee table in his room, it was not long before Gusde fell into a state of trance. His wife, with pen and paper in hand, jotted down his every word. Gusde spoke in a tongue I had never heard before and it was clear that he had entered another sphere. The air in the room became opaque and the atmosphere heavy until he roused from his dream state, returning to normal.

Gusde asked his wife to read back the words he had spoken while in trance, so he could translate them into English for me. The whole process was mystifying, and I was intrigued.

'Gusde, what language were you speaking?' I asked.

Without a pause, he replied, 'Lemurian.' My mind went blank, as this was not a word or culture I was familiar with. When Gusde elaborated it took me by surprise, part of a lost underwater realm.

Like Atlantis, presumed to lie beneath the Atlantic Ocean, Lemuria too was a lost continent, somewhere below the Indian Ocean. While Atlantis was home to an evolved scientific race, the Lemurians were believed to be highly advanced spiritually.'

It seemed so implausible but Gusde was not a man to dismiss lightly. Had Lemuria truly existed, and if so, who spoke Lemurian now? It appeared, both Gusde and his wife, adding to the enigma.

'You have been chosen,' Gusde said, conveying a message, 'To one day make a difference to a world in need of enlightenment. Your life has been leading up to this, and your time will soon come.'

Even though I wanted to protest, there was no denying the incredible synchronicity that had brought us together. In a strange city, sitting in the room opposite mine with my mentor and his wife, on the same two days they were here. In a country with a population of over 277 million, the odds of this happening were zero.

Years later while cruising across the Pacific to New Zealand, the captain announced that we were sailing above the lost continent of Zealandia. Research revealed that a continent was submerged far below, in the ocean depths, extending from the Pacific, east of New Zealand across to Australia. It had broken away from the Gondwana supercontinent, about 180 million years ago. It sounded like a mythical tale but it was not. So who is to say that Atlantis and Lemuria, yet to be discovered or proven, did not once exist? No one.

CHAPTER TWENTY-THREE

DARK PASSAGE

Terror knows no bounds, impacting on a personal level and more broadly when it affects the world. Australia largely escaped the brunt of it but deranged people exist everywhere with only evil on their mind. They lurk in dark tunnels, carved deep within the earth, just like rats that hide in the dim shadows and carry plague and pestilence. They plot destruction for as minions of the underworld, theirs is a cruel master who presides over the gateway to hell.

In astrology, Pluto is the ruler of the underworld and Hades is his Greek counterpart. The dark planet, Pluto, prefers to remain unnoticed in space, deceiving observers to believe it is insignificant. In truth, Pluto packs a mighty punch. Taking 248 years to complete an orbit around the Sun, the full impact of this planet can be deadly.

When Pluto combines forces with other harsh planets, the impact can cut deep and be long-lasting. Mars, the god of war, strong in its sign of Aries, adds fire and turmoil, while Saturn leaves grim consequences. As the Greek god, Cronus, who ate his sons to prevent them from seizing power, Saturn has no conscience.

On the afternoon of 23 December 1982, a bomb exploded outside the Israeli Consulate in the heart of Sydney. The building was significantly damaged and several people were injured from the impact of the explosion. Later that evening another bomb went off in a car parked in the basement of the Hakoah Club, the Jewish club in the eastern suburbs of Sydney. It was packed with hundreds of competitors for the Maccabi Games. Thankfully, no one was hurt as the full potential of the bomb was not released. Police investigations concluded that both attacks were acts of international terrorism. After the case was reopened in 2011, the reward for information was raised to $1 million but no one was ever caught.

Overseas at the time I was crushed to learn of the attacks. Lunch at the Hakoah Club had been a weekly treat for my family. I enjoyed watching well-dressed ladies wander by one hand grasping a chilled glass of soda water and the other balancing the most delicious slice of cake. Not one for alcohol and with a love of dessert, it was my point of connection with my people. God wants us to enjoy His gifts, especially the sweet ones.

It was a chocolate café that was to be the scene of another terrorist attack in Sydney, years later on December 15, 2014. The siege took place at the Lindt Café in the heart of Sydney in Martin Place, when a lone gunman, an Islamic State operative armed with guns and explosives, held 18 people hostage – customers and staff – for over 16 hours. Twelve people managed to escape but tragically the brave café manager was executed and another hostage was killed when the police stormed the scene. Hatred exacts a heavy toll.

On the morning of the siege, I was on a train heading for Martin Place, with a specialist appointment nearby. Just as I reached the city, an announcement was made that the station at Martin Place had shut down. No explanation was given. I got off the train at the next stop, where everyone was panicking. Rumours abounded, some that terrorists were running through the streets, others that bombs had been placed in the Opera House. Neither was true but the damage was done and people were scared. I quickly headed home.

One of my friends worked in an office in the adjoining building to the café and was evacuated. Each week we met for lunch, choosing a different venue every time. I loved to indulge at the Lindt Café on Sydney Harbour but for some reason, I refused to set foot in the one at Martin Place. This was months *before* the siege but as I passed the entrance to the café, a sense of dread overcame me. Darkness shrouded the doorway, barring me from entry.

It was a similar case in Bali. Agus and I occasionally enjoyed the nightlife in busy Kuta but, on the back of his motorbike, as he tried to negotiate the heavy traffic through the streets, an ominous cloud gathered as we passed the Sari Club. Each time, my skin bristled, and I exclaimed, 'That is the gateway to hell!' I refused to step foot inside it. The surrounding energy felt dark and sinister and, trusting my instincts, I stayed far away.

This sense of disaster was warranted. On the night of October 12, 2002, a bomb exploded in a van outside the Sari Club, and earlier across the road at Paddy's Bar by a suicide bomber. In the carnage, 202 people were killed, including 88 Australians. Another 209 people were injured. A dreadful shudder rocked the island, with a ripple effect of shock and sadness. How could such a wicked event take place on this holy island? Shock turned to horror as the true impact of the tragedy unfolded – the human toll impossible to gauge.

I was home alone in Sanur on that fateful night in Bali. When I stepped out onto my balcony to gaze at the moon, I heard a dreadful bang. Even though it was distant, it was disturbing enough to jolt the earth and alert the world to the depravity of man. Such a brutal loss of life and such a senseless act. That morning I had been swimming in a nearby hotel, chatting away in the pool with an Australian lady who was holidaying in Bali with her daughter. That night they went to the Sari Club. The daughter ducked into a shop to buy cigarettes and was saved from the bomb. Her mother was not so fortunate.

The following morning, as news broke of the tragedy and horrendous scenes flashed across the TV screen, a state of shock prevailed and silence enveloped the island. Roxy rang me in a panic, adding to my anxiety, by repeating rumours that there were more bombs planted around the island. There was little choice but to leave Bali, as prompted, until some sense of calm returned, and order was restored. The flight to Sydney was full of dazed people trying to make sense of an event that was senseless, each one stunned.

It was announced on the plane that counsellors would be available at the airport for those who needed them but I was in no state to discuss my feelings. Rather I needed to quell the rage and confusion inside my soul, at those perverted few who wanted to rip the world apart and any sense of moral decency along with it.

With so many unanswered questions, my mind caved in. I wondered if it was possible to sense danger before it happened. Not in predicting the actual event but in its *planning*, tuning in to a plot that had already been hatched and was alive in the conniving mind of the perpetrators. Was their energy whirling around the cosmos, thought giving form to reality and shape to misery? Were my warning signs a premonition, alerted by my psychic sensitivity?

When we reached Sydney, it all proved too much for me. As I walked through the airport terminal, my legs gave way and I slid down the wall onto the floor. 'It could have been me.' The words repeated over in my head as I realised how lucky I was to be alive and how guilty to have survived. My life could have ended in the blink of an eye. Then came an inane reply, the message ridiculous. I needed a message that was as profound as it was comforting. Instead, I was given these simple words,

'But did you eat enough ice cream?'

Spirit messages do not manifest as a voice but rather as thought transference. No sound is necessary but the message is clear. Now, as I questioned the fragility of life, the response seemed trivial until the deeper meaning was conveyed.

Simply put, 'Did you enjoy life?'

Despite all the challenges and obstacles, '*Did you have a good time?*' It was a basic Jewish tenet. While some religions demanded penance and sacrifice and were bound by restrictions, Judaism rejoiced in life. Song, sweets, dance, love and lots of music.

Not familiar with the ways of my faith, I inherited the core values. Sprawled out on the airport floor, that's when I got it. When I truly understood. *Life is a celebration.* It should be grabbed with both hands, embraced and squeezed until the last drop of happiness is extracted and the final opportunity seized. Yes, it can be hard at times and the going is sure to get tough but when you climb that mountain, stumble past the rocks until you discover the diamonds, it will be worth it. And the view at the top will be magnificent.

CHAPTER TWENTY-FOUR

THE ETERNAL FLAME

Standing on a stage on a cruise ship, with the lights shining down upon you in a three-storey theatre filled to capacity, is hard to beat. It is also difficult to process. All eyes are on you, with your strengths and weaknesses exposed. There is little time to assess how you got there and how your life has led to this moment, so many years later.

Over the decades, learning through experience made me bolder and more confident. Looking at the faces among the audience, some were eager in anticipation, longing to learn and add substance to their life, while a few feigned bored disinterest. The callous cynics longed to be proved wrong despite their protestations otherwise. Each person was on a journey, each progressing at their own rate.

I was born to shine with the Sun and Neptune on the Ascendant at birth, but Mercury retrograde in the 12th house was guarded and reclusive. With each passing year, I became more accustomed to the recognition. No more jitters, just gratitude and appreciation. The spotlight felt more radiant, even more deserving, because of the obstacles I overcame to be standing there in all my glory.

One of the worst of these happened while I was at the peak of success. The day was just like any other until it wasn't. In a single dramatic moment, my spine caved in and my world fell apart. All my hopes for the future were dashed. Fortunately, it did not occur on the ocean, where help was far away, but at home. Alone. Rushed to hospital by ambulance, I was barely able to move. The pain was excruciating, the kind that makes death a luring proposition.

After emergency surgery for spinal decompression, I relied on heavy drugs to cope with the aftermath. Added to the pain was the indignation of dealing with a heavy-handed nurse who burst into the room and ordered me up so she could make the bed. I ordered her out of my room and out of my life forever. I needed sympathy from kind-hearted souls and not scorn. My body and soul were suffering.

My neurosurgeon, in all her wisdom, said I could go home from the hospital after two days. Even though it appeared the surgery was a success, I could barely move, had a complex underlying neurological condition and lived alone. So in an act of benevolence, she settled on three days. The physio managed to get me up, barely, but as my health fund didn't cover therapy in a private hospital, I was apparently of no further use and so off I hobbled.

How I managed to get into my building and up to my apartment was a miracle, but there was no way I could get off the bed to get a glass of water, medicine, or go to the bathroom. To be alone in acute pain, helpless and isolated, is the worst kind of confrontation. I barely made it into a taxi to get to a respite home where the nurses declared that I should never have been discharged from the hospital. It took two weeks to recover and take my first steps.

In the meantime, emails came from the cruise company offering me positions as a guest speaker. There was no way I was well enough to accept, but when a cruise was offered in several months, heading from Fremantle to Bali, I was tempted to re-enter the world of the living. Deciding to set it as my goal, I accepted the cruise.

It was no easy feat to start walking again, and it took every ounce of strength to get back on my feet. The pain was persistent but my determination even more so. After several weeks I grew more confident, using shopping trolleys at the local mall to practice. Taking the first steps to freedom, and relying on a walker to stay upright, I was ready to board the long flight to Perth.

Doused with painkillers, once on the plane, I closed my eyes and drifted off. I was shocked when the pilot announced that we were commencing our descent. I thought we had turned back but we were landing in Perth. Time swallowed up in a welcome daze.

Boarding the ship and settling into my cabin, it was wonderful to be on the ocean again and hear the sound of the waves. No more endless buzzers in hospital corridors, beeping monitors or blood tests ... just the sound of the waves. The soothing song of the sea.

Reminded of my wanderlust and fuelled by the desire to trace my ancestry, I embarked on a half-world cruise the following year. It was only fitting that it was on board P&O UK's *Arcadia*. My first cruise in 1965 was on the original *Arcadia*, as was my half-world cruise in 1970 through the Panama Canal to London. Now I was about to complete my circumnavigation of the globe cruising via Asia, through the Suez Canal and the Mediterranean to Europe.

The cruise departed Sydney on 28 February 2018. It was the first anniversary of my father's death. This trip was fuelled by my desire to delve into his Spanish ancestry, most of which was shrouded in mystery. To that purpose, I had permission to disembark the ship in Cadiz in Spain and not Dover in England, our final port,

As part of the cruise, performers were flown into ports, along the way, to ensure variety. I became friendly with the first headline act to board the ship. A gifted couple, one was a talented musician from the UK and his partner an Israeli tenor, with the voice and heart of an angel. There was an immediate rapport between us.

I asked a special favour of Simon, the singer. *A song for my father*. In keeping with his character, my father passed away at the age of 92, within two days of falling ill – just the way he wanted it. Weakness was not part of his repertoire. Till the end, he believed he possessed superpowers and would live forever. There were only a handful of people at his funeral, for he had few friends or relatives.

A simple Jewish ceremony was performed but there was no music, no spiritual overtone to cling to or wish him on his way. In the solitude of the ship's chapel, Simon chose a Hebrew psalm to sing for my father. My soul soared with the splendour of his voice, the psalm haunting in its essence. I prayed my father was listening.

Deflated when the duo left the ship, I immersed myself in the ports we visited, all fascinating in their own right. From Malaysia to Hong Kong and Shanghai in China, my eyes were opened to a different reality. No bonding took place, no ties that bind or real desire to return, but odd moments still lingered in my mind.

In Sri Lanka, the coach driver spoke no English. A humble man, we gestured in sign language and laughed as I sat in the front row. After a visit to a Hindu temple, our last stop was at a hotel for afternoon tea. With a long queue, I was surprised when a smart young man in a uniform, brought a tray out to me on the bus to save me getting off. Back at the dock, when negotiating the steep bus steps with my stick proved an ordeal, three drivers rushed to my aid.

This kindness, or concern, was rare. In Vietnam, I was left behind on the side of a highway. Tagged another *easy* tour, the guide took off with the group across a four-lane highway and vanished down an incline. There was no way I was fit enough to follow, so I sat beside the bus, in a park. We had 30 minutes to return but when I turned around, I was horrified to see the bus take off down the highway, the driver deciding to wait by the river for the group.

With cars whizzing past I was forced to make a dangerous dash across the highway, race past fast lanes of traffic, scale the median strip and scoot across the other lanes using training I had learnt in Bali, praying they would avoid hitting me because as a foreigner it would be costly. Then I almost tumbled down the steep ramp, without a handrail, and narrowly avoided landing in the river.

It was a miracle I made it back to the ship. When I reported my ordeal, I was given a complimentary tour in the next port, but it was a waste of time as I fell sick and collapsed onto my bed. Still on strong pain medication, I decided to stop taking them, reluctant to carry the pills across Europe. Three days were swallowed up in an intense fever, wiped from my calendar, but now I was drug-free.

The rest of the voyage whizzed by, propelled by the whirling dervish dancer on the dinner cruise in Dubai. Then came lunch in a Bedouin tent in Jordan, where I nearly passed out from the heat of the desert. In Oman, our tour guide Omar was a sweet young man, helpful to all those who required aid. When women lined up to hire a hijab to enter the Grand Mosque, Omar was shocked when he saw me. 'You look like a local lady,' he said, taken aback. Even though the country was new to me, it was full of fascination and appeal.

That was to wane in comparison to the feelings that swamped me when we reached Spain. The port of Cadiz was my first hint of the seductive Spain that awaited. There was a vibrant energy here, steeped in centuries of culture and history, reflected in the sharp blue of the sea and sky. I took time to stroll through the colourful plazas and along the shoreline, enjoying the local food and rich ice cream.

Once settled into my hotel, I found a taxi driver willing to take me on a tour of the surrounding countryside. After passing through green fields and navigating steep cobblestone roads, the car barely squeezing through the old buildings, we stopped for lunch. The view, perched on the restaurant's terrace roof, was serene. As we basked in the sun enjoying fresh fish and crisp salad, the driver spoke of his life in Spain and his love for his country.

On the way back, we passed the remains of an old castle and other clues to the region's history. In the lobby of my hotel, I stopped to chat with the receptionist, Lucia, eager to share my travel plans. When I explained that my father's family originated in Spain but had been expelled from the country during the Spanish Inquisition, she remained silent, listening intently to my words.

Between 1478 and 1834, around 160,000 Jews were expelled from Spain or forced to convert to Catholicism under threat of torture, some burning at the stake. With over 32,000 executions, it was a dark period of Spanish history, flawed by religious extremism. Lucia had recently watched a documentary on the expulsion of Spanish Jews and to my surprise, she took my hand and bowed, 'I'm sorry' she said humbly. Those words could move mountains.

Despite the plight of my ancestors, their eternal flame and determination never wavered. That flame was to ignite as I travelled across southern Spain, hiring private drivers from one city to the next as the easiest way to avoid the inevitable stress of travel. My first driver Luis was polished and spoke English. He was a kind man who related the history of the Andalucia region with a subdued sensibility and with the hindsight of his years.

There was one stop along the way to Seville. A cathedral, it was not as grand as many that studded the country with Catholicism. Most were dripping with pomp and wealth, lashed with ribbons of gold. As we looked up at the stained-glass windows, a reflection of its stoic past, Luis asked about my family. When I disclosed that both of my parents had been in Auschwitz, he stopped in his tracks, turned to face me, and apologised. Perhaps, on behalf of humanity. His words were a heartfelt gesture, made by an evolved soul.

Spain is a land of contrasts with a lavish history steeped in layers. The city of Seville was its bright shining diamond, and my arrival was perfectly timed. It was the week of the April festival and the mood was electric, with many people dressed in bright flamenco outfits. The horses were magnificent, proud and embellished, their carriages in matching colours to the families who rode in them.

Weaving through the streets of the old town, full of character and charm, I tracked down a small museum, one of the last remnants of Seville's Jewish past, searching for a clue to my identity. The prominent folk on display had played a large part in the region's history, but it was the photo of a young woman that captured my attention. The stack of bangles on her arm, and the Moorish nature of her dress, were all so familiar and she looked remarkably like *me*.

My next stop in the ancient town of Córdoba added strands to the mystery. Once the meeting place of Jewish intellectuals, some holding high posts in the caliphate, it was a rich mix of cultures. Centuries of Moorish Berber rule proved to be a boon for Sephardic Jewry, with a mutual exchange of knowledge between faiths. Although conspicuous displays of religious rituals were discouraged, Jewish communities were free to practise their faith. It saw the emergence of prominent scholars and many valuable texts.

The streets of Córdoba were a masterpiece of history, with the fragrance of emerging jasmine and orange blossoms filtering through the air. I stayed at a small hotel close to the gates of the old town and after indulging in some delicious flaky pastries at a local café, I headed off in search of the past. The maze of small streets and colourful squares led to the Great Mosque, one of the largest sacred buildings in the Islamic world. In the 13th century, conquest demanded change and it was converted into a Christian cathedral. Wandering through the cavernous halls, I felt dwarfed by its history.

The Jewish Quarter of the old town was a maze of laneways and the small synagogue there was closed for repairs. Between the 10th and 15th centuries, this area had a thriving Jewish population but now the brooding bronze statue of the great Jewish philosopher Maimonides was one of the few homages to the past. It is hard to resurrect what was deliberately destroyed, and the loss was great.

In the Jewish museum, the House of Sepharad, there were few traces of the original Judaic presence. One document, handwritten in 1598, served as testimony to the grim days of the Inquisition. Even after converting, Jews, and their offspring, were not granted the same rights as Christians – unable to 'behave like a nobleman, ride a horse, bear arms, dress in silk, or wear silver and gold for five generations.' There was one woman who defied the rules.

In the museum's courtyard, images of several prominent Jews were displayed, including that of the honourable Dona Gracia Mendes Nasi. A family tree compiled by one of my father's relatives showed her maiden name, Benveniste, as part of our maternal lineage. Of noble Portuguese heritage, Dona Gracia was no ordinary woman but one who saved many lives and enriched others.

After her husband, a rich trader and banker, died, she became one of the wealthiest women in Europe in the 16th century, using her conversion to Catholicism as a shield to hide fellow Jews during the Spanish Inquisition and devise an escape route out of danger. A woman with a heart of gold and nerves of steel, one of the world's first woman philanthropists, she left behind an enormous legacy.

As I learned more about the great lady, it dawned on me that perhaps she was the reason I lingered in Tiberias, on the Sea of Galilee in Israel, so many years before in the 1980s. That impossible pull that I could not define, the driving force, all started to make sense. After making her home in Constantinople, at the invitation of the Sultan of the Ottoman Empire, Suleiman the Magnificent, who was one of the few leaders who accepted Jews, she devised a plan.

After endowing funds for schools, hospitals and libraries, Dona Gracia was desperate to establish a safe place for her people and turned to the Jew's traditional home of Israel. Offering a great sum, she convinced the sultan to grant her a long-term lease for Tiberias in the Holy Land, which the Ottomans controlled, with a permit to establish Jewish autonomy there and create a secure home for the displaced Jews of Europe. She was a true visionary.

Dona Gracia bore the title of Nasi or 'Prince' in Hebrew, a reflection of her status as a descendant of King David, the monarch who united all the tribes of Israel in biblical days. Could it be that this illustrious matriarch took pleasure in one of her descendants roaming the streets of her town, so she cleared the way for me to stay a while? A museum in Tiberias is devoted to her legacy.

More clues to my heritage lay in the magnificent city of Toledo in central Spain. Getting there proved an ordeal, as my driver turned up in a battered taxi with a loose cable on the roof, It clattered all the way along the highway. Despite all his efforts to fix it, we were forced to drive for hours behind trucks to Toledo, to lower the wind blast. *Instant, unrelenting headache.* The trip was an ordeal.

When we reached the outskirts of Toledo, the medieval city provided a sumptuous backdrop to the Spain of old. This was history at its most grand, most ornate and bold. As we drove through the streets I was swept away in the innuendo of the past, each turn or bend in the river a page from a treasured manuscript. Known as the 'City of Three Cultures', the influence of Christians, Muslims and Jews has moulded its character over the centuries.

My hotel was located in the old Jewish section of the city, so I could best explore the area. When my guide Irma turned up that afternoon, we headed off to visit Europe's oldest intact synagogue, Santa Maria La Blanca. It was also one with an identity crisis because its 25 horseshoe arches and intricate plasterwork, were more reminiscent of the mosques of that era. Converted to a church in the 15th century, it was later used as an oratory and barracks. Few remnants of its Jewish past remain, the memories lost long ago.

A billboard, across the street from my hotel, had more impact. On it, was a copy of a letter written by Don Isaac Abravanel, advisor to King Ferdinand and Queen Isabella, along with an image of him kneeling before the royals. In his letter, Don Isaac declined the monarchs' offer to remain in the royal court and escape the fate of his fellow Jews. Instead, he fled Toledo, aware that his life was at risk.

With a possible ancestral link, his words resonated with me. With his title of Nasi, Don Isaac was a descendant of the tribe of King David of Israel, and as such was related to Jesus Christ, the person of their adoration. 'How could they worship one', he argued, 'while damning the rest?' His arguments fell on deaf ears.

Don Isaac was the royals' trusted advisor yet they refused to be swayed. At least he had his say, a chance to air his grievances. Most Jews chose exile rather than abandon their faith while others converted, Conversos, still conducting their Hebrew prayers in secret.

This was evident when my guide Irma turned the key to the cellar of an old house. The musky rooms were used to hide in during the bleak days of the Inquisition when the Jews clung to the last vestige of their faith in darkness. There was little air inside, only the scant remains of candles that burned centuries before to illuminate an eternal flame. The flame of a faith that refused to be extinguished.

These were my people. Noble, resilient and defiant.

Most of all they were learned, willing to share their gift with all those who were open to receive it. Refusing to bow to pressure or the threat of torture or death, they clung to their belief in one true God. The God who created them. Rebel or academic, wise man or hero, bold yet tender, they had endured the curse of centuries of cruel persecution to remain buoyant and thriving to this day.

After exploring the voluptuous art and culture of Madrid, Spain's capital, I joined a coach tour to continue my journey through Portugal. The trip was rushed, and my fellow travellers were bland. It was impossible to absorb the many sites, as the tour swooped back across Spain, to the sunny Costa del Sol and Valencia.

The city of Granada proved a highlight, especially the rich grandeur and gardens of the Alhambra Palace. It was not only the exquisite Islamic architecture, serene pools and perfumed blossoms, or the fact that Christopher Columbus bowed down before the

Spanish royals, Isabella and Ferdinand, here in 1492 and received approval to set sail for the New World, which made it memorable.

Rather, it was the shrieks of our local guide, Carlota, that remain etched in my mind. Trying to hurry me along to keep up with the rest of the group, she goaded me up a mountain of stairs in record time, until my body felt broken. My spirit had given up with the first few steps. Her antics gave me a clear view of the Inquisitors of old.

When we reached our final destination, Barcelona, the guide hailed me a taxi and told me to meet them at La Sagrada Familia, the unfinished cathedral of architect Gaudi. Lost among the massive crowd, and dwarfed by the splendour of his artistic genius, I wandered off to see the sites of this visually stunning city. An artistic orgy of colour and imagination, it stood alone in the world.

The next day, hiring a scooter on the beach, the driver waited while I ate lunch at a café by the ocean. A homeless man staggered by, scooping his fingers in my plate, which sent the restaurant manager into a state of apoplexy. After thrusting him out of sight, he offered me a glass of liqueur. It was time to start drinking.

From Barcelona, I boarded a cruise to the Mediterranean, just in time to catch the Cannes Film Festival in France before a pleasant jaunt to Nice on the French Riviera. No time to gamble at the casino there because, that evening, we set sail for our next port of call, Rome.

Weighed down by its history, it was impossible to digest a fraction of it. Rather it was Florence with its exquisite artwork and architecture, that I loved. I had not thought to book ahead for the Uffizi Gallery and bask in the genius of Botticelli, so I missed out.

Instead, most of my time was spent trying to find our Italian tour guide, who was swallowed up by a sea of waving flags in the town square. After a kamikaze drag race through the medieval streets on a motorised scooter driven by a mad Serbian, dodging masses of Chinese tourists, I was dropped back at the square from where I started. There was an interesting church to visit, one strangely embellished with a Star of David, but first I needed sustenance. Exhausted, I headed for the closest café.

A charming waiter, Gino, was quick to appear. 'Table for one?'

'No, *two*,' I replied, gesturing to a chair. 'Please join me.'

He quickly sat down and bounced back up, laughing. 'No, my boss will kill me!'

Crammed among the tables, I sat between a stoic Swiss couple and a dull American pair. Their looks were so dry, that their faces were in danger of cracking. My brain was screaming for the Italian waiter so I could be reminded that I was still alive. The heavens, wanting to break the human drought, opened up and it began to pour.

With the canopy above us sagging from the driving rain, Gino ran to my rescue while the gruesome foursome retreated inside. Then came a massive bolt of lightning followed by the menacing growl of thunder. It immediately triggered a song in my head.

'Galileo!' I screeched, trying to compete with the storm.

Gino sang along and then replied blankly, 'He's over there.'

'*Who's* over *where*?' I asked, at a loss.

'Galileo.' Gino said as if I should already know. I travelled so far and so often that I had little idea where I was going on any given day, instead relying on the universe to point me in the right direction.

Like a scene from an Italian opera, with props provided from up above, the body of Galileo was *over there*, originally placed in a small room outside the Basilica of Santa Croce. Now inside, he was in good company because the church was also the burial site for Michelangelo, Machiavelli, Marconi, and other famed persons.

Gino took my hand and kissed it when I rose to leave, while the lot inside snarled at me for my song and laughter. The rain was bucketing down and the cobblestones in the square were so slippery that I never made it into the basilica, ten metres away. Instead, I went off in search of an umbrella and what was left of my tour group.

The Star of David at the front of the basilica was the work of the architect, Nicolla Matas, a Jew from Ancona who incorporated the large star as decoration. It didn't click that he was Jewish, even though his contract specified that he would not work on Saturdays. Or maybe it just didn't matter. Galileo, the great astronomer and physicist, was found guilty of heresy by the Roman Inquisition in 1633 and placed under house arrest, where he remained till his death in 1642. All this for offending the Catholic church with his outlandish theory that the Earth revolves around the Sun.

It doesn't pay to be different or have an original thought.

Here's the problem with travel – people, lots of them. Forget any lingering scent of the past, no whimsical scenes of bored aristocrats and mystical castles. Stunning cities, like Venice and Dubrovnik, were consumed by a mass of tourists. I did collar an electric bicycle man in Split, Croatia, for a solitary carriage ride around the old town. Then, splashing out, I hired a private driver in a Mercedes for lunch on a pristine blue lake. It was quite a jolt to inhale fresh air and feel your lungs expand, to realise what you've been missing out one.

Swapping one cruise ship for another, this time to sail around the Greek islands, it was off to stunning Mykonos, Rhodes and

Santorini. The spectacular sunsets, *the crowds, the buses*, the azure sea, the stark white houses against a cobalt blue backdrop, the pink bougainvillea, the fresh plump tomatoes, *the crowds, the buses*.

Decades before, I cruised from Crete to Alexandria in Egypt. During my day trip to the city's fascinating sites and museums, the tour company director sat beside me on the bus. When we passed plush apartments overlooking the Mediterranean, he offered to set me up in one if I wanted to stay. All with a sly nod.

It was never going to happen. I wondered why men felt the need to proposition me, at odd times of my life and in strange parts of the world. They also felt the need to hoist me onto the back of a camel, at the pyramids in Egypt, when the coach driver ignored my pleas to remain on shifting sand. My one attempt to ride a horse, ended in a tortuous trek under barbed wire fences while the horse waited for me back at the farm. Elephants were another story altogether.

Greece, my birthplace, was the highlight of my trip. Athens was overwhelming, in the wealth of its classical history. There were simply no words for the view from my hotel rooftop while I ate dinner overlooking the Acropolis, as the full moon rose, bathing the Parthenon in a stream of light. Couples were dining around me, and groups of people celebrating, but I sat alone, content in my solitude. This was how I appreciated life, in the stillness of beauty.

There were many moments of inspiration on my tour of Greece. The Temple of Poseidon, perched on Cape Sounion, on the southern tip of the Attica peninsula, was hypnotic. A 20-foot bronze statue of the ocean god once stood in pride of place here, but only remnants remain in the Athens museum, along with other ancient treasures.

As the sun set over the marble pillars of the temple at Sounion, the dusky pink sky reflected the annals of time, etched in every fold of the sea. So moved by the scene, the English poet Lord Byron carved his initials in a marble column there, in an early act of romantic vandalism. He became a Greek folk hero, dying in its name.

Our tour included the odd, unexpected treat. At one of our lunch stops, among a parade of olive trees, Stavros the owner, ignited his waning spirit by throwing a stack of white plates around the restaurant. While everyone ran for cover, his wife, Effie, who had witnessed his crazed antics for years, was running out of patience and crockery. She gave him a look worthy of Medusa. Nothing quite compares with a wild Greek, especially one pickled on ouzo.

It would have taken more than strong alcohol to fortify the hermit monks who built their monasteries up high in Meteora, on the plains of Thessaly. These Orthodox Christian monks, in search of isolation, found sanctuary in caves hidden among the many cliffs and, over the centuries, more than 20 Byzantine monasteries were built on top of steep black rocky outcrops. Six are still in use today, two inhabited by nuns, the others by monks.

Gazing up at one soaring monastery, clinging precariously to a peak high in the sky, I wondered how they had the strength and perseverance to carry out such an enormous undertaking. To live isolated, suspended in air, as high as 400 metres in the sky, was unreal. The view from up above, with rising clouds adding to the spiritual illusion, was a grand testimonial of the need to be alone and to be lost in a world of devotion, closer to God.

Like the monks I needed peace. Even more so a comfortable bed. In the next hotel on our tour, the bed was so low that I couldn't get onto it, let alone get up again. When I complained, housekeeper

Toula flung herself headlong into my room, swearing in her mother tongue, as she ran off to find an extra mattress. My life was like a scene from *Goldilocks and the Three Bears*, with chairs, beds, racks, and baths, too high or low. Add to that the fairy tale, *The Princess and the Pea*, and I always packed my pillow and blanket.

In this hotel, compensation came in the form of the hunky baggage porter, Alex, who was the most exquisite example of manhood I'd seen in a long time. With the build of an Olympic athlete, or a Greek statue, he was more tempting than baclava. Dazed, all my attempts to remember the Greek word for 'crazy' to get him to eject Toula, the mad maid, were for naught. Alex was the embodiment of irresistible Adonis, so it was hard to speak.

Legend has it that mortal Adonis died in the arms of Aphrodite, her tears mixing with his blood, from which sprang the anemone flower. Yet another Greek myth, to inspire one with pathos. In the battle between head versus heart, mine would be a tough choice between Athena, the goddess of wisdom, and Aphrodite, Venus to the Romans, the goddess of beauty. Presiding over both Libra and Taurus, Aphrodite was ultimately the ruler of my birth chart.

In northeast Greece, we skimmed past the fabled Mt. Olympus, the playground of the Greek gods. Zeus was in charge of this pantheon of twelve gods. It was only fitting that Zeus was the ruler of Sagittarius, half-man and half-horse. With his might, he insisted on the biggest planet in our solar system, Jupiter.

Hermes, or Mercury to the Romans, claimed both Gemini and Virgo. Ares or Mars, the god of war, reigned in headstrong Aries. Cronus, or crochety Saturn controlled rigid Capricorn. Leo likes to shine so it scored the Sun while reclusive Cancer was content with the Moon, ruled by the goddess Artemis, or gentle Luna.

Poseidon or Neptune, ruler of Pisces, was off contemplating his fate, and that of mankind, while staring deeply at the ocean. Pluto was guarding the gateway of hell, as Hades, and it took both this dark lord of the underworld and aggro Mars to coerce the sign of Scorpio. The dominant Romans lent their name to the planets but eccentric Aquarius chose as its ruler Uranus, god of the sky, the only Greek god among our planets. The word zodiac, like most things in the world, *comes from the Greek* meaning 'circle of animals'.

The place that inspired me the most in Greece was Delphi, the spiritual centre of the ancients. Here lay the sanctuary of Apollo, where people came to honour their gods. Among the green pine trees, on a rocky hillside, was the site of the mystical oracle, the woman with special powers consulted by military commanders and kings alike before any crucial battle. Inhaling the potent fumes of the gorges, she was transported to another place and time to see beyond, a woman with incredible power, able to predict the future.

While others raced towards the temple to plunge themselves into history, I sat in a quiet grove to absorb the energy and ease myself back in time. Closing my eyes, I visualised the past. Who was this woman, the mighty oracle, who possessed the 'gift' of prophecy? Was it a great blessing to be chosen as the oracle, or was it rather a curse, for the future lay in her hands? If her predictions did not come to pass, was she condemned, or easily replaced?

That evening, I relaxed on the balcony of the hotel gazing out over the peaceful valley, consumed by the aura of a timeless magic. When the rest of my tour group bounded up a hill to head for a restaurant for dinner, with all the vigour of people who had not eaten for a week, I stayed behind. I had no intention of breaking the spell.

While standing in the hotel lobby, watching the last of them disappear in the distance, the manager came out of his office. 'You're not joining your group?' he asked. His concern was refreshing. Learning that I was born in Salonica, the second largest city in Greece, he asked about my family. 'Are you visiting them?'

His words brought back a harsh reality. 'No one in my family is left there,' I replied. 'They were all murdered by the Nazis during the war.' Situated on a sweeping bay in northern Greece, Salonica was once the only city in the world with a majority Jewish population. Tragically, around 95% of its 43,000 Jews were murdered in World War II, most on arrival in Auschwitz.

The manager's response was instant, and he swept me up in a warm embrace. With his arm around me, the manager led me downstairs to the restaurant buffet, shouting to the staff. 'She is my guest and does *not* pay for anything,' before hugging me once more. This man possessed the kind heart of a Greek.

It was Greece alone during the Second World War that wrote a letter of protest to the Nazis, signed by many academics and the Archbishop of Athens, declaring that Jews were Greeks and would not be handed over. The Archbishop promised that the Greek church would issue false baptismal papers for the Jews. A ransom was raised for the release of the Jews but the Nazis took both the money and the Jews, as unscrupulous as they were evil. As history teaches us, time and again, *never make a deal with the devil.*

It is an honour to be born in Salonica in Greece, so close to the abode of the gods of Olympus, just over 100 kilometres away. When I took my first breath, was it their whispers that lulled me to sleep and inspired me to see a mythical reality few can recognise? Alexander the

Great came from this region too, a statue of the great explorer on his horse, in all his glory, on the esplanade by the sea. The city is named after his half-sister Thessaloniki. Cleopatra too, the mighty Egyptian queen, was of almost pure Macedonian Greek lineage.

My father's Sephardic paternal line had a heritage as grand as his mother's ancestral side. Hours of searching revealed that many of his forefathers were respected doctors in Salonica, several climbing the ranks to become personal physicians to the sultan of the Ottoman Empire, of which the city was once part. They suffered from the plague of honesty, expelled from the royal court for advising the sultan that to regain his health he would have to end his drinking and orgies. It did not go down well, but at least I was endowed with their forthright manner and possible need for discretion.

CHAPTER TWENTY-FIVE

INTO THE ASTRAL

It's all about energy. For years I tried to figure out why people felt the need to touch me, in particular my right arm. It seemed to emit some sort of force field. It was hard to judge whether they were trying to assault or heal me. It was my right arm that was targeted years before in Bali when the louvre window exploded one night. As a constant reminder, the scar on the fourth finger of my right hand, cut by a jagged piece of glass, throbbed at odd times.

Going out was not without its risks, so I became defensive and steered clear of people most of the time. On my weekly outing with my friend Ingrid, she remained untouched, not even the slightest of taps from anyone in the many years we were friends. For me, not a day went by without a gentle pat on my right arm, as a measure of affection, or a rude knock which invariably led to an argument or confrontation with people who were as hostile as they were mean.

This mysterious magnetic draw led to some funny moments too. One day, on a crowded tram, I sat with my right arm safely against the side so no one could touch it. Then I realised that someone was stroking my left arm. I turned to see an almost toothless gentleman, beaming broadly at me. I nearly choked when he said, 'I'm 70 and

I'm available.' He couldn't stop grinning. His smile was infectious, in so many ways.

'Sorry, I replied. 'I don't date toy boys!' We both cracked up laughing while the rest of the people in the tram were stonily stoic.

The proof that my energy was powerful came when I attended a spiritual function one evening. As part of her readings, a psychic medium handed out metal divining rods to all those in the audience, asking that they be held in one hand. Most rods remained stationary, with the occasional flicker. When she passed one to me, the rod went berserk and started spinning in circles. It was like the rod had a will of its own and it whacked anyone in proximity. 'She has *very* strong energy,' the medium coughed, yanking people away.

There were many markers in my birth chart of a strong spiritual thread, one that dated back to past lives. The alignment of Neptune and the Sun when I was born was conjunct to the Moon's South Node, a measure of my past life. All within one degree of each other, there was no doubt I had been on a mystical path in previous lifetimes. Mercury in the 12th house, the secluded site of spirit, acted as a communication channel to the other side. Add the Moon in the 8th house of the occult and it was a spiritual trifecta.

The connection with spirit was so intense that by simply asking for guidance or a wish, it soon manifested. At times it felt like I had my own genie. Missing the lorikeets that once came to my hotel room on the Gold Coast, to eat from my hand, I 'requested' that two of the lively red and green parrots visit me in my new unit there.

Within *minutes* I heard a shuffling noise and when I went to investigate, two lorikeets were walking around my kitchen without a care in the world. I was left shaking my head, especially when one left a fine feather as a souvenir. It was surely a gift from up above.

Spirit messages often come through song, usually in the first line I hear. When I turned on the music one day, it was a line from my favourite song, about birds appearing whenever you are near. As I turned around a solitary bird was staring at me on the windowsill. It did not budge for hours, its eyes soulful and deep, like those of a wise old man. While it might be a coincidence, there was more to it. It felt like a smile beaming down from heaven.

Music remained a source of inspiration throughout my life and I took full advantage of it. Whenever a superstar came to Sydney, I was there. Tina Turner was stunning in 1977, a powerhouse of energy with the spirited style and fabulous legs of a Sagittarius horse gone wild. Few words can describe Whitney Houston's concert in 1986, a powerhouse Leo presence. Two favourites were Cher, the ultimate Taurus icon with the velvet voice, and sassy Bette Midler, with her fiery Aries ascendant, who visited Sydney on her Divine Miss M tour, selling out 34 shows. Stylish Virgo Beyonce came in 2009, in a class of her own. I was overwhelmed by their star power.

In 2010 came the thrill of winning tickets to the Oprah show, on the forecourt of the Sydney Opera House. With an audience of over 6,000 for each of the two shows, and with guests like Bon Jovi and Hugh Jackman, it was a special moment in time. I still treasure the pearl necklace, circled in silver with the letter O, presented as a gift on the occasion. The Opera House was a perfect setting in 2016 for a master of voice, Josh Groban, who brought a fleeting type of magic, as he performed with the Sydney Symphony Orchestra.

The Sydney Opera House was always stunning, magnified by the avalanche of talent who performed there. My love of ballet was consistent until one night. Peering over the balcony close to the stage, I watched as the male dancer attempted to lift the ballerina from behind. Then I heard a crunch, as he fell to the ground moaning. The curtain was abruptly closed. He had broken his arm, and years of training and devotion were gone in a second.

The musical overtone that shaped my soul had not yet reached its zenith. Forced to leave my beloved cat behind when I moved back to Sydney, I was consoling myself over a cup of tea one day in the local mall. Drawn to a pleasant lady sitting at the next table, I started a conversation. She lived in a street close to mine and invited me over to her place to play with her two ragdoll cats, Jerry and Felix.

It became a weekly occurrence. After one play date, Marie had to rush off because she was late for a rehearsal. A singer, it turned out that she was a member of the Sydney Opera House company. The lady I chatted to over a cup of tea at the mall was a star. Even more wonderful, she gifted me a ticket to the dress rehearsal at the Opera House for every opera she performed in, over ten shows.

Knowing I had issues climbing stairs, she ensured that my ticket was in the front rows of the theatre. It was close to heaven as I watched my new friend, with the voice of an angel, owning the stage. Performances like *La Boheme*, *The Mikado* and *Carmen*. The toreador's grand entrance on the stage on a black horse adorned with gold was hypnotic, as were all the exciting performances.

Marie opened up a whole new world of music to me – opera. Superb voices, grand costumes, fabulous sets and breathtaking music. What better gift to be blessed with? After evening performances, it was pure magic as I walked by the twinkling lights of the Sydney Harbour Bridge in the afterglow of greatness. Under a sky dusted with stars, I was reminded of the sheer wonder of life.

Spirits love rising to a challenge and have a great sense of humour. A friend found her 'dream' man on a dating site but I preferred to stay single. Sitting back on my recliner chair one night, I thought of all the men in my life and issued a cosmic dare. 'In this world of over 8 billion people, there is not *one* man I would be remotely attracted to.' Then it occurred to me that I had yet to add a man from South America. I had cruised around the continent years before but it was too brief to make any connections, and the time was not right.

The cosmic cogs sprang into action. The very next day, there was a buzz on my intercom. It was a delivery, with much more than I expected. He was tall, dark and very sexy, and from Brazil. *Very funny, universe.* You're testing me or else just showing off.

The vision spoke with a dreamy accent. 'I see you're very artistic' he said, looking around my apartment. 'And spiritual,' he added, after spotting some astrology books on the table.

This was a mighty test because this man shone like the sun. My first instinct was to barricade him inside but instead, I remarked, 'You have a lot of Leo energy.' He smiled, confirming that he was a Leo, born in mid-August. Ah, a missing sign in my collection.

It was cruel to tempt me this way. Urges I believed were long gone, roared back into life. Several days later, on my way downstairs, I turned the doorknob three times to leave, only to go back inside because I'd forgotten something. The receptionist was on the phone when I went down so I decided to go outside for some fresh air. When the sliding doors opened, in walked the Brazilian.

At that *exact* moment. It *was* a cosmic conspiracy.

'Can you wait until I come back down?' he asked, anxious to be relieved of his load. It would prove to be a quick delivery and several minutes later he returned.

'Can I have your number?' he asked. I tried hard to look nonchalant as I handed it over, emphasising that if he wanted a chart reading I wouldn't be available for a few weeks. That was not on his mind because *that* night he rang and asked me out for a drink. I was shocked that he was so keen and I invented some excuse not to go. In his 40s, there was a large age gap. Besides, the man worked out and was in great shape. My body had assumed a shape of its own.

One hot breath from him and I was sure to keel over. Over the weeks he persisted, and in the end, I gave in. When he came over, we had an interesting conversation about life paths and fate but sitting on a two-seater lounge, the heat was building up.

In the battle between passion and philosophy, there was no contest. Our liaison was brief but memorable, as his visa ended and he returned to Brazil. My one consolation is that on the fateful day I meet my maker, I will pass over with a satisfied smile on my face!

Not all my wishes were fanciful. One day I blurted out to a friend, 'I want a journalist to contact me!' It was a random thought but that *very* afternoon an email arrived from a journalist. With stories scarce during the pandemic, he'd been searching the internet. Spotting an article about me in Bali, he arranged a phone interview and after sending some photos, a two-page spread appeared in the magazine, with a rather racy title on the cover. '*Wedding shocker. He already had two wives!*' Inside, '*Odyle's surprising story.*'

It was set to get even more surprising. A year later, over lunch with Ingrid, I yelled out, 'I want to do a show on TV based on astrology.' It echoed my frustration at the lack of interesting viewing. That evening Ingrid called me, breathless. 'I just saw a competition to come up with the best original idea for a non-scripted TV show. Entries close in two days!'

I worked hard to enter the contest, along with thousands of others, but I heard nothing the day the results were announced. Then came a 'cosmic urge' to check my Junk mail. There it was. 'Congratulations. You are one of our finalists.' I was ecstatic and quickly worked on the requirements for the next stage of the contest. Even though I didn't win, I received encouraging words from the director of the Australian Academy of Cinema and Television Arts to develop the idea because he believed it could attract a large audience. It provided proof of the power of manifestation, and it is an area to be pursued when the time is right, and the planets align.

Astrology remained my guiding light. On a cruise as a guest speaker at the end of 2019, I shared my prediction that 2020 was set to be a dreadful year. It was inevitable with the volatile merging of fiery Mars, Saturn in its 28-year cycle, and Pluto on its 240 orbital tour de force, sure to upset the cosmic balance. The negative energy engendered by these three powers joining forces ensured destruction, illness and death, and did not bode well.

The outbreak of COVID-19 proved me right as the world shut down. On reflection, I wondered if anyone in the audience had heeded my warnings. I was at the local mall a year later when an elderly woman approached me. 'Are you the lady who did the talks on the ship?' she asked. 'My friend and I loved them. We enjoyed the cruise and were going to book another one in 2020 but you said it was going to be a bad year, so we waited. Thank you so much.'

Such was the accuracy of the astrological predictions that I advised my contact at the shipping company of the date when cruising would resume in Australia. It was a slow return, but I predicted 17 April 2022 as the fortunate date, because beneficial Jupiter joined Neptune, the ruler of the ocean, in its own water sign of Pisces.

Months later, the government gave the green light for cruising to recommence in Australia, on the exact day I predicted. Enough said.

Whatever the quest, spirit stepped in to light my path. While researching material on my family following my parents' death, I was unsure where they first 'met' amid the brutality of the Holocaust. Vital pieces were missing. They had both been in Auschwitz but not at the same time. As Allied troops closed in on the Nazis, inmates were forced to move to concentration camps in Germany. I pored over maps of campsites, to piece together their movements.

Just as I was about to give up the search, an email arrived the same day from an ancestry site, enquiring if the attached document belonged to my family. It was the answer to my prayers – my mother's discharge paper from Dachau concentration camp in Germany, even recording her home address in Hungary. With records rarely kept by the Nazis, or destroyed in an attempt to mask the truth, it restored my faith once more that I was not alone.

The document was so accurate that it even named the sub-camp in Dachau she was confined to – Kaufering 7. Checking the layout and maps it seemed that my father first saw my mother there, while he was on work duty at the same camp. A young girl whose gentle soul still shone through the horror she endured, theirs was a profound love story, a fated union that illustrated without a shadow of a doubt, the power of divine intervention.

When it came time to sell the family home in Sydney after my parents' death, spirits stepped in once again. My parents built their modest home in a nice area of Sydney, on the north shore, in the 1960s, when I had just enrolled in high school. It backed onto a vast bush reserve, on a very steep block of land, with a nice view over the water. The area had been rezoned, so finding the right buyer would be hard because it was not an easy plot to rebuild.

The real estate agent mentioned there were three interested buyers, one an investor, and two couples, and one was the right 'fit'. On the day of the open house, a spirit message came through. 'The book. Put it out.' There were only a few books left on the bookcase and the one that caught my eye was *The History of the Jews* which I placed on the coffee table in the living room. A stack of people walked through the house that day but the agent brought only one couple to meet me, the ones I had chosen.

The husband was buoyant as he said, *'I saw the book.'* The irony was that he hadn't noticed the big picture book added on the coffee table, but one tucked away on the shelf I hadn't seen. A small book, *Jewish Mysticism*. His wife was involved with the Sephardi synagogue in Sydney, akin to my father's roots, and her husband's specialist subject was the Holocaust. When he learnt my parents were Holocaust survivors, it was a done deal. My parents would have been smiling down from heaven, their home in the right hands.

My high school years were spent in that house, with a garden that spread down three levels. It came with the odd poisonous snake and spider, a loud kookaburra with a crazy laugh and a pair of cockatoos that shared breakfast with us on the balcony. Our next-door neighbours were a godsend, Jewish, but without the drama of my own. They became my refuge in times of stress.

The father, Eddie Jaku, became known as *The Happiest Man on Earth*, writing his inspiring book when he turned 100. He devoted his life to rising above the wrongs of the past, receiving an Order of Australia in 2016 and a State memorial when he passed away in 2021. Eddie was an inspiration, and in all the years I never saw him without a twinkle in his eye and a radiant smile. His belief that life is beautiful if you allow it, was his commitment to a better world.

It was the Jewish mantra. *Leave the world a better place because of your presence in it.* As I travelled across the globe, I tried to make sense of a world that failed me at times and exalted me at others. With so much love to give, and so many people of different races and faiths who accepted and loved me, I was blessed. The unlikely bond I shared with Bali, embossed on a map of the world and tied by planetary lines, was lifelong and its roots were deep.

On board my many cruises, the Balinese crew called me 'Jero Mangku', a title of respect as 'wife' to a Hindu holy man. It was an acknowledgement too of my connection to the island, as the author of three books about Bali. One young Balinese man was so moved he shed a tear, never before having heard a foreigner speak his language or share a close bond with his people.

My Balinese waiter on one cruise was shocked when I spoke about the privilege of meeting the King of Blahbatuh and viewing the sacred masks. He exclaimed that he came from that same regency in Bali and had helped make the massive preparations for the esteemed king's cremation. With no idea that the king had passed, I was reminded of his warmth and kindness. Ketut had never seen his king, so when I showed him the photo of the king with me at the book launch for *Bali Magic* he was truly overwhelmed.

On that same cruise, I reunited with the guys in the rock band. They were Indonesian, as many were, super talented and humble, and we restored a strong connection. When the singer spotted me for the first time, seated in the audience in the lounge, he jumped down from the stage and came over to me, placing his forehead on my hand. It was the ultimate gesture of respect to an elder and he had no qualms in doing it openly. The rest of the band followed suit after their set, a reminder of an indelible bond, tinged with mutual respect.

On the Muslim island of Lombok in Indonesia, I recall a conversation with two sisters who had a stall where my cruise ship docked. They sold pearl jewellery and were gracious and sweet. When one tried to guess my age, they both looked amazed as we passed each milestone. The sisters were open-mouthed when the truth was revealed, and taking hold of my hand, one said,

'You are blessed by God.'

'Yes,' the other agreed, 'blessed by God.'

CHAPTER TWENTY-SIX

COME SAIL AWAY

The ocean provided my greatest point of connection to the earth. The urge to cross the seas and discover new places remained, but with age came the fear that I would run out of time to explore them all, or worse still, that my body would collapse under the weight of my eternal longing. How many times had I traversed the earth and how many steps had I taken on my lifelong journey? Perhaps it was not so much the fear of running out of time and energy but rather the dread that there was nothing left to excite me.

In 2023 I set sail once more, determined to circle the globe by ship. As soon as I opened the door to my cabin on *Coral Princess,* I was surprised to find a beautiful arrangement of flowers, along with a plate of canapes. The card read, *'Bon Voyage. P&O Australia.'*

As a guest presenter for the company, I was always spoiled with a fruit basket and bottle of Prosecco on ice in my cabin but this was so unexpected, especially on a sister cruise line, and I felt valued. Sitting on my balcony in the sunshine, the ship's horn blasted as we departed Brisbane on the way to another adventure, a world cruise.

Each morning, with the curtains flung open, I was treated to a different sight. Bound for our first destination, the Indonesian island of Komodo, there was no desire to go ashore after my rat-dragon faceoff decades before. I did not need a rematch. A tender port, it required a trip by lifeboat to get from the ship across to the remote island. Those passengers not on a tour were not allowed to go ashore unaccompanied, for obvious safety reasons.

Our route across Asia, from Singapore to Sri Lanka, was a sweltering heat wave. In Dubai, it was over 45 degrees and the heat soared further in Jordan. Many people on tour to the lost city of Petra were dazed with heatstroke while I sensibly opted for an ice cream resort under palm trees, where I fed a stray cat I named Ringo. Fluffy George, already a hotel fixture joined in for a share of my chicken lunch. Around us, decadent rich ladies on the terrace in veils were smoking *hookah* waterpipes. Presumably, it was flavoured tobacco, but in the past, it had been used with hashish or opium.

Each day spent in port was fascinating, but it was impossible to gain anything but a snapshot of each place. Sadly, we missed out on Oman because of engine trouble, which was just as well because we would have fried in the heat. The Suez Canal, with its miles of parched desert and a queue of ships, was a gateway to another world. The passage through the Mediterranean to Europe was a cultural kaleidoscope, each place embedded with its distinct character.

At our first port, the ship was still experiencing engine issues, so we were forced to bypass Mykonos in Greece. I was craving the sound of my language and a meal of fresh fish and Greek salad at a café by the sea. Instead, the captain tried to make up for the loss with an unexpected stop in Messina in Sicily. There I hired a somewhat battered taxi and portly driver who spoke no English, with saints, churches and cannoli on the agenda.

Dropped off at the town square I chanced upon a wedding inside the cathedral. Sitting quietly in the back pews, I tried to remember a time when I was young naive, and in love for the first time. The bride was radiant, as they most often are, and the groom was grateful that he had found his one true love. Life doesn't always imitate art, but there is poetry in the soul of the Italians, reflected in their lyrical speech and song, so the odds were with them.

Once the young couple made their getaway in a convertible, I took time to explore the interesting façade of the cathedral. The impressive clock in the bell tower struck loudly at midday, capturing my attention. Decorated with a circle of zodiac signs, the clock is the largest and most complex astronomical clock in the world. Apart from its splendid artistry, it was awe-inspiring that the astrological signs were displayed in all their glory on the face of a cathedral.

Rome once again proved too formidable for me. It began when the tour guide on the bus insisted, with her first words, that we didn't forget to tip them. Noted. We were dropped off on the edge of the Vatican, and escorted through a tunnel, with strict instructions that we be back at the meeting point in an hour. The extreme heat caused a brain drain and once in the square, I decided I *had* to see Michelangelo's superb La Pieta statue in St. Peter's Basilica.

The long steep queue was daunting, and ambulances were carting off the feeble. Like a woman possessed, I charged past every bend in the line, shouting '*Mi scusi.* Excuse me.' Even the tough Italians had enough sense to stand aside because I appeared to be a deranged woman suffering from heatstroke, or one who had lost her bag, mobile or grandson. Clearly, I *was* mad for even attempting this feat, but I was rewarded with a flash of artistic genius.

Luckily, my blood pressure dropped by the time we reached France. A lovely jaunt in the French countryside with pretty floral displays, fresh croissants, quaint villages and the scent of roses restored my balance. Sitting outside in a café in Marseilles, a pompous group of men smoking cigars ignored me but when I glammed up with lipstick, a stunning Algerian waitress came over to tell me how beautiful I was. We posed for photos together.

How wonderful it felt to be visible again. Someone *saw* me. It must have been catching because when I returned to the dock, a guy in uniform gave me the 'wink', followed by a come-hither smile. It took me a while to register that I was in France where people had a different perception of life. *Toujours l'amour.* Love always.

It happened again in our next port of Barcelona in Spain, in the duty-free shop, when I got another wink from a rather pleasing Argentinian. At first, I thought the whole region was suffering from an eye affliction but then hid my stick behind the pillar to enhance my glow. I wondered what it would have been like to grow up in a country with men of charm and inherent romance.

With many Australians descended from English and Irish convicts, and proud of it, they were not known for their gentility or courting skills. Still, there was a common bond. In Wales, I was greeted by the town crier and walked arm in arm with a nice young chap who guided me to the church. There the choir was singing the Welsh national anthem and later one of the singers asked if I was a descendant of the American Indians. I bore no resemblance to the Celts, with their red hair and green eyes, so it made sense.

In the rustic seaside town of Cobh in Ireland, the driver took me to the cathedral and then to a cemetery, where some victims of the sinking of the RMS *Lusitania* lay buried. A British ship torpedoed off the coast of Ireland in 1915, during the First World War, and a memorial stood proud in the town square. There were none of the large crowds in Belfast Northern Ireland for the *Titanic* exhibit.

When the waitress in town complained that it was too hot, I laughed. We'd weathered a heat wave and it was quite brisk by comparison.

There was no chance of a walk in the highlands of Scotland and little opportunity to spot any monsters in Loch Ness, smell the blooming roses along the way or sing a plaintiff song about taking the 'high road'. Just as I made it to the lake's shore, it was time to turn around and limp back to the coach before it left, abandoning me on a 'low road'. There was not even time to buy an ice cream, to give me the sugar high I needed to sustain life.

In a small, crowded café in Dover, England, a sweet elderly lady insisted I sit beside her and then went to the counter to stand in line to order my lunch. My stick was wedged behind a pot plant and I was trapped behind some foliage. Then she told me about her life as we sat in the welcome sunshine. She may have been lonely but instead of wallowing in it, she made a point of chatting to strangers and being the epitome of English gentility and kindness.

Dover was the halfway point on our world cruise, with new people boarding. It was a relief because there were so many downcast faces among the first lot of passengers. Most were past their prime and had taken their disillusion with them, along with their luggage. Others were content with an ordinary life and we had nothing in common. Their conversation mirrored the loss, 60 days on a ship comprised of subjects that gathered no more glamour for being on the ocean. Nothing saucy, nothing to sink your teeth into. Surely there was a raunchy episode to provide the occasional bright spot.

One day in the dining room I was enjoying afternoon tea when a group, fresh off a farm in rural Victoria, sat down near me. Just as I was about to bite into my ham sandwich, farmer Jack launched into a loud monologue on the best way to kill a pig. *'Knock them on the head, stun them and then skin them.'* Almost choking I decided it was God's retribution for not being a good Jew, as Jack went onto the part about how to slaughter a rabbit.

The next onslaught came over dinner that evening when three Aussies at a table close by held three Americans hostage with their in-depth dissertation about endoscopies and other invasive procedures in which to discover the contents of your bowel. Jolly Bruce kept the other Aussies rapt with his entrails, sorry, tales, while the Americans surprisingly remained polite, secretly praying that an iceberg would hit the other half of the table and submerge Bruce and the other two into the bowels of the earth and consume them.

At this stage, I buried my head in my serviette, and retrieving my phone as my salvation, played the sensual version of 'I Love It When You Call Me Senorita' into my ear, to quell any words that could potentially ruin my soul. I practised seductive dance moves to the song, in my mind, to ignite a passion inside me slowly dying.

Redemption came later in the cruise, in Ecuador, after the joy of being called young lady, or *senorita*, in Spanish. I was impressed when local men, including security in balaclavas, took my hand to help me get down the curb. These polite gestures in a country where a presidential candidate had just been shot and killed, did not go unnoticed. There was no way that Jack or Bruce would have taken my hand, and there was no way I would accept theirs considering where they had recently been. Such are the vagaries of life.

The ship's captain, trying to make up for not stopping in the Shetland Islands, sailed through the glacial passage from Iceland to Greenland. On a picture-perfect day, I sat spellbound on my balcony as huge chunks of ice drifted by. I feasted on snacks and drank icy

Coke, as icebergs and giant white slabs fell off the mountains and tumbled into the sea. It was one of those rare moments where you focus on a scene that will remain with you forever.

We were blessed with the weather, each day sunnier than the last. The contrast of the white snow against the blue sky became sharper as did my senses, energized by the crisp fresh air. It was spring and Iceland was in full bloom. My morning in Reykjavik was spent at the botanic gardens, replete with arctic blooms, a cavalcade of pink, mauve and white flowers and subtle alpine scents. This was followed by a tour of a nearby town which was so clean and pristine it looked like a painting perfectly executed in watercolour.

The tender boat ride over to the shores of Greenland was on smooth seas and the stroll to the small town nearby was pleasant, especially as it was a day of celebration. There were balloons, music and games. The local people were mostly Inuit, some mixed with Danish, and they remained distant, understandable with the constant stream of ships. When I entered the small church, it was surprising to find a Jewish menorah, a seven-branched candelabra, on the altar. The pastor explained it symbolised the Jewish roots of Christianity.

During our voyage, we crossed the Arctic Circle and received a ship's certificate to add to one celebrating our crossing of the Equator on our first leg to Singapore. Later, as we cruised across the Pacific, came the final accolade for traversing the International Date Line. Ours had been an incredible journey. The highs had been fabulous and some of the lows had unexpected outcomes.

CHAPTER TWENTY-SEVEN

I'VE GOT THE MUSIC IN ME

It all began on my tour of Dubai when a small, mad blonde banshee pushed into the front seat of the coach next to me. Deranged Milicent, clutching her straw boater, refused to let me out of my seat.

'There are *other* people who have to get off,' she barked, like a rabid corgi, before treading on my foot and throwing an empty water bottle at me. I was in imminent peril so I needed to escape.

When I finally broke through, trying to get down the steps, an old fellow shoved me from behind. 'Just get out of the way!' he yelled, causing me to lose my balance. This man was obviously on a serious mission. Probably a meeting with a rich oil sheik, or a local bitcoin dealer. *Enough was enough.* No one was ever going to harass, or abuse, me again and I was fed up with rudeness.

Getting on and off tour buses is one of the riskiest feats one can undertake in a lifetime. Steep steps, better suited for a frisky athlete training for a decathlon, are the first hurdle to overcome. A wooden box would suffice to give you a leg up but is not permitted because of 'liability' issues, which is ridiculous because the risk of injury is much greater if you do a swan dive headfirst onto the ground. You are in danger of breaking a leg, jolting your new hip or losing your dignity. A walking stick is essential for staying upright on tricky bits or fending off a feral mob heading straight for you.

Out there in the real world, there is no time to be delicate or precious. Our guide in Dubai, in his bid to get to the gold market, raced ahead leaving several people with limited mobility behind as he bolted down two flights of stairs. It was the only way to get across the highway and there were another two flights on the other side. With no choice but to rejoin the coach, we turned to see the driver take off, and Milicent waving from the front seat. It was Vietnam all over again but this time I had company, which misery prefers.

Ready to expire in the extreme heat we spotted an enclosed air-conditioned bus stop. It was crammed with smelly sweaty people. I collapsed on top of a group of Indian boat drivers, who finally gave up one of their seats. By the time we were reunited with our coach, even Milicent had the sense to shut up and move over. At least this episode led to greater things. And his name was Raoul.

Raoul, one of the ship's officers, was the sort of man to put a smile on your face. He had inherited the charm of the Latin American people, and there was an energetic attraction between us. His warm touch had a healing effect, alerting my hormones to the presence of a real man. The man you would marry if you had to do it all again, or at least dally and flirt with behind the hacienda and dream about later that night while dancing to 'Bésame Mucho'.

When Raoul heard my tale of woe, it became his mission to protect me. Allowing me to disembark before the rest of the mob, he helped me onto the waiting coach and waved goodbye with a smile that made my heart soar. When he turned to see me heading his way, he touched his heart and gave me a giant hug when I reached him. Raoul was not afraid to carry on this charade in public, our own racy telenovela, and I loved playing the part.

A splendid rare few souls in the world possess a healing touch. Their aura is bright, and their touch sensational, a reflection of their character. Raoul often gave me a giant hug when least expected, reflecting the breadth of his energy. My angst subsided as if by magic. You know you are in the company of a special person when their presence is enough to uplift your spirit. Raoul became my champion, my Ivanhoe and my knight in shining armour. My link to humanity.

Among the blossoms and maple trees of our next five ports in Canada, there was a refreshing sense of space and nature and it was wonderful to ease the pace for a while. The scent of fresh air was invigorating, as was the serenity. Our time in Quebec was far too rushed to be fully appreciated but it was embedded with history and culture, its French flavour adding class. I was beginning to feel balanced again and the country commanded a return visit.

Our next port of call was New York. Having visited the city decades ago it was a daunting prospect, too rushed and raw for me. This time I was meeting my second cousin, Shirley, after many years. She was coming down by train from Connecticut so I had something to look forward to. We last met in the 1980s in Israel, and with relatives scarce, I was happy for this opportunity to catch up.

Anxious about meeting her on time, and the process of clearing US immigration, with busy terminals involving long distances and crowds, I approached the Guest Services desk to see if there would be any assistance available at the port. Traumatised after some dreadful experiences in the past, any help would be appreciated.

Airline terminals were the worst. At times, my pain was so intense it triggered heat sensors, leading to dreadful pat downs and confrontations with officious airline and customs staff, in full view of a long line of irritated passengers. It was humiliation at its worst.

In Singapore, on this cruise, an elderly lady in front of me in the queue, waiting for immigration, collapsed in the extreme heat and hit her head on the cement. She was carted off by ambulance. I was about to pass out too but when I finally reached the terminal door, the port authorities allowed me to bypass the line. There was no ship's crew close by to monitor the situation, as was often the case.

Now, when I enquired about assistance, the Guest Supervisor was gruff. 'You have to get a ticket and wait like everyone else. Our wheelchair guys can only take you as far as Immigration anyway.' This rude gent could not be swayed to show any humanity. Then he fired the final arrow. 'You seem to be standing up all right now.'

My pain was overshadowed by the anger rising inside me. Was this man so ignorant and arrogant to dare assume the state of another person? I was proud of how I continued to travel despite the mounting challenges. While I may be smiling on the outside, my inner issues were confronting and taking their toll.

When Raoul passed by soon after, he saw that I was upset. 'Wait here,' he said after I poured out my heart. Then he went into a back office, and emerged a short time later, with the Guest Manager. He apologised and promised to sort it out.

When we reached New York, I should not have worried. The universe had my back. I was met by an unlikely vision – Reggie, in a halo of light, strode off the gangway and walked straight over to me as I got out of the ship's elevator, with a welcoming smile.

'Hi there ma'am, would you like a ride in my wheelchair? I can take you through Immigration, the terminal and across the road to the taxi stand.' Angelic music surged around me and although Reggie nearly dropped me onto the busy highway on the way to the taxi, he was, no doubt, sent by heaven as earthly angels often are.

New York was not as threatening as I remembered, and the city's energy was dynamic. After admiring a string of vibrant art galleries, I strolled through Central Park with my cousin Shirley as we reminisced on the past. Ours was a wonderful reunion over lunch. My taxi drive back to the port did not disappoint my expectations, the driver erupting into an aggressive tirade at the policeman who booked him for inching over a pedestrian crossing.

Back on board the ship, I sat on my balcony overlooking the naval museum, with the US flags a reminder of the country's might. The fighter jets and submarines had been the setting for a party the previous night, and I sang along to the live band while sipping on a fruity mocktail. As the ship pulled out of the dock, we sailed out of the harbour past the iconic Statue of Liberty as a silvery sun set over the horizon. Few moments in life can compete with such a vision.

It is not only sights but also sounds that define a place and time. Music has the power to shape memories and uplift or calm the spirit. However, heavy rock for breakfast at the buffet in the morning was my worst nightmare. Noise had the power to crucify my soul. No, *my beds were not burning*, but my cabin *did* flood at times.

Most of those in charge were receptive to my request for something soothing to shape the mood and not trigger a headache, an odd rude one was belligerent and unyielding, while a special few went out of their way to be gracious and kind, like Stefan from Serbia.

The maître d' of the dining room, charming Stefan took the time to find me a quiet table where I could sit alone by the window and not be disturbed. Next to the window, the wall behind me offered security from being bumped. The lights were subdued and I was not seated under a speaker. My hearing was super acute, and I had a decibel rating similar to that of a cat, or a bat in a dark cave.

Over dinner one night, I counted over 20 sounds. Conversations from the surrounding tables, clinking glasses, cutlery chucked into a drawer, footsteps, trays, revolving doors, plates dropped in the kitchen and the occasional singing waiter. As for raucous Maureen at a far table, anyone as distant as the lobby could not fail to hear her hysterical laughter. Her cackle could outdo a demented cockatoo or a flaming galah in labour. Her laugh would repel a hurricane and propel it onto another course in the opposite direction.

It was my habit to make a grand entrance into the restaurant for dinner, preferring to hold onto a gentleman's arm, particularly when the boat was rocking. Stefan, in his crisp white jacket, was my escort of choice. As we passed by tables, he smiled as ladies whispered, 'Who is *she*?' Having lost any shred of romance with their partners, they were jealous of the attention. For me, touch broke down formal barriers allowing a welcome level of intimacy. Besides, I was reliving a scene from *Hello Dolly* and making a stirring entry.

It was Stefan who started my search for identity through music. With his love of the blues, one night he suggested my song be, 'The Sensitive Kind'. He couldn't have been more accurate for he understood that life could be hard for someone so delicate and that I needed to be treated gently. His concern proved that he too was sensitive, to recognise my needs and then go the extra mile to *care*.

Inspired, I approached Raoul the next day. 'What song do you think personifies me?' I asked, hoping it wasn't some desperate dirge or a mournful ballad about jumping off a bridge. I was grateful that afternoon when he handed me the lyrics of his chosen song. 'Happy'. 'You make my day light up,' he said with a smile.

When I put the same question to the spirited young Columbian, Carlos, at the Guest Services desk he mulled over it. We engaged in conversation whenever he was not busy, and I learnt that he was not familiar with Western music, except for more recent songs. There was a mistaken belief on my part that everyone had heard of the Beatles. Spanish music had its own rich and dynamic catalogue.

The song Carlos chose for me was 'Vivir Mi Vide', translated as 'Live my Life'. I loved that he perceived me that way, living life to the fullest. Yes, I am going to dance, laugh and enjoy life. I smiled when Carlos said, 'Apart from my ex-girlfriend of seven months, you are the longest relationship I've ever had with a woman.' His definition of a relationship was dubious at best but I had been on the ship for months, so at least we'd bonded!

When it came to the crew on the ship, they all had an obvious affinity with the ocean, the realm of Neptune. They all came from different backgrounds searching for something that eluded their earth-bound friends. Theirs was a special vibration, the sound of the waves crashing and receding into the chasm of their soul.

Also ruled by the Neptunian vibration were musicians, and those performers who came on board at each port embodied the essence of their culture. A group of male singers from Jordan with their poignant melody were at odds with the sensual belly dancers in Dubai. A guitarist from Greece, with hands bestowed by the gods, strummed his instrument with grace, while a singer from Spain had a supreme voice, followed by a troop of fiery flamenco dancers. Then came the lively Irish jig, singers from Wales in ancient dialects and bagpipes from the highlands of Scotland, along with a touch of English rock. They were all so different, and so talented,

A brilliant pianist, Julian, a young man from Romania, was on board for the entire world cruise. A child prodigy, he held the audience captive each evening, pouring his emotions into the piano. His genius was so overwhelming that it consumed him, and when he played he transcended into an altered level of consciousness.

When we first met, Julian was a victim of his beliefs, ranting religious platitudes and conspiracy theories, most involving 20 powerful Jews who ruled the world. I sighed, having to deal with such irrational bias once more. He seemed so closed off and stubborn.

Despite the odds, our friendship evolved. He was born in Transylvania, but while scanning a map of the region, it was a shock to find that he was born only a short distance from my mother's family home. There seemed to be a strange karmic bond between us.

Fate pushed us together, and in a small town in Canada, I found Julian sitting alone on the rooftop garden of the municipal chambers. After our usual banter, we headed off on a bus going to Walmart. Shopping days on the cruise were rare so this was a real treat. It was surprising that Julian chose to remain close while I shopped. When we got to the cashier counter I panicked, realising I'd left my wallet on the ship. Julian paid for me. He then went off to find a taxi when I was about to pass out in the long queue for the bus.

Over time, the bricks and mortar surrounding Julian came tumbling down. He still retained his gruff exterior, exchanging witty retorts, until it became part of a game we played. I had never met a man who I wanted to slap so much. No doubt he would have enjoyed it. We were always finding ways to touch or pretend not to, the force between us overpowering. That energy even showed up in photos.

One evening, in fine form, Julian got up after his last set to mingle with his 'fans'. As he walked by me, I grabbed him. 'Don't touch me, woman,' Julian said, with a flurry, swirling an imaginary cloak. I laughed but then turned around to face Medusa, a grand dame in her 80s, looking down her fine aristocratic nose at me as the wrinkles on her face turned to granite. After clearing her throat decisively, she muttered. '*Outrageous*. Simply outrageous.'

'Madam, don't be so judgemental.' I replied. 'It doesn't become you.' Her elderly husband lay back on the lounge and said nothing, used to her scorn after umpteen decades. Later I ran a thousand responses through my head, as we all tend to do after an altercation to see whether we could have done better. Then a giant gong went off in my head. In reality, this abysmal woman had paid me a huge compliment and put me back on the right track.

Outrageous. Yes. Not dull, dreary or normal. All my life I'd been outrageous. How else could I have met all those fabulous pop stars way back when, bluffed my way into press conferences and television studios? Or become a top fashion designer, been lauded by spirit, acknowledged by kings and politicians, and flown to Jakarta for a press conference, all the while repelling dangerous spells.

How else had I outlived brain and spinal surgery, a deadly dose of dengue, all alone and isolated? Despite the pain, I travelled around the world and gave talks in theatres, with the capacity to change lives and paint smiles on young girls' faces. And what about those amazing men who fell hard for my love? Yes. *Outrageous*.

As for Julian, he went from an arrogant young man who accused me, as a Jew and an astrologer, of consorting with demons, to an advanced level of maturity. Responding to my request to play a song for Jewish New Year, he resisted, in his usual petulant stance but on the night, he looked at me from behind the fort of his grand piano and played a lively version of 'Hava Nagila', the Jewish folk song of celebration. It was followed by a stellar rendition of one of the greatest songs of all time, 'Halleluiah', by Jewish composer Leonard Cohen. When Julian finished, he looked over at me and smiled.

Afterwards, I invited him to dine with me to celebrate the New Year, expecting a brusque refusal but he surprised me when he said yes. Stefan had gone out of his way to meet my request for Rosh Hashanah, the chef making round challah bread with raisins, and apples dipped in honey, symbolising the wish for a sweet year ahead. I had looked it up in my mission to be more Jewish, the auspicious date marking the creation of the world and the start of a new cycle.

Over dinner, I asked Julian to choose 'my' song. Without hesitation, he said 'Kiss from a Rose'. He was so accurate and astute for this was my song with Agus. I *was* the light on the dark side of him, apparently having the same effect on Julian.

He didn't flinch as he came up with the next song, 'Black Velvet'. I loved that song, the music flowing like melted molasses. 'You're soft like velvet with a dark edge,' Julian explained. 'Velvet is smooth and sophisticated; black is dark, solid, impenetrable and deep. You are the juxtaposition of light and dark. You have surmounted so many obstacles, so much darkness, to *be* the light.'

There could be no greater compliment. Nor could the pointed stares from Raoul when I was in deep conversation with Julian, and the glances from Carlos pretending to look the other way. The energy was invigorating and there was definitely the glimmer of lust.

The weather remained perfect for the rest of the cruise, and the seas were rarely rocky. Each day I stared across the vast ocean, looking for signs of life. Apart from the occasional bird and fleet of flying fish, it was only near Peru that there were several dolphin and whale sightings. This vast underwater kingdom that covered most of the earth preferred to remain a mystery and provided few clues to its silent wanderings and the elements that ruled over it.

Our passage through the Panama Canal was in stark contrast to the Suez. It was lush and green with American crocodiles sighted along the shore while the Suez was dry and chalky with few signs of life. Our first stop in South America was Manta in Ecuador.

There I hired a taxi driver, one regulated by the port. He spoke no English so instead we sang songs in Spanish to pass the time. As we drove through an eerie part of town, where many homes lay deserted, the feeling was dark and desolate. Manuel used gestures as we stood outside a church, to mimic a soaring plane and then an explosion. Twenty years before a cargo plane clipped the bell tower of the church, crashing into the houses below with many casualties.

In Lima, Peru, there was a strange vibe near the port, with police standing guard at the crossroads. The edginess lifted in the swanky suburbs by the ocean, as another side of the city was revealed. This was a place of contrasts with so much more to explore.

At the next port of Pisco in Peru, after a drive past endless stark dunes, I sat at a café overlooking the bay, indulging in spicy chicken and rice and a large fresh strawberry shake. After browsing the stalls, I stopped to chat with a young man sitting on the sea wall. He was striking in looks, many of the people here were a mix of Quechua Indians, descendants of the Incas and Spanish-speaking *mestizos,* along with a blend of European and Asian races.

When we set sail across the Pacific, the ocean seemed endless. The ocean had her moods, serene and majestic, turbulent and mighty, but when she merged with the heavens it was God's tapestry. Clouds peppered the sky in a kaleidoscope of colour, the vivid sunsets leaving a trail of silver stars in their wake. Each night proved more hypnotic than the last.

We cruised for days until reaching Easter Island. As a tender port, it was tricky to reach. With rough seas, the captain announced that only those who were fit should attempt to make the journey across because of the large swell. I already had my tender ticket, number 47, but after the captain's warning, I went back to bed. Announcements could *not* be heard in the cabin, so I drifted off to sleep. Several hours later, I was awoken by a voice calling out number 47. It was a sign. I jumped up and headed for the lower deck.

Luckily, the sea had calmed so I braved the trip across by boat. Then it was a stroll along a stretch of coastline, stopping to rest beside one of over 1,000 massive stone megaliths unique to Easter Island. These moai statues were created around 1400 by the Rapa Nui, the natives of the island. Each moai, with its prominent head, depicts the spirit of a deceased person, usually a chieftain, placed so they can continue to watch over their people.

Dogs roamed free on the island, and one, Pedro, nuzzled up beside me and followed me as I watched turtles hover in the shallow water. After a delicious batch of fresh prawns and chips in a local restaurant, Sofia, the hostess, helped me down the steps outside, where Pedro was waiting for the next stage of our journey. We were both happy just basking in the sun, soothed by the sound of the rolling waves on one of the most remote islands in the world.

The next stage of the voyage took us across a vast expanse of ocean to Papeete. The beautiful islands of Tahiti, studded in the ocean, are the soul's poetry. Captain Cook had science on his mind when he arrived on these islands in 1769 to record the transit of Venus on his first voyage around the world. During this transit, Venus appears as a small black disc travelling across the Sun and only occurs every 243 years. Cook's efforts were in vain because the haze or shadow around Venus blurred his images, and his quest failed.

The goddess Venus guards her secrets well, making them far more alluring. The night before Tahiti, I had the strongest urge to go out on the balcony at midnight. In the still silence, the ship carved a delicate path through the water, like a blunt knife cutting through butter. There was no line of separation between the ocean and the heavens and the two merged into a veil of soft indigo velvet, concealing the earth in the softest shades of serenity.

Stars twinkled up above but there was one that lit up the sky. It shone like a beacon, salvation to a lonely sailor or pod of dolphins. Was this bright star the planet Venus, the capricious goddess who spun the sky with magic? A tempting mistress, she blessed lives with love and enchantment and lured both young and old into liaisons too alluring to resist.

After landing in Papeete the next morning, I wandered through the streets to the marketplace. There, beautiful girls performed the 'Ori Tahiti'. With their pink straw skirts and long black hair, they danced sensuously to the beating of the drums. In my mind I swayed along with them, grateful that I shimmied while I could. The dance is so provocative that the missionaries banned it, but luckily Venus passed it on in secret through the generations.

Days later our ship reached Pitcairn Island, one of four volcanic islands that form the sole British Overseas Territory in the Pacific. Only Pitcairn is inhabited, with about 50 residents, descendants of a handful of mutineers and their Tahitian consorts. In April 1789, the mutiny on HMS *Bounty*, saw Captain Bligh, along with 18 loyal crew, set adrift in a small boat. Incredibly they survived a turbulent trip of 3500 nautical miles to reach Timor Island.

Pitcairn had heavy rain for two weeks but we brought the sunshine. No one was allowed on shore but a relative of the people of Pitcairn was on the ship and she chatted over the loudspeaker to the locals, giving us an insight into their existence. New Zealand was our final stop. I was in such a glorious state, I didn't want it to end. Fortunately, there was a cabin available for the next 21-day cruise to Hawaii, so without hesitation I booked it.

It would be foolish to end this marvellous journey, and the lure of the Hawaiian islands was too tempting. Add the stunning island of Moorea in Tahiti, untouched American Samoa, and then Fiji, and the Bay of Islands in New Zealand and there was little doubt. Besides, my birthday was coming up and I wanted to celebrate in style.

Nothing could replace the sense of peace I felt in my cabin. Many hours were spent alone with my thoughts, inspiring bouts of writing and reflection. It was interrupted only by breakfast or room service, and the urge to go out on my balcony and soak in the view.

Bliss, except for one morning when I awoke, still sleepy, and put my feet on the carpet. They were underwater. Worried that the ship had sprung a leak, or worse still that it was sinking, there was no need to panic. A water pipe had burst during the night, and mine was one of three cabins affected. Through adversity and challenge, love and sheer wonder, it was a trip to remember.

The cruise was not to end without a final climax, one that I could never have imagined. When planetary forces kick in, anything is possible, and Venus hovering overhead ensures a sociable time, lots of fun and happiness. Add Mars, and an explosive burst of sexual tension, then prepare to turn up the heat. Nothing could have prepared me for what lay ahead.

The compliments on formal nights were welcome, as were the furtive looks and the occasional 'wow' as I walked by, all sequins and glamour. It had been a long time since I'd attracted such attention. Then the icing on the cake – an anonymous note left on my dining table. Written on it was, 'Your song'. Inside was the title, as raunchy as two words can be and I was reeling in anticipation.

After dinner, I retreated to my cabin to listen to the song. The lyrics were all sensual innuendo and blazing passion. The object of this man's attention had no clue how sexy she was or the effect her eyes had on him. She kept him burning hot, flush with desire. The words kept me awake as my mind whirled with possibilities.

After all these years, now over 70, was I still *hot*? The object of men's fantasies. Did I still have the power to ignite, excite, and burn bright? Even with my walking stick? With all the trials over the years, my flame was just a flicker. Yet despite all I'd been through, I was still *desirable*. I was sexy, sweet, sane, sultry, seductive and sensitive. My nerves may be on fire but I could still incite passion.

According to society, wasn't this the time to be put out to pasture or motor through remote deserts in a caravan? No!!! My hair was still dark, long and shiny, not grey and thinning! My skin was soft and smooth and my spirit was effervescent, forever 18.

Mars was having a field day when I stumbled upon my secret admirer in the atrium, and his look said it all. It is one thing to be undressed by a man's eyes but his were making mad passionate love to me. My body reeled from the impact of his fantasies.

The burst of sex appeal was about to detonate a few days later when we reached Auckland in New Zealand, hardly considered the sex capital of the world. After the ship docked, and a brief dalliance with Raoul when I exited the terminal, I took a stroll along the water's edge until reaching a string of restaurants and loud pubs.

I sought refuge in the café at the Maritime Museum. A guy came in at the same time and grabbed a coffee, and we shared a table and started to chat. In his 40s and an attractive man, fair with hazel eyes and a wry smile, James was polite and well-read and wanted to learn more about my books. It was rare to have an intelligent exchange. He was also a music fan, impressed when I spoke about the pop stars I met during the '60s. I could see his mind ticking over as he calculated my age but it didn't seem to faze him.

When it was time to go, James helped me into a taxi and fastened my seatbelt. Then he rushed off to the movies while I headed back to the ship. The driver was not so cordial and demanded $30 to drive me to the pier close by. I previously had issues with offensive taxi drivers in the city, so I decided to walk back to the ship.

Resting along the way, I paused several times to admire the harbour view. When I finally made it to the entrance of the terminal, a solitary man stood at the doorway. It was James. 'I thought you went to the movies,' I remarked, surprised to see him.

James must have been standing there for some time considering how long it had taken me to get back. The mystery unravelled as the conversation heated up.

'It's so rare to find a kindred soul,' James began, 'I feel very connected to you.'

'That's so nice,' I replied, wondering where this was leading.

'You're a very sexy lady. If I weren't married, I'd invite you to dinner.' Words escaped me, as my mind hit the pause button. With the ship set to depart soon, dinner was highly unlikely and besides, he was married, but James had laid all his cards out on the table.

'That's most flattering,' I replied, taking a step back.

'I couldn't help notice when I helped you into the taxi that,' his voice tapered off. James diverted his gaze to my cleavage which appeared to have fuelled his fantasies. Never one to flaunt my assets, I could not understand all the attention or strange obsession.

Still, the searing look in his eyes said it all. James made it clear that he wanted to take it one step further. Perhaps his latest read was *50 Shades of Grey* but there was no intimidation involved or coercion, but rather two adults making their own decisions. Not in the mood for a casual fling and far too fragile for a quick grope behind the shipping terminal, I replied, 'I think you may have just crossed the line,' and then turned and walked away.

In a way, it *was* flattering, in another strangely disturbing.

This influx of interest from so many men was something I had never experienced before, certainly not at the same time. Mars was on full throttle in the heavens, boosting enough pheromones to last lifetimes. This was a well-needed tonic for a woman who believed the best had passed, the scandals of my youth only a faint memory.

CHAPTER TWENTY-EIGHT

HOLY OF HOLIES

Each Friday on the ship there was a Shabbat service at sunset for those of the Jewish faith. I resisted at first but then decided it was worth another try to connect with my people. Up till now that innate sense of belonging eluded me, and mine was an identity forged by adversity and loss. Wine, candles and twisted loaves of bread on the table of the small chapel set the mood.

Twelve people sat in a circle but few of them looked Jewish. After introductions, I was correct. Two were Seventh-day Adventists wishing to observe, while several were Christian. Wild redhead Rhonda, flush with tattoos, announced she was a bikie from Melbourne interested in discovering different faiths, having already been to the Hare Krishnas. Kudos to them for wanting to learn, but I felt more like a specimen than a Jew. Especially so when a rather dull lady, lacking in spirit, read Hebrew prayers aloud.

Years before on a cruise to New Caledonia, I stood on the deck of the ship immersed in a stunning purple sunset, when a feeling of sadness swept over me. It was the holiest day of the Jewish year – Yom Kippur, the Day of Atonement. It follows nine days after the Jewish New Year, Rosh Hashanah, and marks the end of the High holy days. It is a time of reflection, as God seals your fate for the coming year. I had yet to recognise my purpose let alone my fate and on this, the most sacred day, I felt more lost than ever.

Absorbed in my thoughts, a song came onto the big screen on the deck that could not have been more apt, 'Losing my religion'. A single tear erupted into a flood as the words resonated in my soul. I looked up at the first star to bless the night sky. In Judaism, days begin at dusk, not dawn, so Yom Kippur had begun. More stars lit up a pathway to heaven and I felt the presence of the divine.

Images of my first visit to Jerusalem in Israel were mirrored in the calm ocean, casting me back in time to when I prayed at the Western Wall, the only remnant of the retaining wall of the Temple Mount. This was the site of the First Temple of the Jews. Built in 957 BCE, during the reign of King Solomon, it housed the sacred Ark of the Covenant that held the Ten Commandments.

The Temple was destroyed by the Babylonians in 586 BCE and the Jews of the Kingdom of Judea were exiled. They returned to build the Second Temple on the original site in 515 BCE. Centuries later, in 70 CE, the Romans destroyed the temple and renamed Judea, Syria Palestina in the 2nd century, to humiliate and remove any trace of its original Jewish presence. This term referred to the Philistines, early Greeks who inhabited the south of the Land of Canaan.

History, like the remnants of the wall, is cast in stone. The Western Wall, all that remains of the two destroyed temples, is a sacred place of prayer and is the holiest site for the Jewish people. The Islamic shrine, the Dome of the Rock, stands on the top of the mount, its golden dome glistening in the piercing sun. It was built centuries later, on top of the original site of the Jewish temples.

Within its walls, the wails from the Al-Aqsa mosque echo the faith of the Muslims gathered inside in prayer. On the other side of the old city of Jerusalem stands the Church of the Holy Sepulchre, one of the holiest sites in Christianity. It is believed to hold the tomb where Jesus was buried and then resurrected. This fusion of faiths in Jerusalem is profound and is rarely replicated.

While there is grandeur in these buildings, the Jews had to be content with the remains of a wall. Still, there is godliness in simplicity and a block of stone embodies more than its physical presence. A stone beneath his head triggered Jacob's dream of a ladder that led to heaven. A single stone enabled David to slay the giant Goliath, and stones, not flowers, are placed on Jewish graves because of their permanence, and as a mark of respect.

Enveloped in a cloud of pious devotion at the Western Wall, swarming with young girls and women, I placed my note into a stony nook. Separated from the men, they recited from the Torah while placing slips of paper into the rock crevices, scrawled prayers of hope. With their hair covered, many were in a state of rapture, while part of me felt like a fraud because I was not familiar with the holy book of Judaism. My wish was a timeless one – peace in this land of hope and heartache, and in all places of war and conflict, along with closure for my family and forgiveness for those who sinned.

It was hard to comprehend the significance of the wall, but it became clearer when I joined a small group for an underground tour. There was a palpable energy in the tunnel beneath the wall as if the past were embodied in an ancient literary script captured in every block of stone. The Foundation Stone is the heart of the Holy of Holies and is believed to have once held the sacred Ark of the Covenant. Some believe that the Ark now lies beneath the Stone, in a cavern known as the Well of Souls, but it can never be excavated.

In ancient times, only the High Priest, in white, was permitted to enter the Holy of Holies, and only on the day of Yom Kippur. The Ark, gilded in gold, contained the two stone tablets of the Ten Commandments, a pot of manna, protection for the Children of Israel, and the staff of the first High Priest. The wings of two angels, sculpted in gold, were outstretched on the top of the Ark, raising the holy presence for this was the spiritual junction of Heaven and Earth, the hallowed place where God could dwell on Earth.

The stones in the wall were laid out in perfect alignment without any need for cement, one slab so huge that it was impossible to fathom how it got there. Pausing to absorb the energy, and to rest, the tour leader's voice became a faint drone in the distance. I followed the group along the narrow underground trail, dodging rocky ledges to navigate the path, but by the time I reached them, they were already retracing their steps back to the Jewish Quarter.

The guide advised me there was an exit further along, a doorway into the Muslim Quarter. She warned it could be crowded but it was the fasting month of Ramadan, and most people were praying or resting in the heat of the day until the fast was broken at sunset. The door between the Jewish and Muslim Quarters was locked at night for security. The street was deserted when I exited.

Deciding to walk in the other direction, I rested while watching a film about the history of the area in a monastery close by. Now in the Christian Quarter of the old city, I walked slowly along the cobblestone street, sipping my water, while shielding myself from the glare of the hot sun. Looking up at the sign above me, I was shocked to see *Via Dolorosa* – The Way of Sorrow. It was the path that Jesus took en route to his crucifixion and death.

Silence. Sheer silence. There were no muffled screams or stirring protests from the ghosts of the past, or echoes of the Roman soldiers as they drove Christ onwards. There were no Christian faithful re-enacting history, carrying the burden of the crucifixion cross. Not the tremor of a single footstep, the surge of righteousness, rampant tour groups or the solitary call of a bird. I took time to reflect because few places in the world had such an impact.

Overwhelmed, I carried on till I reached a crossroads of narrow laneways crammed with busy market stalls, pulsing with people of all races, faiths and costumes, many heading towards the Armenian Quarter of the old city. It was not the shops of rare jewels that caught my eye but rather the stalls packed with stacks of delicious halvah – crushed sesame seed and sugar, streaked with pistachio and chocolate. I extracted enough energy from a large chunk to climb the steep path that led to the Christian gateway out of the old city.

My final stop was the Church of the Holy Sepulchre. Inside were priests of many denominations and worshippers overcome with emotion. Some, shaken to their very core, were draped over a slab of rock near the entrance where the body of Jesus had been laid out. Being in the presence of such a powerful relic, I knelt to touch the stone, but unlike the others who were prostrate with grief, there was no divine revelation or surge of energy.

Several priests at the doorway yelled for us to move because a religious procession was entering the church. The pilgrims scurried away while I slowly made my way around the church corridors, past the Rock of Calvary, encased in glass at the Altar of the Crucifixion.

When I joined the queue to enter the shrine where Jesus was believed to be buried before his resurrection, a Russian couple pushed in front of me. Instead of lashing out, I repeated '*forgiveness*', over and over, in keeping with my blessed surroundings.

It begged an age-old question, one that deserved an answer. Years ago, on a bus tour in Sydney, a short, mediocre woman asked me over tea, if 'I felt guilty for killing Christ', a Jew himself. I wasn't sure if she meant personally or collectively.

I muffled my response, for she was Italian and shirked the responsibility of the Romans in his death. It was only the Romans who used crucifixion as punishment but facts rarely matter. The idea of the collective guilt of the Jews for the death of Christ was officially repudiated by the Second Vatican Council in 1965, and later in a book written by Pope Benedict.

Two questions loomed large in my mind. As a Christian, why didn't she practice its basic tenets of love and forgiveness? It would prevent a lot of the hatred and racism that exists in people who profess to be righteous. Beyond that, I wondered if *she* felt guilty for killing my family. Italy was a staunch ally of Nazi Germany during World War II and thus complicit in their murder. We only see what we choose to see when it suits our purpose.

Discrimination *can't* have it both ways. The Jews were accused of killing Christ in the year 30 BCE, over 2000 years ago, yet others claiming land rights, argue that the Jews first came to Israel in 1948, when Israel was declared a nation by vote in the UN. In truth, the Jews were the only indigenous people to *rule* this land, beginning with the Jewish patriarch Abraham, and his great-grandsons who formed the 12 tribes of Israel in 1200 BCE.

When it came time to enter the tomb of Jesus, I stooped low to get inside the crypt and then stood in silence, gripped by the gravity of such a holy site. The Russians were in an altered state, moved by the tremor of its sanctity and the accumulated power of all the prayers of the faithful who entered before. Such power is far too great to dissect. It simply exists. So does bigotry, hypocrisy, intolerance, hatred, envy, revenge and rage. None have any place in the Holy Land, nor anywhere in the world, for we are all part of God's creation.

As I stood on the ship's deck that day in New Caledonia, on the rim of the mighty Pacific Ocean, the vivid sunset was a tribute to the Almighty. What wonders I had seen, how privileged I was to have experienced so much of the world. Was I any closer to understanding my place in it, probably not. On this, the holiest day, I longed to talk to a fellow Jew. It was a big ask on a remote tropical island.

The following day, I wandered along the pier in Noumea looking at the stalls. A piece of jewellery caught my eye and I started chatting with a pretty French girl, Hannah, who later disclosed that she *was* Jewish. Ask and you will receive, time and again. Divine providence is the greatest blessing one can receive.

As proof, she showed me a large tattoo on the back of her calf, in honour of her grandfather. An eagle's head with a dagger stuck through it, his symbol as a member of the French resistance against the Nazis in World War II. Some battles are won undercover. Like a single drop of water in a raging current, the silence is deafening.

This young girl understood what it meant to lose her loved ones and to search for meaning. It was only after my mother's passing that I was able to watch her film interview, made by the Shoah Foundation in our home in Sydney, as part of their archival records.

Founded in 1994 by Steven Spielberg, its goal was to preserve individual testimonies of the *Shoah* – the genocide of the Jews, as proof for posterity of the atrocities committed. There are those deniers of the Holocaust who are so blind that no amount of proof will ever be enough, nor are they deserving of any. They are so bigoted they prefer not to see, blind ignorance their ticket to notoriety.

My mother was hurt that I refused to watch her interview, but I argued that I had no stomach for a cruel truth, one that I had heard over and over. As she fell into the bottomless pit of dementia, she became immersed in the dismal memory of the camp. I advised the staff at her nursing home to never mention the numbers tattooed on her forearm, so as not to catapult her into a deeper depression. My father refused to be interviewed, despite the need, because so few Greek Jews survived. He remained tight-lipped until his dying day.

My mother passed away a year later, in the early hours of the morning, in her nursing home. When the phone rang I refused to answer it. I did not want to hear the words. So final, yet welcome. Her peaceful passing in her sleep was a blessed relief from the torment that crippled her. Not a day went by in the time following my father's death that she did not tell me how much she wanted to die. It took a dreadful toll on her and drained my soul.

When the nurse finally got through to me, she asked that I choose a funeral home. I opted for one run by ladies, to ensure my mother was treated with dignity. The following morning I received a call, saying they were unable to bury my mother because they could not carry out the Jewish rituals needed before burial, and informed me of the only place on the coast that could. So my mother had one final drive, a lap of honour, around the area.

Trying to sleep that morning, after receiving the news of my mother's death, was impossible. Even more so because of the raucous celebrations going on in heaven. I could *see* and *hear* it, so clearly – the warm hugs and kisses from the family lost to her in the war. She finally had her wish to be reunited with her loved ones. They all danced in a circle, embracing her, with plates and glasses smashed in rapture. The plates were a Greek thing, so I knew my father was there, the glasses were more Jewish. I shared in their joy.

There are those moments in life that need to be cherished and those special people who shed light on your journey, if only for a fraction of time. The surge of love that encircled me at the end of the world cruise, was beyond affection. It felt like it emanated from a higher source, a tie that bound people together on so many different levels.

One evening, a crew member sped towards me and wrapped me in a heartfelt embrace. Mira was from Chile and she had called me into her office one day as I was passing by. She had read the notes of my struggle for port assistance and recognition of special needs.

'Not every disability is visible,' she said, emotionally. Confessing that she too had brain surgery, Mira lived with the trauma of the pain and worse still, the *disbelief*. She took a deep breath, a measure of her anguish, and hugged me once again. I had touched a nerve and we were united in a cause, to be recognised and afforded respect.

Nearing the end of the cruise, two of my favourite crew returned to the ship. Frank from Botswana was the first to greet me with a broad grin that lit up the room. He had the same exuberance as the ship's photographer, King from Zimbabwe, who always joked and laughed. Although we were brought up continents apart, we were united in the vivacity of life. Our goal, despite our different backgrounds, was to spread humour and joy all around.

Aldas from Ukraine was my sensitive other half. We shared a gentleness of spirit and vulnerability that being an evolved soul in a harsh world entails. The biggest hurdle of this sensitivity is the isolation that separates you from the rest of humanity, simply because you *feel* the world in colours they cannot see. Your greatest strength becomes your greatest weakness and only the presence of kindred souls can ease the sense of alienation.

As soon as Aldas heard I was still on board, he raced over to me in the dining room and gave me a giant hug. Then he held my hand and smiled, like a docile deer, with his big blue eyes. He had returned from his break, unable to go back to Ukraine because of the war. Staying with his cousin in Croatia, his family reunited with him there. Ours was a bond forged in adversity, for to be the innocent target of another's ambitions and quest for power, brings unimaginable heartache. There was so much more sorrow yet to come.

Ukraine was not only a beacon of light in a sea of darkness but also the place where my grandfather's body lay buried in a mass grave. From the one treasured photo of him, my mother's only memento of the father she adored, he looked so kind and learned. He was the grandparent I always wanted but I was robbed of them all, on both sides of my family.

Taken from Hungary to Ukraine by the Nazis in 1944, for forced labour, he never returned. Whether he died of typhoid or was shot in the back of the head and dropped into a giant hole in the ground, his loss was enormous. This dismal fate was shared by more than one million Jews who were forced to dig their own grave, in a horrendous act of mass murder in Ukraine. The gunshots paralleled the throbbing wound at the back of *my* head. The constant ache in my skull was the cry of humanity, as it pleads for world order.

There was no end to the tyranny in the world, wielded by the forces of darkness. A dreadful massacre took place in Israel on 7 October

2023. Over 1,200 innocent souls – infants, children, young adults in the prime of their lives, and older folk who deserved a peaceful end, were ravaged and slaughtered at a music festival where they were revelling in life, by those working at the hands of the devil.

There was limited coverage of the news on board the ship, but enough carnage on social media to make my soul shudder. How could this onslaught be repeated time and again through the pages of history? Once again the dark overlord, Pluto, attacked the very core of spiritual Neptune – *music*. A music festival, like concerts targeted before, where the vibration of the earth could be elevated. It was all so sadly predictable, so pitiful and so poignant.

A veil of despair consumed me and the only words of consolation offered were, *'Don't watch the news.'* As if ignoring events would erase the truth. The world was guilty of that time and again. While most high-minded leaders condemned the hideous act of terror, others like the United Nations remained mute and mindless, stirred into moral bankruptcy by their personal agenda.

Two days after the attack on October 7, was my birthday. It was on October 9 that I watched, horrified, as a large unauthorized protest took place at the Sydney Opera House, its sails lit up blue and white in respect for the massive loss in Israel.

At first, I thought it was a protest against the inhuman rape, mass murder and mutilation that took place there, and for the 251 souls who were taken hostage. How could I be so naive as to think that sympathy and sorrow were the normal response? Rather it was quite the opposite. Rage at the *victims* and calls for more violence. Calls of hatred that wounded the sky and catapulted back to earth.

Oh, no you don't! Not in my city, the progressive city of Sydney where I grew up and lived most of my life. Where I cruised across the blue waters of the harbour and caught a glimmer of paradise. *Not* at the Opera House, a place of culture, where enchanted notes bounced off the sails of its roof and echoed across the open skies. The hallowed halls of ballet, opera and concerts, it was the fulcrum of creativity and could not be defiled by chants of people who later demanded sympathy but were incapable of showing any when it counted. The very definition of corrupt moral decay.

And *not* on my birthday. October 9, a birthday I shared with John Lennon, the voice of peace and love. Birthdays are a time of celebration and joy, not of horror as you are forced to face the cruelty of humankind. Libra is a sign of peace, so it should never be corrupted by acts of brutality. Just 'Imagine' if we all lived in harmony and the world was united as one. Just imagine.

And most of all, *not* with my people. The Jews have been innocent targets throughout history. *Never again* would they go silently to their graves. Antisemitism, resentment against the Jews, dates back throughout history. The Jews were targeted as scapegoats for plagues, and natural catastrophes, blamed for economic decline, or simply coveted for their wealth, land and most of all for their knowledge and light, very threatening to vain despots. Perhaps that was the defining connection with my faith, united in indignation.

And *not* with my *clan*, the good people of the world, of all races and creeds, who are wise enough to discern lies from the truth, and good from evil. Those evolved souls who seek knowledge as the source of their decisions. People who don't rant and rave and preach hatred and division, pretending to fight for a cause they have no inkling of. Worse still are the hypocrites who preach vengeance when they are guilty of the worst of crimes. It is up to good people with a conscience and a moral compass to restore the balance.

In the ultimate battle between the dark forces of Pluto and the uplifting light of Neptune, while one is consumed with hatred and destruction, the other chooses to *dance*. To hear the music of the heavens and rejoice. Music is the ultimate link with the divine, so join hands and dance. Project a stream of healing light around the world, one that echoes words of love and peace, in so many languages, sung by a huge magnificent earthly choir.

Can you hear it? The voice of angels drifting up to heaven?

I was not in the mood to celebrate my birthday but the universe stepped in to remind me of the good people in the world. It was quite extraordinary – lots of hugs and warm wishes from friends among the crew and officers. Carlos joined me for dinner and the dining staff sang 'Happy Birthday', presenting me with a luscious cake while the Indonesian waiters came over to sing their version of the song, *'Selamat Panjang Umur'*, wishes for a long life.

Earlier I had returned to my cabin to find two vases of roses on the table. Pink ones with flutters of white blossoms were sent by my friends at the Guest Services desk, along with a lovely card signed by all the staff. The stunning red roses and chocolate-covered strawberries were sent from Anya, from Moldova, who had already left the ship. She worked in one of the offices and we celebrated her birthday a week before, over afternoon tea. The card she wrote was exquisitely worded with love, a measure of her tender, caring soul.

When I walked into the atrium, Raoul spotted me and darted out of his office with a recorder blaring 'Happy Birthday' in Spanish. With another card signed by the Shore team and lots of hugs, it was impossible to stay depressed. Then came the crowning moment. While chatting away with a lady officer, the captain and staff captain approached on their daily rounds. The Irish captain was both open and warm, and we had met several times before on P&O cruises when I was guest speaker. We had shared a few tales along the way.

Posing for a photo together, all of us in a fond embrace, the captain put his cap on my head, leaving me in charge as the imaginary captain of the universe. With all of us chuckling, Raoul heard all the commotion outside his office and emerged with a machine blowing bubbles at us. Everyone erupted into laughter, and for a precious moment in time, the world was happy and carefree. All our troubles blew away in a stream of magical crystal bubbles.

If only life was that easy, but anything of consequence rarely is.

CHAPTER TWENTY-NINE

SEA OF HEARTBREAK

Life is a never-ending source of inspiration but travel was becoming increasingly difficult with too many demands and stresses involved. I had reached the point where even cruising was daunting, each port viewed in terms of strategy rather than wonder. While I was lucky to have lasted so long, my body was becoming a total of all its parts, each one feeling the strain of longevity. Worse still, things that had once excited me were now seen as ordinary.

There *were* moments of humour along the way. On a cruise headed to the island of Timor-Leste, I opted for a tour on a hop-on bus. It turned out to be a rusty old van with holes in the side for ventilation. Unable to get up the steep step into the back seats, the driver came up with an ingenious solution. He grabbed a box of water bottles and placed it on the ground so I could step on it. During the trip, all the water was drunk so there was no choice but to ungracefully slide out of the van, and land in a heap on the gravel.

On my adventure in Papua New Guinea, I bravely hired a car and driver to take me on a one-hour tour. We got less than one block on a road pitted with massive potholes when I told the driver to turn back. The only bitumen road led up to the lookout, so at least I got a good view. Later I managed to get on a yellow minivan heading for the cultural centre. It was nowhere to be seen on my return. After many attempts to board other vans, a nice local lady yelled out to a guy in the garage, and Obi drove me back to the ship in style in his vintage truck.

Now, unwilling to compromise my comfort, it was luxury travel all the way. With over 55 voyages completed in my lifetime, and more than two years spent at sea, I could not resist another cruise to see places I had not yet visited. It was no surprise that there was a higher purpose involved, one that invariably helped define my path.

In April 2024, I boarded the *Coral Princess* once again but this time I would cruise only as far as Dover. The original itinerary through Asia and the Mediterranean was changed because of world events, and now we would set sail across the Indian Ocean around Africa. It suited me as Asia had been my playground for years while Africa was far more alluring and distant.

Our first port of call was Fremantle in Western Australia, and my friend Roxy drove down from Perth so we could spend the day together. It was a long overdue reunion, years in the making. Roxy had been one of my closest friends in Bali and we shared many escapades. Over lunch we reminisced, so much had happened over the years and our lives had gone in different directions. Walking along the beach, we soaked up the energy of the vast ocean.

There was another meaningful reunion in Fremantle. The P&O Australia cruise ship, *Pacific Explorer*, berthed beside us in the harbour, made a sharp turn before it manoeuvred out to sea. The captains sounded a celebratory horn, as passengers yelled and waved. It was a last goodbye, a sad end to a rich history. Months later the brand's demise was announced after 90 years of cruising in

Australian waters. No more would I see the logo of a company that had inspired me all my life. So many memories, a wealth of ports and a fleet of ships that were dear to many people's hearts. Precious highlights that will always be remembered.

On board the *Coral Princess*, I accumulated an eclectic bunch of comrades. Most were crew, some a welcome reunion. It was the broad smile of Carlos, my carefree Columbian, that welcomed me. Many of the other crew were now scattered around the world, cruising on different ships, gaining experiences that shaped their lives.

My bestie among the passengers was Miss Pamela, a 93-year-old lady who often came to sit with me as I lingered over dessert at dinner. Thankfully, I had been placed at the same table as on my previous cruise, next to the window with a wall behind me for protection. My overzealous waiter Rizzo from the Philippines was sent into a tailspin one night when he tripped over Miss Pamela's walker while juggling several platters but, after several pirouettes, he managed to remain upright, if not badly shaken. He was never the same.

Miss Pamela was a feisty Aries, my perfect match, and each night after dinner we went to the Guest Services desk to engage in some witty banter with the staff, sing a few oldies, and sway as much as we could. We still had the music in us, which seemed to have eluded the younger generations. They simply did not have rhythm.

The new Guest Services manager was a godsend. Marcos came to my rescue when my cabin flooded *five times,* usually in the early hours of the morning when no one was around. There is no greater feeling of panic, or helplessness, as you watch water cascade from your toilet in a tidal wave into your cabin. Only *my* cabin. It happened before on the previous cruise, but it was already a fait accompli with my feet underwater when I woke.

My deck supervisor from Bosnia was way out of his depth and I could feel my spirit dwindle every time he appeared. With his blunt haircut and vapid look, he reminded me of a medieval peasant planting oats in a field of wheat. When the hairdryer attached to the wall expired in my cabin, and the new one began to talk to me in the middle of the night, making strange sounds, I knew it was a curse! Electricity and water are not a good combination.

It was difficult to infiltrate the source of this ancient curse, so I gave up trying. Clearly, I was a person of some magnitude to have the dark side go to so much trouble to irritate me, so I simply stopped reacting. When it came to the more serious elements of life, my efforts to bond with my faith did not go as planned. There were only seven Jews at the Shabbat service, and no prayer ritual despite the prompting of the two Christians who attended. The Jews just wanted to chat and find comfort in numbers, and some sense of belonging.

Miss Pamela was even more disappointed. One Sunday morning I found her wheeling around in circles, looking for the Christian service but there was no one to be seen. When no one turned up the following week, she was distraught. A fine Protestant lady, she had attended church services diligently since she was young. Granted the ship was in port much of the time and people had whizzed off to explore. There was also a choice of churches and cathedrals along the way. Or maybe people had simply outgrown religion.

As we crossed the Indian Ocean, the vast expanse was moody and uninspiring. Seven days passed before we reached the island of Mauritius, which despite the lush greenery and fascinating culture, took the prize for the worst drivers I'd ever come across. The roads on the island were riddled with speed bumps. Not one, but three in a row in quick succession, and I could feel my back shudder. Despite my pleas, the driver refused to slow down.

After five more days of cruising, we reached Cape Town in South Africa, now forced to round the Cape of Good Hope because of the trouble in the Red Sea. This was not the first time conflict had brewed in the vital sea passage leading to the Suez Canal. Somali pirates were an ongoing risk, but now it was a rat pack of militant rebels who had nothing better to do than stir up strife that was more menacing. Life can be disappointing when you amount to nothing.

In 1985, four men representing the Palestine Liberation Front hijacked the Italian cruise liner *Achille Lauro* off the coast of Egypt, as the liner sailed from Alexandria to Ashdod in Israel. The grisly newspaper headline, along with a graphic image of an elderly Jewish American man in a wheelchair who was shot in the head, and then thrown overboard, was too confronting to forget. History demands a heavy toll from its Jews. Ironically, the date of the shooting was October 7, the same day marred by mass murder in Israel in 2023.

In South Africa, many Jews were uneasy as to their place in society, feeling diminished and at risk after the carnage in Israel and their country's stance on the issue. It was all very hypocritical considering its racial past. With Table Mountain looming in the distance, I walked from the ship to the Marina at my own pace and reached a quiet mall, early on Sunday morning. Fate was at work when I was drawn into a private art gallery.

A demure young lady was sitting at the desk. After admiring the art, we talked for the better part of an hour. I felt a strange connection and was prompted to ask, 'Are you Jewish?' She nodded yes. There was no doubt that this meeting had been orchestrated, just like my encounter with Hannah in New Caledonia years before.

After we spoke about my book, tracing the lineage of the Jews, *People of the Stars – Astrology and the History of the Jewish People*, she virtually begged me to publish it.

'You don't know how important this is,' she uttered, the light almost extinguished from her eyes. When I spoke of the astrological thread in my books, I expected her to recoil as she seemed conservative, perhaps orthodox, and had studied Hebrew holy books in depth. Instead, she surprised me. 'Moses was the first astrologer,' she said staidly, before scribbling down a reference book to support her statement. The cosmos had outdone itself.

Some passengers disembarked in Cape Town, so at the Friday Shabbat service, we were down to five. When I brought the leftover challah bread to Guest Services, wanting to spread the love, they were more than happy. To ease my dejection, clever Carlos pointed out, after I told him that Jews make up only 0.02% of the world's population, that their expected presence on a ship of 2000 was 0.4 people. We had exceeded our target.

The ship continued to plot its course around the west coast of Africa, heading for Europe. Namibia was our next port of call. It was a country that I had never aspired to visit but after the shambles caused by our late entry and a new dock, I finally hoisted myself into the front seat of a van. With six others on board, we headed straight into an endless void of desert and sand dunes, and a lake full of faded pink flamingos, strutting in the distance.

A few days earlier, news came of ten passengers left behind by another cruise ship when they failed to return in time from a private excursion off the coast of Africa to the island of Sao Tome. The ship sailed off without them. The news struck a nerve with me.

Did anyone else realise the dreadful history of this island, centuries before? It was hardly the place for a day trip. But then again, the past is often buried in the interests of the present.

During the time of the Inquisition, in 1496, King Manuel I of Portugal punished those Jews who refused to pay a head tax, by wrenching their children from their arms. Close to 2000 children, 8 years old or under, were forced onto a ship headed for the island of Sao Tome, off the coast of Africa. Many young lives were lost on the awful voyage, the rest were dumped on an isolated beach on the island. Fending off crocodiles and giant lizards, many were lost to sheer desperation, and after a year only 600 survived. Forcibly raised as Roman Catholics, they worked in the sugar trade,

I sighed when I read of their plight those many centuries ago. Now as I stood on the peak of a barren isolated cliff in the Cape Verde Islands, the facts were even more confronting. Staring over the ocean, all alone in the middle of a vast emptiness, my Reggae driver was not interested in history, swamping me instead with tales of his recent breakup rather than anything more sinister.

In Las Palmas in the Gran Canary Islands, I decided against a taxi, instead sliding around in the back of the hop-on hop-off bus. As I made my way back to the ship, the local mall was deserted as it was Sunday and the shops were closed but luckily a few fast food outlets were open. So began a strange interlude.

Back in my cabin, I slept. *And slept*. I was shocked when I woke up at 4 pm the next day. This had never happened before. Rather than being refreshed, I felt odd, like a radio that wasn't quite on the right channel, or frequency. Turning on the television, there was a fuzzy screen with the message, 'no signal'. Everything was wrong, or at least not quite right.

It only occurred to me days later, that there had been a cosmic shift during that time. Just before sunrise on 3 June 2024, there was a powerful alignment of six planets, with the orbits of Mercury, Mars, Jupiter, Saturn, Uranus and Neptune, all lined up on one side of the Sun. The cosmic pull was tangible, and this 'parade of planets' is rarely replicated. The Moon passing over this lineup for the first week in June, illuminated their effect on Earth.

It followed a total solar eclipse on 8 April 2024, visible across most parts of North America, the last one to cross the United States until 2044. In the sign of Aries, this alignment of the Sun, Moon and Earth ensured change on both an individual and global level. It followed a full Moon eclipse on March 25, in the opposite sign of Libra. Aries, as the aggressor, pitched against Libra, peace, ensured a mighty battle and countries reeled.

The solar eclipse took place at 19 degrees of Aries, triggering my life purpose, or natal North Node. Aries is a spirited sign, so my life purpose was to gain strength and independence. When others marvelled at my daring, venturing out alone across the globe, it seemed natural to me. Protected, I set out with few misgivings.

It was the lovely young cruise director Rebecca who inspired me on this voyage. Perky and impossibly wise for her age, we sat down for a deep and meaningful talk the night before arriving in Europe. Without bringing up my past, she told me that a week before the cruise, she visited a concentration camp in Germany. *Dachau.*

I shuddered for it was the camp where my parents were imprisoned, where they saw each other for the first time. Rebecca was deeply moved by her visit to Dachau, rocked to her very core by the suffering that took place there. The fact that she wanted to go there in the first place spoke volumes. Rebecca had matured through her experience, adding to her soul's evolution. This was another in a long list of 'co-incidences' that cemented my search for identity, along with the realisation that a true understanding of history only comes to life when revisited.

On a rainy day in the Netherlands, the taxi drivers at the port jostled for a fare but I chose a gentle one hovering in the background. He agreed to drive me to a nearby town, and he took lots of photos along the way to save me from getting out in the rain. On a whim, I asked him to drive to Amsterdam, stopping for hot croissants and tea along the way. The cost of the trip scarcely mattered because it was clear that I would never pass this way again.

The driver, Naim, was from Morocco, a country I shared an affinity with. This cruise provided my second visit to Tangiers and I headed straight for the narrow streets of the kasbah for lunch. Then it was off to the park where cats roamed free. I spent much of my day on a bench stroking a cat that had curled up right beside me. A litter of kittens were resting in a cardboard box nearby, with food and water left by locals, a measure of their kindness.

On my previous visit to Tangiers, the year before, I read of an old synagogue within the walls of the kasbah, and I asked the guide about it after I got off the shuttle bus into town. He happily directed me to the kasbah and told me to ask one of the locals for directions, once inside. Halfway down the narrow busy laneway, I stopped to ask an old man sitting in front of a stall, and he pointed to a sign on the wall directly above him, *Rue de synagogue.*

He insisted on showing me the way, down a narrow path to the small synagogue where a caretaker allowed me entry. The beautiful carvings, chandeliers and holy books dating back to the 1500s spoke of a time when Jews were welcomed into Morocco during the dark days of the Spanish Inquisition. The Sultan of Morocco, Mohammed V, protected his 250,000 Jews from the Nazis during World War II, refusing to bow to Hitler's demands.

As Naim drove through the streets of Amsterdam, past the well-worn canals and city sites, I asked if he could drive by the house of Anne Frank. A queue had formed outside so we did not stop. 'This is the place most tourists taking a taxi want to visit when they come to Amsterdam,' Naim said, adding 'then the red light district.'

'Do you know the story of Anne Frank?' I asked Naim. He had no idea. So sad, the ordeal of this young Jewish girl who hid in the secret annexe of her father's business, with her family, for two years, during Nazi Germany's occupation of the Netherlands. From the age of 13, Anne wrote daily in her diary, recording her fears and hopes to one day be a writer, an ambition she never achieved but her words were more powerful than she could ever know.

Food and other supplies were smuggled in by friends, but in August 1944, after a tip-off, the family were captured by the heinous Gestapo, and Anne was sent to the Bergen-Belsen concentration camp where she became ill and died at the age of 15. In her diary, Anne wrote that despite everything she still believed that people were really good at heart. Forever innocent and trusting.

When the ship anchored in the port of Warnemunde in Germany, many passengers headed off by train for the long trip to Berlin, some even choosing to visit the Holocaust museum. I had no desire to remember something I had worked so hard to forget, discounting messages from friends who commented how hard it must be to step foot on the land that caused me so much grief. I cast their concerns aside but when I passed the stern faces of some of the locals and the arrogance of the young man serving me at a café – tall, blond and icily cold, I was swept back to the war, imagining him in a Nazi uniform. Then it was blood-curdling, and confronting, buried deep within a collective consciousness.

When we cruised out of Riga in Latvia, the sea was sullen and bleak, the woods barely daring to whisper of the past. As I sat on the balcony of my cabin, the ship carved a path through waters that trembled with silence. During the Second World War, these woods provided the last breath of oxygen for 25,000 Jewish souls who were shot there, the trees the only witness to the massive sin. Jews praying in a synagogue nearby were locked inside by the Nazis and the building was set alight. All inside perished. If only my tears could extinguish the flames but there weren't enough tears in the world.

That evening, as the tainted woods flowed by, I ventured into the chapel for the Shabbat service. I was the *only* one there. I could not have felt more isolated. Taking a sip of the blessed wine, I prayed for the souls of all those lost in that forest, for the spirit of the trees forced to witness it and the sea that was awash with the ashes of all those who were burnt alive. They had yet to recover because the pall of sorrow still hung over this place, like many sites in Europe where the atrocities of the past were impossible to erase.

During the night, as we cruised towards Sweden, a dense fog descended on the ocean. Grey mist swamped my balcony with zero visibility. No stars, no hint of the moon, or the sound of the lapping waves against the ship's hull. All night the ship sounded the fog horn to alert any approaching vessel to steer clear. It was eerie, as the low and threatening boom echoed through the void. Stern warnings, bouncing off the ether, like scenes from an old movie in black and white, or the moans of seafaring ghosts yet to find their peace.

The mood intensified when we reached the port of Aarhus in Denmark, on a dismal day. After a visit to the cathedral in town, I headed for the Occupation Museum to learn more about what happened here in the Second World War. A small building, it was more intense than I could cope with because it was the actual former Nazi headquarters in the town. The beastly energy of the interrogation and torture rooms, and the Nazi flag in deadly red and black reeked of the devil's decaying breath and demanded a heavy toll on all those who entered. Mine was a rapid exit, spurred on by a heavy pressure in my chest and a rising dread.

Copenhagen proved a happy distraction when I caught up with an old friend, Craig, and his two daughters. Last seen as pretty girls, they had blossomed into beautiful young women. I first met Craig in Bali, on the dance floor of a night club, and with his wacky sense of humour there was an instant rapport. We shared good and hard times, and it was decades since we last met but there was still a bond.

In the faces of Craig's daughters, I saw youth and expectation, carving out a good life filled with ambition and dreams. It was time to hand over the baton, to another generation. The 1960s were never going to repeat with its Neptune in Libra love vibe. It was mine to treasure, along with those fortunate enough to have experienced it.

Over the years Neptune drifted through the astrological signs, branding each age with a different energy and musical imprint. In 2011 Neptune entered its own nebulous sign of Pisces, but in 2025 there will be a brand new start as Neptune's transit begins again through Aries, marking the beginning of a new 165-year cycle.

The cosmos is a place of mystery, with secrets we are not privy to. The evening before my cruise ended in Dover, as we were nearing the coast of England, I was drawn out onto the deck. There were only a handful of people there, most gone to dinner or a show. Never before had I seen such a superb sight. It was sheer magic. The sky had melted into the sea, as the sun dissolved into drops of gold, pink and orange and slid over the horizon. Like silk, the ship glided across the water, through gentle folds of gossamer, until there was no distinction between the earth and the heavens. There were no lines of separation, only peace. Peace.

CHAPTER THIRTY

OCEAN OF LOVE

I heard it whispered one day, overheard by the sun and masked by the moon, that I was on a quest. A child of the universe, connected by stars to the beating heart of our world, rivers of red ran deep within me while shades of blue and green filtered through my eyes. The ocean and nature provided oxygen to breathe and those exquisite starry, starry nights, the space to connect to a higher source.

The planets circling above in the sky lent reason and rhyme, in a kaleidoscope of light. Eternal poetry, their energy resonates through the heavens, casting notes and scales that unite to form music. The music lifted me to the height of angels and celestial beings.

I have inhaled the breath of many faiths, the seal of their kiss a merging of our energies. The force of two souls that become one, echoes the dignity of unconditional love. A tapestry of ancestry streaks my soul with colours. The eternal wanderer, like my forefathers who were forced from one place to another, created a remarkable DNA. This genetic roadmap formed a historical timeline, constantly updated in the struggle to discover my identity.

I was cut from a vast piece of cloth – a mix of Ashkenazi Jews from Central and Eastern Europe and Sephardic Jews from Spain and Portugal. Over 20% of my DNA comes from Southern Italy where they rested along their way in their passage of exile, and 6% from the Aegean islands of Greece. Anatolia and the Caucuses form another 4%, during their retreat to the Ottoman Empire. Add a dash of North Africa, Morocco, Egypt, Cyprus, Germanic Europe and the Levant of Israel, moulded centuries before, and I am a citizen of the world by necessity and design, ensuring the survival of my people.

There is a wrong belief that ancestry cannot reveal one as Jewish. Some argue that religion does not show up in DNA. No, it doesn't but ethnicity does. Judaism is embedded in the heart and soul of each person who is born Jewish. They may choose not to follow the religion but they cannot erase their Judaic roots, for it is integral to their being. It dates back thousands of years, to a heritage of prophets, holy men and kings, and they should be proud.

The word 'Jew' stands prominent in the word 'jewel' symbolising the gifts they share with the world, far greater than their numbers. If not blessed, how else does a single faith that constitutes only 0.02% of the world's population, contribute so enormously to the spheres of music, film, literature, medicine, physics, economy, technology and almost every other field of advancement? So to those who are jealous of their achievements, be grateful instead.

While negative powers try to tear the world apart with their anger and chants, it is the positive energy of those who uplift it with their tolerance and kindness that raise the vibration of the earth. From the earliest days of the Old Testament of the Bible, the Jews were deemed God's 'chosen people', the bearers of light, and it is for that very reason that the forces of darkness have repeatedly tried to destroy them. However, the Jews are divinely protected, escaping centuries of persecution to enhance the world with their presence.

As God pledged, 'I will bless those who bless you, and whoever curses you I will curse; and all peoples on earth will be blessed through you.' Genesis 12:2-5 (NIV Bible)

There *was* magic in the air the day I was born, for I was given the chance to explore the galaxy. What an amazing ride I've had, privileged to feel the love from so many different lands and see life, not through the veil of illusion, but through the eyes of a broader reality. Oceans have washed over me and I have sailed upon them to the far reaches of the globe, and to the ends of the earth.

Born into an extraordinary lineage, I have been gifted my ancestors' strength and wisdom, gleaned from my diverse heritage. To my adopted country, Australia, you provided the *opportunity* to grow and glow, the *encouragement* to learn and the *freedom* to be who I am and to chase stars, both real and celestial. To ride under the banner of your flags and to be acknowledged by Australian Consuls and dignitaries in a foreign land, is priceless.

With marriage, I gained a wonderful extended English family and a goddaughter who grew up to follow her bliss to become a Christian pastor. It was in England that I discovered my psychic gift, and had it recognised for the first time. Its spiritual seal helps define and express who I am. The country also produced the fabulous British rock gods who inspired me in the '60s and kept my soul singing, and grooving, for the rest of my life.

To stand beside a regal Hindu king, on the enchanted island of Bali, and record its history was a true privilege. What an honour to be loved by two of its sons, one a Hindu holy man and the other, half Chinese Buddhist, and to have his precious daughter named after me. To my spiritual mentors, an esteemed Hindu priest and priestess, I bow with respect. On the special island of Bali, and in mystical Java, spirits singled me out and chose me to be privy to their secrets. Spirit does not segregate according to faith but rather is part of a stream of consciousness where there are no lines of separation or superficial restrictions.

To be flown to Jakarta, the capital of Indonesia, the biggest Muslim country in the world in terms of population, for a press conference because my voice deserved to be heard, and being chosen to meet political heads and acclaimed mystics of many faiths, was extraordinary. As was travelling through such a vast country and bonding with people of all tribes and persuasions. With no common background, we were united in curiosity, goodness and sound intentions. The spiritual tie with that country and its people is irrevocable.

My Nepalese brothers are forever treasured, as is the love of a special man in the jungle and his gentle welcoming family. My elephant sister, my guardian cats and the pack of dogs that followed me, symbolise my affinity with animals because they don't know, or care, what faith you are. They sense your spirit and what lies in your heart. Soaring to the base of the highest mountain in the world, to bask in the light of the stunning full moon, was magic. As were the Buddhist monks who circled me while etching secret mandalas of protection.

Little can match the canopy of starlight over Masada, the holy site of ancient Israel. It was a tale of sacrifice and freedom, a persistent theme that plagues my people, but still, they are steeped in love and create a beautiful symphony woven from the stars. Blessed by the glow of Neptune, the spiritual planet inspires music, dance and an idealistic form of love. The trials of my forefathers, reflected in the eyes of Daniel, were life-affirming.

I have experienced pain so intense that I wanted to dissolve into dust. To the doctors who rose to the challenge and gave me back life, there are no words powerful enough to express my gratitude. To those health workers who have learnt the skills but are yet to develop compassion, many layers to the soul must be restored before true healing can take place.

Even in the dimmest hospital corridor or numb to the sharp blade of the surgeon's knife, nothing could stop the music. In the deepest recesses of my soul and the fertile labyrinth of my mind, I was dancing. An eternal dance that enriched my life.

To search a list of names, desperate to find the family who were lost to me, nothing is more confronting than to track them down to a register of Holocaust victims, at Yad Vashem Museum in Jerusalem. Beside each of their names is one word, as dramatic as a single word can ever be. *Murdered. Murdered. Murdered.*

I have no tears left, for they were shed with far greater meaning by my mother and father who felt the loss more closely. To those countless victims of war and persecution, *wherever* they may be, in a world that strays at times into madness and depravity, you are not lost. These innocent victims who felt the full force of conflict are stars in heaven and their light can, and will, never be extinguished.

God is watching, Beyond all else, there is love. The love of the family lost to me, I know you are looking after me from afar. Your love is tangible. On the earthly plane, the soft caresses and warm kisses, from near and afar, were a panacea for my soul. As were the eyes that enchanted, the light of the fireflies and the ocean at midnight. Love is the saving grace of us all, extinguishing the fire of hatred until it dissolves. Love and light. The two strongest forces to overcome negativity and bring order back to the world.

There were moments of peaceful glow, heavenly scenes and times of magic. Above all, is the presence of a chorus of angels. The spirits who saved me from danger, who guide and listen to my every plea, grant my wishes and propel me on the road to my destiny. These guardian angels wrenched me out of the dark when I plunged into an abyss, lifted me up to guide me along my path, and taught me how to face life with purpose and resolve.

Then there is simplicity. In all my attempts to discover my identity, there was a simple realisation that brought all the strands of my search together. My best friend at high school, Isabel, was my soul sister and although I have been fortunate to have many friends, nothing can compare to the bond we had, when we were young and impressionable.

Together we bravely stalked pop stars and climbed fire escapes, infiltrated TV studios and danced for the camera, spurring each other on. Endless hours were spent talking on the phone and cheeky notes were passed across our school desks. We plastered pictures of the Beatles across our bedroom walls until we were saturated.

Isabel left high school before me and we lost touch for decades. One day, my mother bumped into Isabel at a shopping mall and we made contact once more. Throughout our school days, I knew Isabel as Catholic but over tea, 50 years later, she confided her secret.

Her parents had fled Europe shortly after the war and were so fearful of the consequences, they told her *never* to reveal her true faith. So she became Catholic, in name only. In fact, she was Jewish, and a large part of her life was dictated by fear and secrecy.

United by our love of music, Isabel and I were tied by a bond that was impossible to define. Sitting side by side, clenching hands in ecstasy and screaming aloud at the Beatles concert in 1964, we were forever linked. Such a cosmic force field lasts for an eternity. For some close bonds, there are no words and for most, no words are needed or will suffice. In truth, all you need is love.

And love will show you the way.

ABOUT THE AUTHOR

With a BA in History and Psychology, and Diplomas in Education and Counselling, Odyle Knight has worked as a teacher and school counsellor in Sydney and rural areas of Australia.

Odyle has lectured widely on the metaphysical and holds a diploma in Astrology from the Faculty of Astrological Studies in London. Named Young Psychic of the Year in England, she was honoured to give a public reading with the president of the Psychic Society.

Odyle has travelled extensively around the world. A one-week holiday in Bali turned into an incredible 20 years, many spent on the enchanted island as partner to a Hindu priest. She wrote three books about her experiences there – *Bali Moon, Bali Magic and Bali Hai*.

Her book *Hippos Eat Grass* discusses astrology and its influence on character, shape and size, affirming that we were all created differently and should embrace our differences.

Odyle has lectured on cruise ships as a guest speaker on Bali and astrology, sharing her passion for the subjects with her audience. She continues to cruise the world and enjoy life.

Praise for Odyle Knight's Bali books

'Odyle Knight – Astrologer, Author and Lecturer. It is appropriate that the theme of divine providence is the common thread running through all of Odyle Knight's books. Her belief that a universal force guides us along our journey is fundamental to her life path, as is the call of destiny, the right to make our own choices and the presence of profound spiritual forces that support all of us along the way.'
Bill Dalton, Indonesia Expat magazine, Issue 124

'Books by Australian writer Odyle Knight reveal that beyond its natural beauty lie many aspects few know about the island of the Gods.'
Garuda inflight Magazine

'Combining personal experience, intuition and the deep knowledge of Bali's absorbing mystique and history, Odyle has woven a wonderful story. On the surface, simply a tale of one woman's unusual passage it is much more. Few visitors or even long-term residents have ever experienced the island as this writer has. And fewer still would share it with others.'
Pak Bill, Toko Buku, Bali Advertiser

'My goodness, Odyle's books took me to places and situations that left me breathless, I had to read them one after the other as I just kept wanting to know what would happen next. Well done Odyle, you know how to keep me captivated.'
Frances. Colorado, USA

'I have just finished reading Bali Moon, it was one of the greatest books I've ever read. Your love and passion was so beautiful, I enjoyed your sense of humour too. Overall the book was absolutely brilliant. Well done! I can't wait to read the rest of your books.'
Inge, Melbourne

'Thank you for taking your inspirational story and setting it in my favourite place, Bali. It all came so alive for me. Your books have helped me focus my energy away from feelings of darkness and loneliness to feelings of hope and inspiration. I thought you should know how much your books touch the lives of those who read them.'
Kirsten, USA

'I was visiting Bali and someone said I should read Bali Moon, I went out and found it, could not put it down then bolted out and bought Bali Magic. What an amazing writer, the books were epic in understanding the magic and culture surrounding Bali and its people. Odyle's journey is one that not many of us would survive. Congratulations.'
Carmen, Perth, WA

'Just read your book Bali Moon. Thank you for writing this. It has touched me deeply and reminded me of something in me, and I wonder about my own journey. I can't wait to read Bali Magic and any other books that Odyle writes about her amazing life.'
Mike, Bangkok

'Thank you very much for writing so fascinating books. When I started to read the books, I felt like I'm reading story about myself. It was unbelievable. Your book connects me always with Bali so thank you very, very much.'
Alena, Czech Republic

'As of 30 minutes ago I just finished reading Bali Moon and I'm writing to say thank you. Very few of us get to have an experience such as yours and even fewer of us would share it. You write so beautifully and I love your characters.'
Stephanie, Singapore

'I have just read your books in one day. They were riveting and I could not put them down. I want to congratulate you on your wonderful writing and oh, how I long to be in Bali after only just having left. You take me back there.'
Lauren, USA

'I am a Balinese man living in Australia for over 20 years. I find your book very interesting to tell of my island through the eyes of a Westerner. I'm impressed with your research and can connect with all the places you describe. Thank you.'
Ketut, Sydney, Australia

'Your books are the first books I've ever re-read. I love your unique insight into the Bali culture! I've read Bali Magic at least 3x and Bali Moon. Thank you for writing such awesome books!! I love the adventure of them, and it feels like being in another world while reading. I always look forward to sitting down to read your stories!'
Emmy, California, USA

'As a traveller to Bali and a lover of this beautiful island, you gave me such an insight into their spirituality, I believe my next trip there will be more enjoyable and with a different view thanks to your books.'
Carol, Brisbane

'I loved your books and couldn't put them down. Having spent so much time in Bali I could relate to so many of the stories. Your descriptions were wonderful and your characters were just great. Loved them.'
Lynn W, UK